MEMORIALS

OF

BAPTIST MARTYRS

Baptist Martyrs.

BURNING OF MRS. ELIZABETH GAUNT.   PAGE 300.

MEMORIALS

OF

BAPTIST MARTYRS

WITH A PRELIMINARY HISTORICAL ESSAY, BY J. NEWTON BROWN

THE BEHEADING BLOCK

PHILADELPHIA
AMERICAN BAPTIST PUBLICATION SOCIETY
1854

The Baptist Standard Bearer, Inc.

NUMBER ONE IRON OAKS DRIVE • PARIS, ARKANSAS 72855

Thou hast given a *standard* to them that fear thee;
that it may be displayed because of the truth.
-- *Psalm 60:4*

Reprinted
by

THE BAPTIST STANDARD BEARER, INC.
No. 1 Iron Oaks Drive
Paris, Arkansas 72855
(501) 963-3831

THE WALDENSIAN EMBLEM
lux lucet in tenebris
"The Light Shineth in the Darkness"

ISBN #1-57978-385-6

Sicut lilium inter spinas sic amica mea inter filias

On The Cover: We use the symbol of the "lily among the thorns" from Song of Solomon 2:2 to represent the Baptist History Series. The Latin, *Sicut lilium inter spinas sic amica mea inter filias*, translates, "As the lily among thorns, so is my love among the daughters."

PRELIMINARY HISTORICAL ESSAY.

BY J. NEWTON BROWN.

A MARTYR is a witness—a witness for God, for Truth and Righteousness—a witness tried both by action and by suffering, and found faithful to his conscience and to Christ, through every trial. Such, at least, are those who, by the grace of God, are entitled to the name of Christian martyrs. "To you it is *given*," says Paul to the Philippians, "*in the behalf of Christ*, not only to *believe* on him, but also to *suffer* for his sake."

By usage, however, this title, which belongs to faithful Christians in general, has come in modern times to be restricted to those who suffer *unto death*. Hence, in our English Bible, the only three examples where the term occurs are of this kind :—Stephen of Jerusalem, Antipas of Pergamos, and the prophetic roll of the "martyrs of Jesus," with whose blood the mystic "Babylon" is drunken. Acts 22 : 20. Rev. 2 : 13. 17 : 6.

Martyrdom, in this restricted sense, may be said to have begun with the first generation of fallen man. Then in the world's fresh morning, the blood of righteous Abel, shed by a brother's hand, cried unto God from the crimsoned earth. The first revealed "heir of the righteousness which is by faith," was thus a martyr—a Christian martyr—typically, but truly—like John the Baptist in later time, bearing witness unto death to "the Lamb of God, who taketh away the sin of the world."

(3)

But it is manifest that the testimony of the true martyr must vary *in degree*, though not in kind, *with the measure of Divine Revelation* in different ages, and under different dispensations. Hence, the martyr from the time of Noah to Abraham might die as a witness to the *new* truth revealed to Noah; and from Abraham to Moses for the *new* revelation to Abraham; and from Moses to Christ for the *new* revelation to Moses, or to any one of the successive prophets, by whose anointed lips, "God, in time past spake unto the fathers." The martyrs down to the time of the Maccabees, are examples cited by Paul. Heb. 11 : 35–38.

On the same principle, it is equally clear that, after the coming of Christ, every faithful martyr was liable to suffer *for the new revelations and institutions introduced by Him;* whether in person, or through his Apostles, by the power of the Holy Ghost. (John 15: 18–27. 16: 1–4. 12 –15.) Of this, Christians, from the beginning, were fully forewarned, and especially Christian ministers, (Matt. 5 : 10–12. 10 : 16–42. 16 : 21–28.) and appropriate cautions, counsels, and consolations were provided for their guidance and support.

It behooves us, therefore, to examine carefully *what those new revelations and institutions are*, belonging especially to the New Testament dispensation, and binding upon the conscience of every disciple of Christ, "even unto the end of the world." For it is not every *sufferer* that is a martyr—*though he may be a Christian;* for it is possible that even a Christian may suffer for his own faults, and not for righteousness' sake, or for Christ's sake. (1 Peter 4 : 15–16.) A single fault in the temper and tongue of the meekest of men, shut him out of Canaan. Moses, the noblest witness for God in his time, yet died for his own fault — a warning to every succeeding generation of God's witnesses. Still more striking is the case of the young prophet at Bethel; who died for disobeying the plain command of God, through what might be thought a becoming deference to the authority of a "father" in Israel—a warning too little heeded by those who followed "the traditions of the elders" in after times, and the authority of "the early fathers" in the Christian Church. (1 Kings 13: 20–24.) In like manner, Paul in reproving the Corinthians for their abuse of the Lord's supper, says, "For this cause many are weak and sickly among you, and many sleep." (1 Cor. 11: 30).

Nor is it every one that *suffers in a true and righteous cause*, though he may die with indomitable courage, that wins the crown of martyrdom; for "though I *give* my body to be burned," says the Apostle, "and have not charity, (*i.e.*, love), it profiteth me nothing." Thousands also have been slaughtered for their connection with Christianity, like the infants of Bethlehem, who were rather *victims to cruelty* than martyrs for *Truth*.

Much less, even in the judgment of charity, are they to be justly regarded as Christian *martyrs*, who die in the diffusion and defence of *antichristian errors*. We grant that this distinction may be, and has been sadly abused for many hundreds of years, by many pretentious parties in Christendom; still within proper limits, and with due allowance for all Christian freedom of thought, it is a sound one, and must not be ignored. The opposite opinion—however disguised under the name of *liberality* — involves absolute contradiction. Though often grievously misapplied, therefore, the old maxim is essentially true, "There are no martyrs out of the Church." But then the Church is no narrow sectarian organization, no self-assumed infallible patron of orthodoxy, no State Establishment, whether episcopal, presbyterial, or congregational; but *the universal body of evangelical believers*

of every age — the body which recognizes and adores
Jesus Christ as "God manifested in the flesh," "the pro-
pitiation for our sins," and the unchanging "head of all
principality and power."

It may be well to state explicitly what we conceive
to be the essential and invariable elements of true EVAN-
GELICAL CHRISTIANITY. There may be others, but the
four following we regard as both fundamental and vital.
THE SCRIPTURES ONLY, AS THE SUPREME RULE OF FAITH;
FREE JUSTIFICATION IN CHRIST ONLY THROUGH FAITH;
SPIRITUAL REGENERATION ONLY, AS THE ORIGIN OF FAITH;
PERSONAL SANCTIFICATION ONLY, MANIFESTED BY GOOD WORKS,
AS THE EFFECT AND EVIDENCE OF FAITH. These propositions are logically and inseparably linked together,
and constitute one self-consistent organic system of revealed Truth. This system is "the Gospel of Christ."
No other can be substituted for it. It bears on its front
the stamp and seal of the Almighty. It is the power of
God unto salvation to every one that believeth. And of
this it is the Apostle says to the Galatians, "If we, or an
angel from Heaven, preach unto you any other Gospel,
let him be accursed." The man who intelligently and
honestly believes this—lives for it, and dies for it—wherever found, or whatever name he bears, is worthy to be
esteemed by all mankind, as he is by Christ himself, a
"faithful martyr."

But we go farther. The above formulas of fundamen-
tal truth do not exhaust the distinctive principles of a
PURE CHRISTIANITY. There are others that belong to *the
institutions of Christ*, under the New Testament economy.
Such, for example, are the following. UNIVERSAL FREE-
DOM OF CONSCIENCE ONLY AS A CONDITION OF FAITH; BAPTISM
ONLY ON A CONSCIENTIOUS PROFESSION OF FAITH; IMMERSION
ONLY, AS THE PRESCRIBED BAPTISM OF FAITH; BAPTIZED BE-

LIEVERS ONLY, AS THE PROPER MATERIALS OF THE CHRISTIAN CHURCH—the living Body of Christ.

These propositions—to add no more—may be safely said to shine on the face of the New Testament, and to inhere in the very substance of the revealed dispensation under which we live. They are all organically and logically connected with each other, and are essential to the normal or regular *visible constitution* of the kingdom of God on earth. They are the characteristic features of that " kingdom which is not of this world ;" in distinction from all preceding dispensations ; and in contrast with all subsequent forms of religion, founded on human policy, and supported by civil power.

Now what we wish to be remembered is, that any one who, from a good conscience toward God, suffers for *any one of these " words " of Christ*, suffers as a Martyr. He is bound, as a Christian, "to observe *all things whatsoever* " commanded by Christ, even at the hazard of his life, or the loss of it. Unless he thus take up the cross of his crucified Lord, he cannot be a genuine disciple. " He that seeketh to save his life, shall lose it ; and he that loseth his life for my sake," says Christ, "shall keep it unto life eternal." And " Fear not them which kill the body, but are not able to kill the soul ; but fear Him who is able to destroy both soul and body in hell." Hence, our Lord himself—the King of Martyrs—bore testimony to the truth before the Jewish Sanhedrim, although he knew that his death would be the penalty—a death of public infamy, and of unutterable agony. Hence, animated by His Spirit, Peter and John, when summoned before the same council, and forbidden to preach in the name of Christ, made their noble appeal—" Whether it be right in the sight of God, to hearken unto you more than unto God, judge ye ; for we cannot but speak the things which

we have seen and heard." Hence, the intrepid Stephen
laid down his life, under the hands of violence—praying
like his dying Saviour, "Lord, lay not this sin to their
charge." Hence, John the Baptist, for his faithful re-
monstrance against sin, and James, the son of Zebedee,
that fearless "son of thunder," both fell under the bloody
steel of Herod. Thus began, with names never to be forgotten, the long bright roll of New Testament Martyrs.
And thus, from year to year, and from age to age, that
illustrious roll received accessions, from the violence of
Jewish or Heathen persecutors, for three centuries.

But, with only one known exception, all this time, these
Christian Martyrs were BAPTISTS. Neither Christ, nor his
Apostles have left us a single precept or example of Infant
Baptism. This is a conceded fact. The very first Pedobaptists in history—Cyprian of Carthage and his clergy,
(A. D. 253,) did not plead any law of Christ, or Apostoli-
cal tradition, for infant baptism. They put the whole
thing upon analogy and inference—upon the necessity of
infants on the one hand, and the unlimited grace of God
on the other. Their own language is an implied and absolute confession that their "opinion," as they call it, had
no basis in any New Testament law or precedent. It
confesses, in a word, that in advocating the baptism of
literally new-born babes, they were introducing *an innovation into the Church of Christ*—and they defend it only
on the ground of *necessity*.

In stating this historical fact, we are perfectly aware of
the views of Dr. Wall, in favor of a different conclusion.
And we are perfectly aware of the special pleadings by
which he has darkened the clear light of history on this
point. Honest, but prejudiced to the last degree, he has
propagated for a century and a half a host of delusions
among his confiding followers. He has started wrong at

the beginning; and beguiled his own strong intellect by the most unfounded assumptions. His hereditary idea of a State Church is the first grand error—perhaps the real root of all the rest. Then came the convenient argument of Jewish Proselyte Baptism as the model of Christian Baptism—involving a whole series of false assumptions. Then, the language of Christ and his Apostles is tortured, to draw from it meanings it never can have by any fair interpretation.* Then the language of the early Christian Fathers must be put upon the rack, for the same purpose. Could Clement of Rome, Hermas, Justin Martyr, Irenæus, Clement of Alexandria, Tertullian, or Origen himself, rise from the tomb, they would protest with solemn indignation at the *force* that has been put upon their words, and the absolute perversion of their testimony.† Then follows Dr. Wall's ingenious *supposition* to account for the language of Basil, and Cyril—his grand mistake of the testimony of Augustine and Pelagius—and his miserable attempts to set aside the fact, that every distinguished Christian writer of the first four centuries, whose baptism is recorded, was baptized in adult years, on his own confession of faith—a fact that also holds true of every Christian emperor in the fourth century, from Constantine to Theodosius.

The infatuation of Dr. Wall is sad enough; but it is outdone by a writer in the North American Review for January, 1854; who has the weakness to affirm in the

---

* Even the great Schleiermacher says, "He that will find infant baptism in the New Testament, *must first put it there.*" So, in effect, say Neander, Hahn, Hagenbach, Bunsen, and the North British Review.

† The reader will find the clearest evidence of this in the articles of Dr. Sears, in the Christian Review, for March and June, 1838; and still more fully in those of Dr. Chase, in the Bibliotheca Sacra, for November, 1849, and in the Christian Review, for April, 1854.

face of the world—in a lame criticism on Bunsen's Hippolytus—that the evidence for infant baptism " amounts to *historical demonstration !*" The words of the Apostle to Timothy seem here truly applicable : " Now as Jannes and Jambres withstood Moses, so do these also resist the truth. But they shall proceed no further ; for their folly shall be manifest unto all men, as theirs also was." The accomplished scholars of the North British Review, in several recent numbers, have frankly confessed the want of scriptural and early authority for infant baptism ; and have intimated that even the Archbishop of Canterbury himself, appears to be on this point undergoing a process of " *historical conversion.*"*

But there is one *decisive* evidence that the primitive Martyrs for three centuries were Baptists. We refer to the document prepared by Eusebius of Cæsarea, the ecclesiastical historian, for the signature of all the bishops of the General Council of Nice, (A. D. 325). It is found in his own report of the proceedings, addressed to his flock at Cæsarea, as given by Socrates and Theodoret. We subjoin it in Dr. Cave's translation.

" The form *proposed by us*, and which was read in the presence of the most sacred emperor, and seemed to be liked *and approved by all*, was in this manner :—The exposition of our faith, as we have received it from the bishops, who were our predecessors, *both when we were first instructed in the rudiments of the faith, and when afterwards baptized into it ;* as we have learned from the Holy Scriptures, and both believed and taught, not only when we sustained the office of presbyter, but since we came to the episcopal station, so do we still believe, and produce this as the account of our faith : We believe in one God," &c.†

Here is a testimony from the " Father of Ecclesiastical History," produced on the most public occasion, in the pre-

* North British Review for August, 1852.
† Cave's *Lives of the Fathers*, Vol. II. p. 112, Oxford, 1840.

sence of 318 bishops of the Catholic Church, besides near 2000 other delegates, presbyters and laymen, convened from all parts of the world—in the most solemn form and for the most solemn purpose conceivable—that according to Christ's Commission, *instruction in the principles of Christianity, in all cases preceded baptism.*

We have said that there was *one exception.* Cyprian of Carthage, the father of pedobaptism, was a man of God and a martyr. But we affirm, without fear of contradiction, and invite correction if we are wrong, that *he is the only one recorded in the first three centuries.* Indeed, that the "opinion" of this distinguished man in favor of the baptism of babes before the eighth day from their birth, refers *only to cases of immediate danger of death,* is clear, not only from his own words, but also from the fact that Eusebius does not even deem the opinion worthy of mention in his Ecclesiastical History. And, as we have seen, the custom was unknown seventy-two years afterwards, at the Council of Nice. Yet how often is this "opinion" of Cyprian quoted now, as if it were evidence of the *universal prevalence* of pedobaptism in the first ages!

As now, it appears that pedobaptism had "no recognized existence," even in the so-called Catholic Church, until after the Council of Nice, (nor indeed until the time of Gregory Nazianzen, A. D. 363,) so we have no proof whatever that it ever existed in the Pure Churches, or *Cathari,* who separated from the Catholics in the preceding century, in the time of Novatian, A. D. 251. This large body of Dissenters from the Catholic communion, were called Novatians by their adversaries; but as the historian Socrates testifies, they called themselves in Greek, *Cathari,* (in Latin, *Puritani,*) signifying *the pure;* and the name was designed by them to announce the fundamental principle of their separation, which was the preservation cf a pure church membership, communion, and discipline. They held that the Catholics had so departed from the original constitution of the Church in this respect, as to have forfeited their claim to that honor; and hence invariably baptized all who joined them from the Catholic churches. Hence they are the first in history who were called *Anabaptists*, that is, *rebaptizers;* although, of course, they denied the propriety of the appellation, as they believed the baptism administered by a corrupt church to be null and void.*

Much stress has been laid on the fact, that no catalogue of heresies from Irenæus to Epiphanius, (A. D. 180, to A. D. 380,) enumerates any sect as deniers of infant baptism. The facts already established furnish the answer: there was then no such Catholic custom as infant baptism to be denied. Tertullian (A. D. 200), *did* oppose *the innovation of Quintilla,* who would have given baptism to children too young to give proper evidence of piety ; and his voice was not, what it has been strangely misrepresented to be, even by Dr. Schaff, " a solitary voice, without an echo ;" it was the voice of the then Catholic church,

---

* Dr. Wall says, they did not complain of the Catholics for infant baptism : but, as we have seen, for a very good reason, namely, that it did not come into common use for ages after, among the Catholics themselves. Neither do the Donatists—who seceded from the Catholics about sixty years after the Novatians, and for very similar reasons—make any such complaint; although they chiefly resided in North Africa, where Cyprian lived and died, and might be supposed to sympathize with him in opinion and practice. Dr. Wall takes this for proof that they were all Pedobaptists—a consequence of his own previous assumptions. All the positive evidence he adduces, is the canon of a Council which belongs to the *fifth* century ; when some of them may be supposed to have fallen in with the prevailing practice of the State Church, though contrary to the distinctive spirit and tendency of their own secession.

against which none replied.* How could they indeed, when the catechumenical course was universally established, as necessary before baptism?

It is time that men of learning and candor abandoned all such unhistorical positions, and inconsequential reasonings. Infant baptism is an error from beginning to end; corrupt in theory, and corrupting in practice; born in superstition, cradled in fear, nursed in ignorance, supported by fraud, and spread by force; doomed to die in the light of historical investigation, and its very memory to be loathed in all future ages by a disabused Church †. In the realms of despotism it has shed the blood of martyrs in torrents; that blood cries against it to heaven; and a long-suffering God will yet be the terrible avenger. The book before us is a swift witness against it.

Down to the time of Constantine, with the solitary exception of Cyprian, as we have shown, all the martyrs—and their number has been computed at three millions—were BAPTISTS; though with various shades of error gradually gathering over them from the beginning of the third century — perhaps earlier. Already the corruption in Rome, and Carthage, had become so great — not in the *ordinances*, so much as in the *membership* — as to

---

* This whole subject of infant baptism, and the true theory of the sacraments, in Dr. Schaff's otherwise admirable History, needs, and will, we trust, yet receive from its esteemed author, a thorough revision.

† In no boastful spirit, but in the spirit of a martyr before God—stung by the solemn conviction of duty, after thirty-five years of earnest and impartial investigation on this subject—to speak out "the truth, the whole truth, and nothing but the truth"—we nail these THESES to the door of every Pedobaptist Church in Christendom; and challenge all the Christian scholarship of the age, not to ignore, evade, or deny them, but to face the inevitable trial, summon the witnesses, sift the evidence, and, if it can, disprove all, or any one of them. And may God help the right.

2

have led to two great Secessions, for the sake of purity, namely, the Novatians, and the Donatists.* When Constantine and Licinius first came into power, (A. D. 312,) they gave equal religious toleration to all their subjects. But the attempt to settle the controversy in North Africa, between the Catholics and Donatists by imperial intervention, (A. D. 316,) was a departure from this impartial protection and equality before the law ; and from that fatal moment, persecution began under the Christian name. The Emperors, whether Orthodox or Arian—the Bishops armed with imperial commissions, whether Orthodox or Arian—became the persecutors of their brethren of the opposite faith. The Pure Churches, (*Cathari,*) —confessedly orthodox in all things else—refused all the attempts to bring them into the ROMAN CATHOLIC IMPERIAL CHURCH, organized and established by Constantine ; and although for a long time honored and protected by the Catholics themselves, for their virtues, began in the fifth century to feel the heavy hand of Catholic intolerance. Socrates, in his Ecclesiastical History, (A. D. 445,) though he records their sufferings from the Arians in the fourth century, tells us that Innocent I., Bishop of Rome, in the reign of Honorius, "was the first persecutor of the Novatians at Rome, many of whose churches he took away." The same course was pursued by Celestinus, (A. D. 421,) as well as by Cyril, bishop of Alexandria, (A. D. 412).

If, now, we inquire into the cause of this persecution, we shall find it mainly owing to *the increased zeal for infant baptism,* awakened by the writings of Augustine in this age. Other causes, doubtless, combined with this; but no one who reads the canons of the Council of Carthage at which Augustine presided, (A. D. 414,) one of

* See *Mosheim's Commentaries,* &c., for a careful examination of these Secessions. Also, *Lardner, Robinson,* and *Neander.*

which runs in the following terms : " WE WILL that whosoever DENIES THAT LITTLE CHILDREN BY BAPTISM ARE FREED FROM
PERDITION AND ETERNALLY SAVED, that they be ACCURSED,"
can question this. Other evidence in confirmation, if
necessary, might be adduced from the letters of Augustine
himself. From this influence came, also, the edict of
Honorius, and Valentinian III. (A. D. 413,) forbidding *re-
baptism*, (as it was termed,) throughout the Roman empire, under the penalty of death. This edict, though aimed
especially at the Donatists — whose numerous and flour-
ishing churches were nearly ruined by its rigorous enforce-
ment—was soon applied to the Novatians, whose practice
it had always been to baptize those who came over to them
from the Catholic churches. *From this time, therefore,*
THE PURE CHURCHES, *became the victims of perpetual persecutions from the hands of the Roman Catholics.*

"The first result of the protectorate of the Christian
Emperors," says the Chevalier Bunsen, "was, that in their
codes they converted church ordinances, (that about baptism, for instance,) into statute laws. Thus Justinian,
in the beginning of the sixth century, ordered new-born
infants to be baptized, under a penalty for neglecting it;
*a law which still passes for a Christian principle in the
code of many a Christian State.* Evangelical and Christian freedom thus received its death-blow, from the same
police crutch which was given it for support."*

Under Roman laws like these, enforced as they were
in the Middle Ages, with new and most sanguinary edicts
in all the States of Europe, what multitudes must have
become MARTYRS, may be conjectured from what occurred
at the Reformation, when Baptist martyrs were counted
by tens and even hundreds of thousands.

We are now gravely told by historians that, from the

* Bunsen's Hippolytus, Vol. III., p. 249.

sixth century, the *Cathari* began to decline; and we are told or led to infer, that they ceased to maintain their pure distinctive principles, and gradually merged in the Roman Catholic Church. Not a shadow of proof is offered for this assertion or inference, but that they disappear from the notice of Roman Catholic writers. But the northern "barbarians," (as they are called,) who broke the Roman Empire into ten kingdoms, for a long time refused subjection to the Bishop of Rome, and gave religious toleration to their subjects. Especially was this the case with the Ostrogoths in Italy, under the long and happy reign of Theodoric the Great — when all Italy flourished like a garden. (A. D. 491–527.)

Afterwards, in the East, the Saracens did the same thing, especially to that branch of the succession of the pure churches which went under the name of PAULICIANS. These last maintained themselves, even under the Greek-Roman emperors, amid the fires of persecution, for at least six hundred years, (from A. D. 653, to A. D. 1260,) indeed till lost to view by the conquest of the empire by the Turks. The Free Cities of Europe generally—the Italian Republics of the Middle Ages—the Moors in Spain —and the Princes of Provence, or Southern France—all these at times, and even for long periods, gave protection to the persecuted Baptists; who were known alike by their original name of *Cathari*, THE PURE; and by the subsequent names of Paulicians, Paterines, and Poor Men of Lyons, down to the beginning of the twelfth century—as appears from the successive edicts issued against them.*
At this point of time they were joined by some illustrious

---

* We do not quarrel with Neander for his lamentably distorted and contradictory account of the "Catharists," and some other denominations, of the Middle Ages. He was not satisfied with it himself. His candor would have set all right; but he wanted the real key to the problem.

reformers from the Church of Rome, such as PETER DE BRUIS, (A. D. 1104 to 1124,) HENRY and JOSEPH, his disciples, (A. D. 1116 to 1148,) and ARNOLD OF BRESCIA, A. D. 1135 to A. D. 1156,) with whom the present volume begins its "Memorials of Baptist Martyrs."

From the rapid review we have now taken of the history of Baptist Martyrs from the beginning, we gather some interesting conclusions:

1. That the Baptists have no difficulty whatever in tracing up their principles and their churches to the Apostolic age. It has been often said by our enemies, that we originated in the German city of Munster, in 1534. Lamentable must be the weakness or ignorance of such an assertion, come from whom it may. It were easy to cite eminent Pedobaptist historians, to refute this calumny—especially Limborch and Mosheim, of the last century. But we prefer to quote two historians of the present century, selected by the King of Holland to draw up a history of the "Origin of the Dutch Baptists," for the use of the government. Dr. Ypeig, professor of theology at the University of Groningen, and Dr. J. J. Dermont, chaplain to the king—both of the Dutch Reformed Church—in the authentic volume thus prepared, and published at Breda, in 1819, come to the following deliberate conclusions:

"The Mennonites are descended from the tolerably pure evangelical Waldenses, who were driven by persecution into various countries; and who, during the latter part of the twelfth century, fled into Flanders, and into the provinces of Holland and Zealand, where they lived simple and exemplary lives—in the villages as farmers, in the towns by trades—free from the charge of any gross immoralities, and professing the most pure and simple principles, which they exemplified in a holy conversation. *They were therefore in existence long before the Reformed Church of the Netherlands.*" Again: "We have now seen that the Baptists, who were formerly called Anabaptists, and in later times Mennonites, were the original Waldenses; and who have long in the history of the Church, re-

2*

ceived the honor of that origin. ON THIS ACCOUNT THE BAPTISTS MAY BE
CONSIDERED AS THE ONLY CHRISTIAN COMMUNITY WHICH HAS STOOD SINCE
THE DAYS OF THE APOSTLES; AND AS A CHRISTIAN SOCIETY WHICH HAS
PRESERVED PURE THE DOCTRINES OF THE GOSPEL THROUGH ALL AGES.
The perfectly correct external and internal economy of the Baptist denomination, tends to confirm the truth, disputed by the Romish Church,
that the Reformation brought about in the sixteenth century, was in the
highest degree necessary ; and at the same time goes to refute the erroneous notion of the Catholics, that their communion is the most ancient."*

Let it be remembered that the learned men who say
this, and say it aloud in the ear of majesty, after diligent
investigation, are not themselves Baptists.   It is a confession of the rarest candor.   "Their rock is not as our rock,
our enemies themselves being judges."

But what it has cost the Baptists thus to keep their
churches pure, through all ages, amidst abounding corruption, heresy, schism, tyranny and persecution, this book
of Baptist Martyrs will in some measure show.

2. Baptist principles have always flourished wherever
the ruling powers have allowed them toleration. Baptists, it is true, have often lighted up the darkness of history by the flames of their martyrs, and compelled the notice of Chronicles and of Councils, by the very vastness,
variety, and intensity of their sufferings. Again and
again, as in the primitive times, has the blood of the martyrs been the seed of the Church ; but when a little breathing space has been given them in any quarter of the
world, they have sprung up like the grass from the scythe
of the mower ; or, rather, as the oak which has bowed its
lofty head beneath the axe, again renews its branches, its
towering trunk, its verdure and its strength.   Witness

---

* It is an interesting fact that as a consequence of this, the government of Holland offered to the Mennonite churches the support of the
State. It was politely, but firmly declined, as inconsistent with their
fundamental principles.—See Ward's Farewell Letters, 1821.

their rapid growth in the East, in the seventh century—in Italy and France in the twelfth—in all Europe in the sixteenth—under the English Commonwealth in the seventeenth—and in the United States from the period of the American Revolution.*

3. The Baptists have not only their own Martyrs, but it is clear that from the time of Christ down, they have furnished the purest, the most magnanimous, and the most numerous martyrs of all Christendom. This is true from the days of the Apostles, and throughout the Middle Ages. Hear what a Roman Catholic prelate, Cardinal Hosius, president of the Council of Trent, says on this subject, to the Protestants of the Reformation:

"If you behold their cheerfulness in suffering persecution, the Anabaptists run *before all* the heretics. If you have regard to the number, *it is likely that in multitude they would swarm above all others, if they were not grievously plagued, and cut off with the knife of persecution:* If you have an eye to the outward appearance of godliness, both the Lutherans and the Zuinglians must needs grant that they *far pass them:* If you will be moved by the boasting of the word of God, these be no less bold than Calvin to preach; and their doctrine must stand aloft above all the glory of the world, *must stand invincible above all power,* because it is not their word, but the Word of the living God."†

4. We see another fact, which gives a peculiar and glorious feature to our denomination. Much as the Baptists have suffered from others, *they have never retaliated*—never, when in power, pleaded for the principle of persecution, or put it in practice; but have stood forth, among persecuting sects, solitary and alone, as the fearless champions and examples of liberty of conscience. This they have done, too, on settled Scriptural principles, peculiar to

---

* Those who think to do battle against the Baptists as a modern, reactionary, ephemeral sect, will find themselves greatly mistaken.

† Struggles and Triumphs of Religious Liberty, p. 88.

their views of baptism ; and hen:e have pleaded for liberty
of conscience to the fullest extent.   Witness the periods
of their power in Italy—in Armenia, Syria and Asia
Minor—in Southern France—in the Mediæval Roman
Republic—in Poland in the sixteenth century—in England, Ireland, and especially Rhode Island, in the seventeenth—in the United States at the formation of the
American Constitution ; and since then in the new Con-
stitutions of the States—in several of which States they
were a clear majority as a denomination.   No sect, whose
origin dates back two centuries, can share with them this
glory.   The Quakers, the Moravians, and the Methodists,
are of more recent origin.   The principle of religious
liberty—a distinguishing principle of the Baptists in all
ages—we are however happy to add, is now universally
adopted by other denominations in the United States—
and is fast spreading over the world.

    5. The Baptists—though for the most part of the
poor of this world, rich in faith only, and unknown to
fame, as were the primitive Christians—have yet, in almost
all ages, had of their number men of the most eminent
learning and ability, who died as martyrs to the faith.
From the time of Novatian, indeed, it has been customary
with their adversaries to call the whole body by the name
of its most distinguished leader—as if they were only a new
sect, of which he was the originator.   Thus the *Cathari*
were called Novatians—then Paulicians—then Petrobrus-
ians, Henricians, Josephists—then Arnoldists—Waldenses
—Lollards—Mennonites ; nor were they ever permitted to
bear their present name of BAPTISTS, until after their legal
toleration, in England, in 1688.   Yet to them, as we have
seen, belong all the inspired writers of the New Testament—the sources of our Christian literature—Matthew,
Mark, Luke, John, James, Jude, Peter, and Paul himself,

the accomplished pupil of Gamaliel. To them belong all the Christian writers of the second century, including Justin Martyr, Irenæus, Clement of Alexandria, Tertullian, and in the next age, Hippolytus, and even Origen himself. And from the time of the Pure Secession, in A. D. 251, they can produce names among the noblest. Novatian himself had no superior in his own time—as his remaining writings show. But most of their writings have perished. The same persecutions that robbed them of their churches, liberty, and lives, suppressed their schools, and their books—leaving them only that one Book from which they would never part—the foundation of their principles, the guide of their practice, and the support of their hope, amid the terrors of martyrdom—THE BIBLE. Churches supported by the State, with stereotyped creeds, canons, and forms, could afford to do without the Bible ; but the Pure Churches, in their sublime dissent and protest, could not.

6. We learn that the Baptists have A GLORIOUS PAST, whose history is yet almost unwritten ; and that, rising from the deep roots of the Past, and spreading with the spread of the Scriptures, and of spiritual religion, aided by historical investigation, and by universal liberty, they have in reserve A GLORIOUS FUTURE. All they want now, in every country on earth, is that same freedom which they have ever given, and rejoice to give, to ensure the ultimate triumph of their principles. As surely as many shall run to and fro, and knowledge be increased—as surely as the light of the moon, according to the beautiful figure of the prophet, shall be as the light of the sun, and the light of the sun sevenfold, even as the light of seven days—as sure as the time shall come that the saints shall possess the kingdom—and the spirits of the martyrs shall live again in their successors on earth, and reign with Christ for a

thousand years—so sure, judging from all the past, and all the present, is the final triumph of Baptist principles. Based on the book of God, in a fair field nothing can stand before them. Already they are winning from all others in the United States, in a steady stream of success*—they are reforming more thoroughly the Reformation in Europe—in Africa, and Asia, in the isles of the ocean, and indeed at every point where earnest piety is pressing on to the conversion of the world, they are gaining power—and the prospect now is, that they will soon be spread over the entire East, including India, Burmah, Siam, and China—nations comprising more than half the population of the globe. So, O Lord, let thy kingdom come!

7. But if these things be so, Baptists have a sacred duty to perform; first to themselves, and then to all Christendom. They must seek among themselves to revive THE MARTYR SPIRIT—"not the spirit of fear, but of power, and of love, and of a sound mind." They must present their bodies, with their souls, their hearts and all their substance, a living sacrifice to God, holy and acceptable, which is their reasonable service. They must not be conformed to this world, but transformed by the renewing of their mind and practice in a more eminent degree. They must better estimate the worth of their own Scriptural principles, the glory of their past history,

* It is recorded by Luke, as an evidence of the triumph of Christian Truth in the days of the Apostles, that "the disciples multiplied greatly, and a great company of the *priests* were obedient to the faith."

A competent writer has affirmed recently, that the number of *members* received into the Baptist churches, for some years past, from other denominations, exceeds 2000 *annually ;* and that the number of *ministers* so received by change of conviction, is *equal to one for every week in the year.* This great movement is in principle the very reverse from that of Bishop Ives and the Puseyites. And it is in addition to about 50,000 converts yearly. See *Christian Review*, January, 1854.

.nd the grandeur of their position and destiny. They must examine, and cultivate themselves more perfectly, by the help of the Holy Spirit—"that they may know what is the hope of their calling, and what is the riches of the glory of God's inheritance in the saints." They must more fully honor, love and pray for the Lord's people of every name; and study to do them good, to profit by all the grace that is in them, and seek to supply what is yet lacking in their knowledge, faith, or practice. They must more fully display that charity which suffereth long and is kind ; which envieth not ; which vaunteth not itself, is not puffed up, doth not behave itself unseemly; which seeketh not her own, is not easily provoked, thinketh no evil; which rejoiceth not in iniquity, but rejoiceth in the truth ; which beareth, believeth, hopeth, endureth all things. This is the true spirit of Martyrdom—without which we may give all our goods to feed the poor, and our bodies to be burned, and it profiteth us nothing.

This was the spirit of the BAPTIST MARTYRS, whose memorials will be found in this book. No memorial of this kind has before appeared in this country, or even in England. Though confessedly far from complete—embracing no sufferers for Christ, but those who suffered unto death— going back only to the Middle Ages in time, and limited to Europe as its field, and on that limited theatre preferring the principle of *selection* to that of accumulation —it will be found to embrace a great variety of the most authentic and heart-touching, as well as pure, noble and triumphant examples of the principles of our faith and the power of the Gospel. It gives us names in which, for Christ's sake, Baptists may justly glory, and which the world itself "will not willingly let die." To specify no more—here is ARNOLD OF BRESCIA, the brightest name of Italy in the Middle Ages—JEROME OF PRAGUE, the most

accomplished man of his time—and HUBMEYER OF RATIS-
BON, the friend of Erasmus, the fellow-laborer of the first
Reformers, classed by the Romanists themselves with
Luther, Zuingle, and Calvin, as one of the four great
leaders of the Reformation.   Inferior in rank and learning, but not in interest, is the wise and good HANS OF
OVERDAM—the bright youthful JACQUES DOSIE of Leuwarden—the loving but faithful JERONIMUS SEGERSON of Antwerp—and the sturdy, outspoken, English yeoman, RICHARD
WOODMAN of Sussex, whose mind seems as strong as the
iron that he worked in his daily toil.   Of the softer sex,
nere is the gentle but heroic ELIZABETH OF LEUWARDEN—
MARIA OF MONJOU, happier than a bride in the hour of her
martyrdom—ANNE ASKEW, of the noblest blood of England, but still nobler by her Christian faith and fortitude
—and ELIZABETH GAUNT, the never to be forgotten martyr
to evangelical Christian Charity, whose name has been
embalmed by Bishop Burnet.

Richard Baxter somewhere says, that he "could as
soon die for Charity, as for any article of the Creed."
While he was *uttering* this just and beautiful sentiment,
Elizabeth Gaunt was *exemplifying it in the flames*, at Tyburn.   The picture of her martyrdom forms the appropriate frontispiece of this volume; which is also embel-
lished by engravings of the drowning of Maria of Monjou,
and of the examination of Anne Askew in the Tower of
London, and of her suffering at the stake in Smithfield.

There are many noble names, of Baptist Martyrs, that
we miss here; but we cannot have everything, in a single
volume of the size of this.   We doubt not this excellent
book will be warmly welcomed by every genuine Baptist
in the Union.

PHILADELPHIA, May 1, 1854.

PREFATORY NOTE.

———◦●◦———

THE contents of this volume have been principally drawn from the old works on martyrdom : such as, "FOXE'S *Acts and Monuments*," and "BRAGHT'S *Dutch Martyrology*," together with the more modern sources of CROSBY, IVIMEY, MANN, JONES, BENEDICT, UNDERHILL, TAYLOR, TONNA, PUDDICOMBE, etc., etc. The selections have been made to secure as much of interesting incident, evangelical truth, and enlightened opposition to error, as could be comprised in a moderate sized volume; and the object kept constantly in view has been to stimulate to holy and energetic action the Christians, and especially the Baptists, of these United States.

It will be observed by the careful reader of this volume, that considerable pains have been taken to authenticate its statements, both general and denominational. We believe that no reasonable doubt can exist in reference to any of the principal facts here stated, or as to each and every one of these holy martyrs belonging to the Baptist body

Generally speaking, the evidence of this last fact is overwhelming. To a New Testament Baptist, it must afford no small gratification, and the highest ground of thanksgiving to God, that our scriptural principles have been so fully tested, and have come out pure from "the fiery trial."

To the Historical Essay which precedes the work itself, and which was written by the esteemed Editorial Secretary of the American Baptist Publication Society, the attention of the reader is earnestly requested. He will there find the enunciation of facts and principles which may well lead to serious reflection and persevering action.

The labor given to this volume will not have been lost, if, under the Divine blessing, the spiritual interests of individual readers, and the highest prosperity of our beloved country, are, in any degree, advanced by its instrumentality.

B.

Philadelphia, 1854.

CONTENTS.

———◦●◦———

(27)

CHAPTER III.

CHRISTIAN WOMEN MARTYRS ON THE CONTINENT OF EUROPE.

CHAPTER IV.

CHRISTIAN MEN MARTYRS IN ENGLAND.

CHAPTER V.

CHRISTIAN WOMEN MARTYRS IN ENGLAND.

Engravings.

———◦●◦———

Flung to the heedless winds,
Or on the waters cast,
Their ashes shall be watched,
And gathered at the last:
And from that scattered dust,
Around us and abroad,
Shall spring a plenteous seed
Of witnesses for God.

Jesus hath now received
Their latest dying breath;
Yet vain is Satan's boast
Of victory in their death.
Still, still, though dead, they speak,
And, triumph-tongued, proclaim
To many a wakening land
The one availing Name.

BAPTIST MARTYRS.

INTRODUCTORY REMARKS.

A CERTAIN class of men who have risen up within the last forty years, and whose direct object seems to be, if possible, to lead Christians back to Rome, have spoken lightly of the martyrs of past ages. Over such perversion of mind in such men, we can scarcely wonder, but must deeply grieve; for, as a recent writer on this subject has well said, "If ever men have won for their memories the meed of honest praise, it was those self-devoted and lion-hearted martyrs for the truth, who counted not their lives dear unto themselves, but stood their ground in the forefront of the battle, valiant for the truth even till they fell, and in falling conquered."

Manifold indications show us that both in this country and in Europe, a war of principles—a great moral contest between Protestantism, so called, and Popery, is at hand; and that the opposing parties are likely to engage in the conflict with great energy. We earnestly hope that the friends of truth will show a warm adherence to its simple and powerful principles, and that they will look to heaven for the strength and wisdom they need.

(31)

Among the means employed to animate the
Christian warrior in the battle, and to impress the
minds of surrounding spectators, the presentation
of the examples of the "great cloud of witnesses"
for the truth, who have sung the praises of God in
the prison, calmly submitted to the agonies of the
rack, or gone with cheerfulness to the stake for the
glory of Christ, has always produced a mighty effect. It is true that science, yes, and false religion,
also, have had their martyrs, who thus gave evidence of their sincerity; but did they ever compel
the profligate persecutor to admit the truth, and to
admire the spirit of ardent piety? Did they ever
compel those who had till then been unbelievers
in the Gospel, to seek the pardon of their sins, and
bring them forward to be baptized in the room of
the dead? Look at the results of the death of
Stephen on its immediate spectators, and on the
Church and the world ever since; and see how, in
all ages, the blood of the martyrs has increased,
purified, and elevated the body of Christ.

We cannot read the accounts of martyrs, to
which the reader is now introduced, without a conviction that wherever religion flourishes in the soul
of a man, there is the spirit of martyrdom, evinc-
ing itself in his temper and conduct. Self-denial,
and readiness to bear the cross, will always be essential to a true Christian character. There may
be martyrdom without the rack, the prison, or the
stake; but the spirit cannot exist unless there be
a readiness to endure these things, if need be. "I
am ready," said one of our missionaries, at his or-

dination, "I am ready, if called, to die in the missionary field; unless I enter it I can have no peace; engaged in the labor, I can die in triumph." Such is the spirit which becomes those who are acknowledged by Jesus Christ as his brethren.

It cannot but afford high gratification to every devoted Baptist, that the body to which he belongs has in every age furnished most zealous adherents to the cause of Christ, and that multitudes have literally "glorified God, in the fires." Cardinal Hosius, one of the Pope's presidents at the Council of Trent, says, "if the truth of religion were to be judged of by the readiness and cheerfulness which a man of any sect shows in suffering, then the opinion and persuasion of no sect can be surer than that of the Baptists; since there have been none for these twelve hundred years past that have been more grievously punished, or that have more cheerfully undergone, and even offered themselves to the most cruel sorts of punishments, than these people."

"Anabaptists," says old Bishop Latimer, afterwards himself a martyr, "were burned in different parts of the kingdom, and went to the stake with good integrity."

In reading the records of the martyrs as handed down to the present age, by writers of different persuasions, the Baptist Christian usually meets with some difficulty in recognizing his own brethren and sisters. On the one hand, some of the principles which peculiarly distinguished .the old Baptists, such as the sovereignty of Christ in his

Church, the sufficiency of the Scriptures to guide men into all truth, the right of private judgment in all matters of religion, and the entire freedom of every man to act for himself, under his responsibility to God, have, in whole or in part, been embraced by some who were not immersed; and on the other, very many Baptists have died without their practical testimony to the purity of Christian ordinances being recorded. Good old "Father Foxe," in his "Actes and Monuments," conceals, where he can, the views of our fathers on their peculiarities; and when he cannot do this, he labors to extenuate and excuse what the good old man personally considered "the errors of the anabaptists." Still, however, the facts are sometimes developed, even by himself, and in other instances by contemporary writers; so that no small difficulty presents itself in making a selection from the great number of those who died not only for the Gospel, but also to keep in the Church "the ordinances as they were delivered."

It will be seen by the reader, as he proceeds in the perusal of this volume, that the spirit of martyrdom is distinguished by a supernatural principle, which the apostle Paul calls *faith*, and upon which he suspends the purity, the self-denial, and the sufferings of the illustrious patriarchs, the noble army of martyrs, the persecuted Church of God, from the beginning to the hour when he sat down to write to the Hebrew Christians. This principle does not spring from any known natural source, but is superior to human philosophy, persuasion, and conviction. It is th3 full and entire belief of God's own testimony, produced in the heart by the influence of the Holy Spirit.

Hence, the spirit of Christian martyrdom rests on a supernatural support. God is present to give special help. Hence Latimer, who had long been bowed down by the infirmities of age, stood upright and firm at the stake; and hence the timid and delicate female has forgotten her feebleness, and shown, as the fire has burnt around her, indomitable courage and strength.

This spirit, too, is associated with a supernatural prospect. It embodies, and realizes, and appropriates the invisible things of an eternal world. It presents even the Deity himself present to the mind, who fills from his fullness all its faculties. Like Moses, the martyr endures " as seeing Him who is invisible;" and this makes the present state shrink before the soul into comparative insignificance. Such men have always been " strong in the Lord and in the power of his might."

How different from all this is the spirit of persecution. In all ages " they that will live godly in Christ Jesus must suffer persecution;" but who can survey the monster and his triumphs without the profoundest horror and indignation? The offspring of Satan, the birth-place of persecution was hell. Vile in its own nature, and in its objects, it is cherished by those who delight to scatter arrows, firebrands, and death, wherever they go. Persecution preys only on the virtuous; it grasps after victims of no other kind; and, as

though tired of its own existence, it aims with one
effort to devour them all, and thus like the ana-
conda, with one mighty meal, to finish its work,
and procure its own death. It is driven from the
dwellings of sincerity and truth, and is cherished
only by hypocrisy and falsehood. It converts the
world, as far as it prevails, into a moral aceldama;
but it often defeats its own purposes by exhibiting
its odious features and its execrable allies too publicly. "He that sitteth in the heavens shall
laugh" at the designs of this enemy; He holds it
"in derision," and overrules its operations to purposes of his own glory.

Many who have filled the seat of government,
and who have supposed that their subjects were
bound to submit to their rule, however arbitrary
and opposed to the liberty which is the birthright
of every man, have made the religion of the cross
itself a mere instrument of accomplishing their
tyrannical purposes; thus forgetting their responsibility to God and man. They have linked the
Church to the State, and have sought to make
every will bow to their caprice, or determined to
subdue the opposer by their frown.

It is a wise arrangement of Divine Providence
that persecution is allowed to delight in *public*
cruelty, and to rejoice in what it esteems to be the
disgrace of its victims. A professor of the religion of Jesus could not, in the times of papal
persecution, recant, as, under the influence of the
dread of suffering, some did, without carrying the
badge of it about his dress till his dying day. The

records of persecution describe to us those who abjured the faith of Christ, and who were condemned to bear a fagot during their lives. These persons were fastened to a stake by the neck with towels, and their hands held fast, while they were marked on the cheek with a hot iron, which was called *branding ;* after which they were compelled to wear a fagot of sticks, indicating their near escape from burning, worked or painted on the left sleeve of their outer garment, and if at any time they laid it aside the law adjudged them to be burnt.* What must be the character of the religion which sanctions all this; and which lays claim to its reception by the whole world!

It cannot be otherwise than ˙gratifying to my

---

* It may not be without its use to copy a list of the *expenses* of martyrdom, two or three centuries ago, in our fatherland. The thoughtful reader will not merely regard it as a *curiosity*, but will devoutly thank God that, whatever may be in the future, we have not the immediate prospect of the public money being spent in this manner in our own happy country.

When Strype wrote his " *Memoirs of Archbishop Cranmer*," in the year 1693, he found the book in which the expenses of the martyrs, during their residence in Oxford, were entered by the bailiffs of the city, was in existence; and it is probably still preserved among the manuscripts of that University. The sums paid for the burning of Archbishop Cranmer and his two fellow-sufferers, Ridley and Latimer, appear in the book as follows :—" For one hundred of wood fagots, 6s. ; for one hundred and a half of furze fagots, 3s. 4d. ; to the carriage of them, 8d.; to two laborers, 1s. 4d. ; to three loads of wood fagots to burn Ridley and Latimer, 12s. ; one load of furze fagots, 3s. 4d. ; for carriage of these four loads, 2s. ; a post, 1s. 4d. ; for chains, 3s. 4d.; for staples, 6d. ; for laborers, 4d." The above are exact transcripts from the bills by the person who had charge of the funeral piles.

4

readers, that these introductory remarks should close with the following lines, by the Earl of Surrey, who was called to suffer in the reign of the capricious tyrant, Henry VIII., and who wrote them in prospect of that solemn event, over which, however, he could happily triumph.   We may call it

THE MARTYR'S HYMN.

My life's a shade, my days
Apace to death decline ;
My Lord is *Life*, he'll raise
My dust again, e'en mine.
        Sweet truth to me,
            I shall arise,
            And with these eyes
        My Saviour see.

My peaceful grave shall keep
    My bones till that sweet day
I wake from my long sleep,
And leave my bed of clay.
        Sweet truth to me,
            I shall arise,
            And with these eyes
        My Saviour see.

My Lord—his angels shall
    Their golden trumpets sound,
At whose most welcome call,
    My grave shall be unbound.
        Sweet truth to me,
            I shall arise,
            And with these eyes
        My Saviour see.

I said, sometimes with tears,
  Ah me! I'm loth to die;
Lord, silence thou those fears;
  My *Life's* with thee on high.
    Sweet truth to me,
      I shall arise,
      And with these eyes
    My Saviour see.

What means my trembling heart
  To be thus shy of death?
My Life and I sha'n't part,
  Though I resign my breath.
    Sweet truth to me,
      I shall arise,
      And with these eyes
    My Saviour see.

Then welcome, harmless grave,
  By thee to heaven I'll go,
My Lord—his death shall save
  Me from the flames below.
    Sweet truth to me,
      I shall arise,
      And with these eyes
    My Saviour see.

CHAPTER I.

ARNOLD, OF BRESCIA.

Seven hundred years, seven hundred years,
  Since Truth and Rome together strove ;
Since Heaven beheld Italia's tears,
  And ARNOLD spoke the words we love !

He spoke ;—and Italy arose,
  Thrilled by her prophet's voice of flame;
Religion triumphed o'er her foes,
  And Freedom sung her ARNOLD's name

But ah, the Martyr's voice was hushed,
  His ashes strewed the Tiber's flood;
Truth, Freedom, Right, by Power were crushed,
  And Rome was drunk with holy blood !

                 J. N. BROWN.

ABOUT the year 1137, a reformer appeared in Italy, who proved himself a powerful opponent to the Church of Rome ; and who, in fortitude and zeal, was inferior to no one bearing that name, while in talents and learning he excelled most. This was Arnold, of Brescia; a man remarkable for force of piety and austerity of manners.

In early life he had traveled into France, and studied under the renowned Peter Abelard. On leaving this school, he returned into Italy, assumed

(40)

the habit of a monk, and began to propagate his opinions in the streets of Brescia, where he soon gained attention. He especially directed his zeal against the wealth and luxury of the Roman clergy, and his noble eloquence soon roused the inhabitants of Brescia, who revered him as the Apostle of religious liberty, and rose in rebellion against the tyranny of the bishops. The Romish Church took alarm at his bold attacks, and in a Council condemned him to perpetual silence.

Arnold now left Italy, and found an asylum in the Swiss canton of Zurich. Here he began his system of reform, which was never more needed. For a while he was successful, converting even the Pope's Legate; but the influence of the famous Bernard, Abbot of Clairvaux, made it necessary for him to leave the canton.

The bold man now conceived the plan and hazarded the desperate experiment of visiting Rome, and fixing the standard of reform in the very heart of the capital. In this measure he so far succeeded as to win over the Senate and effect a popular change of the government. The Pontiff struggled hard to maintain his ascendency, but at length sunk under the pressure. Eugenius III. withdrew from Rome, and Arnold, taking advantage of his absence, impressed on the people the necessity of setting bounds to clerical authority. Arnold's sentiments were influential among the people, and on a few of the clergy. But not being prepared for freedom, they carried their measures to an extreme, abused the clergy, and burnt their property.

4*

They required all ecclesiastics to swear allegiance to the new constitution. "Arnold," says Gibbon, "presumed to quote the declaration of Christ, that *his kingdom was not of this world.* The abbots, the bishops, and the Pope himself, must renounce their *state*, or their salvation."

At length, in 1155, the Pope laid an interdict on the city. As the sword was no weapon in Arnold's panoply, the noble champion retired to Tuscany. There he was seized, brought back to Rome, condemned, crucified, and burnt. His ashes were thrown into the Tiber.

The clergy triumphed in his death, and with his ashes, it was thought, that his sect was dispersed. Yet his noble spirit of religious freedom did not die, but was cherished with his memory in the hearts of reforming spirits in future generations, such as Wickliffe, Huss, and their compeers. And even his immediate followers did not become extinct, for the ARNOLDISTS are often met with in ecclesiastical history as a body who were worthy of his name, and of our high respect.

Many very decisive facts show Arnold to have been a Baptist. Bernard accuses his followers of mocking at infant baptism. Evervinus, in Germany, also says "the Arnoldists condemn the [Catholic] sacraments, particularly baptism, which they administer only to the adult; alleging that place, whoever shall believe and be baptized shall be saved." And, in a word, Arnold himself was formally condemned by the Lateran Council for rejecting infant baptism.

JEROME, OF PRAGUE.

THIS remarkable man was the intimate friend and companion of the celebrated John Huss, in the early part of the fifteenth century. He was in early life distinguished for the pursuit of knowledge, and spent many years in the Universities of Prague, Paris, Heidelburg, Cologne, and Oxford. At the latter university he became acquainted with the works of Wickliffe; he translated them into his native language, and on his return professed warm adherence to his views. In addition to the fact stated in a letter written to Erasmus from Bohemia, that the followers of Huss "admit none until they are dipped in water, and they reckon one another, without distinctions of rank, to be called brothers and sisters," and the statement by Robinson, that the sermons of Huss were full of "anabaptistical errors," as they were called, and that many of his followers became Baptists, Orchard tells us that he was baptized by immersion by some of the Greek Church. This view of Jerome's creed, and the fact of his being a layman, will account for many historians omitting his name altogether. But this omission may well be pardoned while we have a full and satisfactory account furnished by some of his strongest enemies.

When Jerome heard, while at a distance, that his beloved friend John Huss was in danger be-

fore the Council of Constance, in 1411, he fled to
his help, and was soon apprehended, and tried in
company with him, and both were sentenced to
death. Huss, however, suffered some months before him. There seems to have been a period
when, like Cranmer, Jerome's faith faltered, and
he recanted; but his adherence to the Saviour was
soon renewed, and he died at the same stake where
his dear friend Huss had been sacrificed to Christ.
"The sanguinary annals of the human race," says
Bonnechose, "do not, perhaps, present any specta-
cle more odious than the funeral pile of Jerome."

Poggius, who was secretary to the Pope, a frank,
ingenuous man, saw and heard Jerome in the
council, and wrote, in a letter to his friend Leonard
Aretin, a eulogium on him in a spirit of admira-
tion and love. He says, "Since my return to
Constance, my attention has been wholly engaged
by Jerome, the Bohemian heretic, as he is called.
The eloquence and learning which this person has
employed in his own defence, are so extraordinary,
that I cannot forbear giving you a short account
of him. To confess the truth, I never knew the
art of speaking carried so near the model of ancient
eloquence. It was, indeed amazing to hear with
what force of expression, with what fluency of
language, and with what excellent reasoning, he
answered his adversaries. Nor was I less struck
with the gracefulness of his manner, the dignity
of his action, and the firmness and constancy of
his whole behavior. It grieved me to think so
great a man was laboring under so atrocious an

accu ation. Whether this accusation be a just one,
God knows: for myself, I inquire not into the
merits of it: resting satisfied with the decision of
my superiors. But I will just give you a summary
of his trial.

"After many articles had been proved against
him, leave was at length given him to answer each
in its order; but Jerome long refused, strenuously
contending that he had many things to say previ-
ously in his defence, and that he ought first to be
heard in general; before he descended to particulars. When this was overruled, 'Here,' said he,
standing in the midst of the assembly, 'here is justice—here is equity! Beset by my enemies, I am
pronounced a heretic. I am condemned before I
am examined. Were you Gods omniscient, instead of an assembly of fallible men, you could
not act with more sufficiency. Error is the lot of
mortals; and you, exalted as you are, are subject
to it. But consider, that the higher you are exalted, of the more dangerous consequence are
your errors. As for me, I know I am a wretch
below your notice; but at least consider, that an
unjust action in such an assembly will be of dangerous example.' This, and much more, he spoke
with great eloquence of language, in the midst of
a very unruly and indecent assembly; and thus
far, at least, he prevailed; the council ordered that
he should first answer objections, and promised
that he should then have liberty to speak. It is
incredible with what acuteness he answered, and
with what amazing dexterity he warded off every

stroke of his adversaries. Nothing escaped him : his whole behavior was truly great and pious. If he were, indeed, the man his defence spoke him, he was so far from meriting death, that, in my judgment, he was not in any degree culpable. In a word, he endeavored to prove, that the greater part of the charges were purely the inventions of his adversaries. Among other things, being accused of hating and defaming the holy see, the pope, the cardinals, the prelates, and the whole estate of the clergy, he stretched out his hands, and said, in a most moving tone, ' On which side, reverend fathers, shall I turn for redress ? Whom shall I implore ? Whose assistance can I expect ? Which of you hath not this malicious charge alienated from me ? Which of you hath it not changed from a judge into an inveterate enemy ? It was artfully alleged indeed ! Though other parts of their charge were of less moment, my accusers might well imagine, that if this were fastened on me, it could not fail in drawing upon me the united indignation of my judges.' "

It appears from this secretary, Poggio Bracciotini, that on the third day of his trial, Jerome obtained leave to defend himself. " He first began with prayer to God, whose assistance he pathetically implored. He then referred to profane history, and to unjust sentences given against Socrates, Plato, Anaxagoras. He next referred to the Scriptures, and exhibited the sufferings of the worthies: and then he dwelt on the merits of the cause pending, resting entirely on the credit of witnesses,

who avowedly hated him; and here his appeal
made a strong impression upon the minds of his
hearers, and not a little shook the credit of the
witnesses. It was impossible to hear this pathetic
speaker without emotion. Every ear was capti-
vated, and every heart touched. But wishes in
his favor were vain; he threw himself beyond the
possibility of mercy. Braving death, he even provoked the vengeance which was hanging over
him. Through this whole oration, he showed a
most amazing strength of memory. He had been
confined almost a year in a dungeon, the severity
of which usage he complained of, but in the language of a great and good man. In this horrid
place, he was deprived of books and papers ; yet
notwithstanding this, and the constant anxiety
which must have hung over him, he was at no
more loss for proper authorities and quotations,
than if he had spent the intermediate time of
leisure in his study."   In his defence, " his
voice was sweet, distinct, and full; his action
every way the most proper, either to express indignation or to raise pity, though he made no affected
application to the passions of his audience. Firm
and intrepid, he stood before the council, collected
in himself, and not only contemning, but seeming
even desirous of death. The greatest character in
ancient story could not possibly go beyond him.
If there is any justice in history, this man will be
admired by all posterity. I speak not of his errors:
let these rest with him. What I admired was his
learning, his eloquence, and amazing acuteness.

God knows whether these things were not the groundwork of his ruin.

"Two days were allowed him for reflection; during which time many persons of consequence, and particularly my lord cardinal of Florence, endeavored to bring him to a better mind. But persisting obstinately in his errors, he was condemned as a heretic.

"With a cheerful countenance, and more than stoical constancy, he met his fate; fearing neither death itself, nor the horrible form in which it appeared. When he came to the place, he pulled off his upper garment, and made a short prayer at the stake; to which he was soon after bound, with wet cords and an iron chain, and inclosed as high as his breast in fagots. Observing the executioner about to set fire to the wood behind his back, he cried out, 'Bring thy torch hither. Perform thy office before my face. Had I feared death, I might have avoided it.' As the wood began to blaze, he sang a hymn, which the violence of the flames scarcely interrupted.

"Thus died this prodigious man. The epithet is not extravagant. I was myself an eyewitness of his whole behavior. Whatever his life may have been, his death, without doubt, is a noble lesson of philosophy."

To this account of Jerome, furnished by an enemy to his faith, we have only to add that he suffered martyrdom, May 20, 1416.

FELIX MANTZ.

THIS distinguished man, a leader in the Reformation in Germany, was a native of Zurich, and was educated in all the learning of the age, his father being a canon of the great minster in the place of his birth. In 1519 we find him studying the Hebrew language with the eminent Zuingle, under the tuition of Carlstadt, and to have been on terms of intimacy with that Reformer, as well as with Myconius, Capito, and other leaders of the Swiss Reformation.

About the year 1522, he began to doubt as to the scriptural character of infant baptism, having many conversations on that subject with Zuingle, who was at first inclined to embrace the same views. The progress of his investigations led him further to object to tithes and usury, and to desire to lay aside the peculiarities of Rome more rapidly than was consistent with the opinions of Zuingle. This led to a separation, and to a final adoption, on the part of Mantz, of the sentiments of the Baptists. In 1523, he began to preach publicly on the subject of baptism, and to urge the necessity of a church constituted in accordance with the word of God. "He wished," says Zuingle, "to form a church free from sin." In this way did the reformer express the sentiment of Mantz—that a church of Christ should consist of believers

5   (49)

baptized into Christ, and of them only. Mantz likewise objected to the presence and use of secular power in the church of God.

In the three disputes held at Zurich during the year 1525, Mantz appears to have taken part, and after that of March, to have been thrown into prison, from which, however, he escaped. His pious reference to the escape of Peter by the assistance of an angel, as in some measure applicable to his own, gave his enemies occasion to assert, that he said an angelic being had likewise opened to him the gates of his prison-house.

He now diligently proclaimed the freeness of the gospel in different parts of Switzerland, and taught the true constitution of the church. He was baptized by Blaurock, a companion in suffering; and in the fields and woods, as occasion offered, with the Hebrew and Greek Scriptures in his hand, he expounded the word of God to the people who flocked to him. As this was contrary to the prohibitory command of the magistrates of Zurich, he was deemed a rebel against legitimate authority, and an exciter of the people to sedition.

Towards the end of 1526, he was seized and imprisoned in the tower of Wellenberg. He confessed that he had baptized contrary to the edict. It was right, he said, to obey God rather than man. Exhibiting no sign of repentance, he was at last adjudged, and on the 5th of January, 1527, was drowned.

Bullinger thus writes, " As he came down from

the Wellenberg to the fishmarket, and was led
through the shambles to the boat, he praised God
that he was about to die for his truth; for anabap-
tism was right, and founded on the word of God,
and Christ had foretold that his followers would
suffer for the truth's sake. And the like discourse
he urged much, contradicting the preacher who
attended him. On the way, his mother and brother
came to him, and exhorted him to be steadfast; and
he persevered in his folly, even to the end. When
he was bound upon the hurdle, and was about to
be thrown into the stream by the executioner, he
sung with a loud voice, 'Into thy hands, O Lord,
I commend my spirit.' And herewith was he
drawn into the water by the executioner, and
drowned. His body was then taken to the Place
and buried at St. Jacob's." "It is reported here,"
says Capito, writing to Zuingle, near the end of
the same month, "that your Felix Mantz hath suffered punishment, and died gloriously; by which
the cause of truth and piety, which you sustain, is
weighed down exceedingly."

Mantz left behind him a paper, written in his
last days, with a view to encourage his companions
in their sorrows, which the reader will be glad to see.

"My heart rejoiceth in God, who giveth me
much understanding, and guideth me that I may
escape eternal and endless death. Wherefore I
praise thee, O Christ, Lord of heaven! that thou
succorest me in my affliction and sorrow; which
Saviour God hath sent me for an example and a
light, who hath called me before my end is come,

to his heavenly kingdom, that I might have eternal joy with him, and love him in all his judgments, which shall endure both here and hereafter in eternity, without which nothing avails or subsists. Therefore are there so many, who not having this are deceived with a vain opinion. But, alas! nowadays, we find men who boast themselves of the gospel, speak much of it, teach and publish it, to be full of hatred and envy; who have in them no divine love, whose deceit is known of all the world, even as we have been told, that in these last days, they that come to us in sheep's clothing are ravening wolves, who hate the godly in the earth, and hinder the way of life and to the true sheepfold. Thus do the false prophets and hypocrites of this world; with the mouth they curse and with the same mouth likewise pray, whose life is bad; these call upon the magistrates to put us to death, and herewith they destroy the body of Christ. But I will praise the Lord Christ, who hath all patience with us. He instructeth us with his divine grace; he showeth, after the nature of God, his heavenly Father's love to all men, which none of the false prophets can do.

"Herein must we observe the difference; the sheep of Christ seek the honor of God. This they choose. They suffer not themselves to be hindered by gain or temporal good, for they are in the keeping of Christ. The Lord Christ forces no man into his glory; but the willing and ready alone enter, who come thereto by true faith and baptism. When a man bringeth forth the true fruits of repentance, for him is purchased and procured, by Christ, through grace, the heaven of everlasting joy, by the shedding of his innocent blood, which he so willingly poured out. Thereby he showeth us his love, and endueth us with the might of his Spirit; and he who receiveth and exerciseth this, groweth and becometh perfect in God.

"Love to God, through Christ, will alone endure and profit; no boasting, railing, or threatening. There is nothing but love with which God is pleased. He who can show no love shall find no place with God. The true love of Christ shall cast off the enemy. It is set before him who will be an heir with Christ, that he must be merciful, even as his heavenly Father is merciful. Christ never accused any one, as the false teachers now do ; whence it appears that they have not the love of Christ, nor understand his word. Yet they will be shepherds and teachers. But at last they must tremble, when they find that eternal pain will be their reward, if they do not amend.

"Christ never hated any, and his true servants likewise hate no one, continuing thus to follow Christ in the right way, as he has gone before them. This light of life they have before them, and rejoice to walk therein ; but those who are full of hatred and envy, who thus wickedly betray, accuse, smite, and wrangle, cannot be Christians. These are they who as thieves and murderers run before Christ, and under a false show shed innocent blood. Thereby may men know them, they take no part with Christ. for through malice, as the children of Belial, they annul the command of Jesus Christ; as Cain slew his brother Abel when God accepted his offering.

"Herewith I will finish my discourse, and request all the pious to meditate on the fall of Adam, who followed the serpent's counsel; and being disobedient to God, death followed him. So shall it also befall those who receive not Christ, but oppose him;—who love this world, and have no love to God. With this I conclude. I will abide close to Christ and confide in him; he knoweth all my distresses, and can help me out of them Amen."

GEORGE WAGNER.

GEORGE WAGNER, of Emmerick, was appre
hended at Munich, in Bavaria, on account of four
articles of faith. First, that the priests cannot forgive men their sins : secondly, he did not believe
that a man can bring God from heaven: thirdly,
he did not believe that God, or Christ, is bodily in
the bread that the priest places upon the altar;
but that it is the bread of the Lord : and fourthly,
he held not the belief that the baptism of water
saves men.

Because he would not retract his articles, he was
put to great torture, so that the prince had great
compassion upon him, personally visited him in
prison, and earnestly exhorted him, saying, that
if he would recant, he would call him his friend
during his life. In like manner the steward of the
prince's household persuaded him to recant, and
made him many promises. Finally, his wife and
child were brought into the prison and placed before him, to move him thereby to a recantation.
However, he could not be moved, but said, that
though his wife and child were indeed so dear to
him, that the prince with his whole land could not
purchase them from him, yet nevertheless he would
not forsake the Lord his God. Many priests and
others also visited him to persuade him to renounce
what were considered his erroneous doctrines, but

(55)

he continued firm and immovable, and was finally condemned to die by the flames.

When he was delivered over to the executioner, and led into the middle of the city, this excellent man said, "This day will I confess my God to the glory of Christ Jesus, that such happiness is afforded me in the sight of all the world." His face was not pale, nor were his eyes distorted. With a smile playing on his lips he went to the fire, where the executioner bound him to the ladder, and hung a bag of gunpowder to his neck; and when he had taken leave of a Christian brother, he was thrust into the fire, and calmly yielded up his spirit to Christ, February 8, 1527.

The historian of this event tells us that the sheriff, whose name was Der Eisen Reich, of Landsberg, wishing, while riding home from the burning of Wagner, to seize some of the companions of the martyr, with a view to their suffering death also, died suddenly in the night, being found dead in his bed. "Thus," saith our author, "he was snatched away by the wrath of God."

A few further particulars of Wagner cannot be uninteresting to the reader. As the day of his martyrdom dawned, two executioners entered his cell, to draw him to the place of burning. At the same time some Franciscan monks entered with them, and forced themselves on the condemned man, in their usual way, to instruct and prepare him for his last hour. But he begged them to return to their cloister, as their services were entirely useless to him. At the steps of the court-house, what they called his erroneous propositions were again read to him, and he was once more entreated to recant: but he still remained immovable.

Among the Catholics who sought to recall Wagner to Popery was one Conrad Schaider, the master of St. Peter's school in Munich, and a doctor of divinity. He asked him, "My dear George, art thou not afraid of the death to which thou wilt so soon be exposed? If thou wert now free, wouldst thou not most joyfully return to thy wife and children?"

GEORGE.—Were the judges to let me go free, ah! to whom would I rather hasten than to my wife and dearest children?

CONRAD.—Recant, then, and thou shalt go free.

GEORGE.—My wife and children are indeed so dear, that the duke, at no price, not even for the revenue of his land, could purchase them of me; but for the great love of God I will willingly let them go.

As they came to the place of execution, Conrad again addressed him: "Believe," said he, "in the mystery of the altar, and do not say that it is a mere sign." "I confess," said Wagner, "that the sacrament is a sign and emblem of the body and blood of Jesus Christ, who suffered the death of the cross for our redemption."

"George, what thinkest thou?" continued the teacher; "thou holdest baptism to be nothing, and yet thou knowest that Christ was baptized in Jordan." George then showed the design of

Christ's baptism, and how it was necessary, in
order to redeem sinners, for Christ to die on the
cross. " Even that Christ," he continued, " is my
Saviour; for faith in whom I to-day yield up myself, and whom to-day with a good confession before all, I will glorify."

Conrad made other attempts to bring George
Wagner to the admission of what he called the
mystery of the altar; and failing in that, to persuade him to open his heart to a confessor, in
order to obtain absolution. After a short time,
Doctor Conrad commenced, in a clear voice, the
repetition of the Lord's prayer, to which Wagner
responded as follows :—

Conrad.—Our Father ! who art in heaven.

George.—My God ! thou art truly our Father,
and no other; to-day I long to be with thee.

Conrad.—Hallowed be thy name!

George.—O my God ! how little and how coldly
is thy name hallowed !

Conrad.—Thy kingdom come!

George.—To-day, I hope, to my great joy, to
enter therein.

Conrad.—Let thy will be done on earth as it is
in heaven!

George.—My Father ! I am willing that thy will
be done, not mine.

Conrad.—Give us to-day our daily bread.

George.—Jesus Christ is the true and heavenly
manna. He will feed me to-day.

Conrad.—Forgive us our trespasses, as we forgive them that trespass against us.

GEORGE.—I forgive with my whole heart, all that my friends or enemies have ever done against me.

CONRAD.—Lead us not into temptation, but deliver us from evil.

GEORGE.—O good God! with out doubt thou wilt to-day deliver me; for in thee alone I trust.

In a similar way Wagner responded to the repetition of the creed. On arriving at the place of execution, Doctor Conrad gave a parting pledge, that if George would only express his belief in the use of prayers for the dead, he would say a mass for him. But George besought his prayers for him while he was yet alive, that God would grant him patience, courage, and a Christian's faith to endure the punishment of death which awaited him.

The executioner now seized him and bound him to the ladder; but he continued to declare to the spectators the chief points of Christian truth. When some Christian brethren who were present, requested him to give them from the midst of the fire some token of his firm and unshaken faith, he answered, " This shall be the strongest mark of my faith in Jesus Christ, that so long as I can open my mouth I will not cease to praise God, and confess the name of my Saviour." When thrown into the flames, he cried with a loud voice, "Jesus! Jesus!" As the executioner cruelly turned him, he often repeated, with a clear emphatic tone, the name of Jesus. **Thus he died.**

LEONHARD KEYSER.

WHILE in the sixteenth century, the believers in Jesus on the continent of Europe, greatly increased in number and purity, as the sanctified result of persecution, there were some instances very strikingly illustrative of the power of the gospel.

Among these we may mention a learned Catholic priest in Bavaria, named Leonhard Keyser. Guided by the Spirit and Providence of God, he was led to study the writings of Zuingle and Luther, and afterwards to visit Wittemberg, and converse with the evangelical doctors of that city, with whom he also communed in the Supper of the Lord. Returning into Bavaria, and observing the doctrines and conduct of the Baptists, as well as of Luther and of Zuingle, he took up the cross, and united with the Baptists, the separated church of the Lord, in the year 1525. And immediately, with great power and zeal, he proceeded in his ministry, undismayed by all the tyranny exerted against the faithful by water, fire, and sword.

In the second year of his ministry among the Baptists, Keyser was apprehended at Scherding, on the river Inn, about eight miles south of Passau, and by the bishop of the last named place, with other priests and prebendaries, was condemned to the flames on the Friday before the day of St. Lawrence, in August of the same year. The chief

(60)

heads of accusation against him were, that faith alone justifies, without good works; that there are only two sacraments; that the gospel was not preached by the papists in Germany; that confession is not God's command; that Christ is the only satisfaction for sin; that there is no purgatory; that Christ is the only Mediator; and that all days, (alluding to feast or saints' days), are alike with God. At the trial of this worthy minister of Jesus Christ, a criminal was brought to swear against him that he deserved to die.

The enemies of truth conducted Keyser to the stake bound on a cart, followed by the priests. They spoke to him in Latin, but he answered them in German, for the sake of the people at large, in which language they would not speak at his trial, though he more than once demanded it.

When he came to the field outside the town, and was approaching the fire, he bent on one side over the cart, and gathered a flower, bound as he was, and said to the judge who rode on horseback by the side of the cart;—"My lord, I have plucked a flower; if you can burn me and this flower, then have you righteously condemned me; but otherwise, if you can neither burn me nor this flower in my hand, then reflect on what you have done and repent." The judge, with three executioners, therefore threw many fagots of wood, more than ordinary, into the flames, in order by a great fire to burn him immediately to ashes; but when the wood was entirely consumed, his body was taken out of the fire unburnt. The three executioners and their servants then took fresh wood, and made a large fire, which being consumed, his whole body still remained unburnt, his hair only had been burnt and his nails turned brown. The ashes being brushed from his body, it was smooth and clear, and the flower was found unfaded in his hand, not the least burnt. The executioners then hewed his body in pieces, and threw the pieces into a new fire, which again being burned out, the very pieces lay unconsumed in the fire. Lastly, they took the pieces and threw them into a running stream called the Inn. The judge was thereby so terrified, that he resigned his office, and left the place. His principal servant, who was with the judge, having seen and heard this, came himself to us in Moravia, became our brother, lived a godly life, and so died. Our teachers took this down from his mouth, and wrote it for a memorial, and now to the honor of God, publish it and make it known.

Such is the account furnished by Van Braght, the historian of the Dutch Baptist Martyrs; which is substantially confirmed by Frank, J. P. Twisck, and the distinguished Martin Luther, who some months afterwards seems to have been induced, by various prevalent reports, to examine into the matter. He says, "They now came to the gravel upon the river Inn. Upon the gravel, near to the gibbet, the layers of wood for the burning were prepared. As an arm of the river encircled the gravel, Keyser was placed on a cart and the executioner with him, that they might cross over it. When placed

in the circle, he expressed his hearty forgiveness
of all those who had brought him there, as he
hoped for forgiveness of God. He exhorted the
people to pray earnestly with him for all his enemies. He entreated the pardon of any whom he
might have offended in his life, or by his example;
also that they would pray for him, that he might
die in the exercise of a firm Christian faith. He
further prayed for those who were not yet enlightened. The sheriff interrupted him, and said
to the executioner, 'Make an end of it, thou
knowest what is commanded thee.'

"Leonhard was soon undressed, and lay down
in his shirt in a small cavity in the wood pile.
He was then bound upon the wood. As they
bound him, he besought the people to sing, ' Come,
Holy Spirit,' etc. A popish priest, who had before been sent away, again approached him, and
said, 'If in aught he had erred, he should pray to
God for mercy.' Leonhard made no reply. The
priest asked, ' Would he die as a pious Christian?'
Answer: ' Yes.' The priest then exhorted him
on baptism. The fire was kindled, and from its
midst, with loud cries, he said, ' Jesus, I am thine,
save me.' After this, his hands, feet, and head
were burnt away. As the fire diminished, the executioner took a pole, and rolled off the body, then
laid more wood on the fire. The executioner next
hewed a hole in the body, then thrust in a sword.
Afterward he stuck the pole in the body, and again,
on the pole, lifted it up on the pile, thus consum-
ing," etc.

Thus abruptly, as Mr. Underhill has remarked, ends Luther's narrative, and some other blanks in it lead to the conclusion, that his information substantially agreed with the first printed one. The same writer very properly adds, "We do not see in Luther's account anything but what may easily be reconciled with the other, allowing for the certain difficulty of any two persons, on such an occasion, pressed on all sides by a curious crowd, being witnesses of precisely the same events, and the consequent discrepancy (apparently so at least) in their accounts which must ensue. Many singular and marvellous events are related by martyrologists of the sufferers of those times, as may be seen in the '*Actes and Monuments of* JOHN FOXE.' They were regarded by the persecuted as tokens of divine favor, and were repeated from mouth to mouth to animate each other in the bitter trials through which they were called to pass." We may add, that, whatever view the reader may take of this extraordinary statement, we see no reason to doubt the credibility of the witnesses.

SICKE SNYDER, OR FREERKS.*

In the month of Frebruary, 1531, the harboring of any Baptist preachers in the Netherlands was forbidden by authority, and a reward offered for their apprehension. An edict was issued immediately after this, directing that those who having been *rebaptized*, as it was termed, recanted, were to be admitted to mercy, but the obstinate were to be punished with the utmost severity.

Soon after this became known, a devoted disciple of Christ, a staunch champion in his Master's cause, usually called Sicke Snyder, separated himself from the ungodly church of Rome, and from her false and fanciful worship. He resolved on walking in the footsteps of the true Lawgiver, and only to hear his voice, as speaking in the Scriptures. Conforming himself to the appointment and example of Christ, he received Christian baptism on confession of his faith, as a token of being a regenerated child of God, and as testifying his holy obedience.

As the consequence of this act, he became a prisoner in bonds at Leeuwarden, in Friesland,

* Freerks seems to have been the proper name of this man, as appears not only from historians, but from the record of his sentence in the court book of Friesland. Snyder, as he was usually called, is indicative of his trade, which was that of a Tailor.

and endured much suffering from the adversaries
of the truth. And as he could not, by the torments
he sustained, be persuaded to apostatize, he was
there put to death by the sword, displaying great
firmness in testifying to the truth, and showing its
power on his soul by the manner of his death.
His sentence is thus recorded in the criminal sen-
tence-book of the court of Friesland:—" Sicke
Freerks, on this 20th of March, 1531, is condemned
by the court to be executed with the sword, his
body shall be laid on the wheel, and his head set
upon a stake, because he has been rebaptized, and
perseveres in that baptism."

The effect of the martyrdom of this poor but
pious man, who does not appear to have been even
a minister, was very important, as it first led the
mind of the distinguished MENNO SIMON to more
Scriptural views of baptism than he had formerly
entertained. He himself says :—" It now happened,
that I heard from some brethren that a God-fearing
pious man, Sicke Snyder by name, had been beheaded at Leeuwarden, because he had renewed
his baptism. This sounded wonderfully in my
ears, that any one should speak of another baptism. I searched the Scriptures with diligence,
and reflected earnestly upon them, but could find
no trace of infant baptism."—See the " Life and
Times of Menno," by the Rev. J. Newton Brown,
recently published by the American Baptist Publication Society.

ELLERT JANSEN.

THE arrival of the emperor, Charles the Fifth, in the Low Countries, in the year 1540, was the signal for the renewal of the grievous persecutions which had already been endured by the Protestants of Holland. Several severe proclamations were issued against both the persons and writings of the so-called Anabaptists, on whom this persecution chiefly fell. It contiuued with unrelenting rigor and barbarous cruelty for more than fifteen years. During this period the faith of the sufferers was strengthened by the Christian ministrations of the eminent Menno Simon, who found refuge in the habitations of his companions in tribulation, from the unceasing pursuit of his foes. The following narratives are but specimens of the courageous piety of that age and country.

In the year 1549, there lay in prison, at Amsterdam, on account of religion, about twenty persons, called Anabaptists, all of whom, but five men and three women, made their escape, by the help of some kind and sympathizing friends.

A certain tailor, named Ellert Jansen, might have escaped with these his companions, but he refused, saying, "I am now so well satisfied to be offered up, and feel myself at present so happy, that I do not expect to be hereafter better prepared." He was lame in one of his legs, and

(67)

thought that though he might escape, he would be easily discovered and retaken ; he therefore stayed behind, and was burnt on the 20th of March 1549, with the other four men and three women, according to their sentence, " For that they had suffered themselves to be rebaptized, and had wrong notions of the sacraments."   As he was being led to execution, he cried out, " This is the most joyful day in my whole life."

EELKEN AND FYE.

In the year 1549, about three weeks before Easter, two excellent men of the Baptist body were apprehended in the town of Olde Boor, in West Friesland; their names were Eelken and Fye. They were brought before the magistrates, and there boldly confessed their faith. They first asked Eelken, Who has given you permission to collect the people together to instruct them?

ANSWER.—God has permitted me.

QUESTION.—What have you taught?

ANSWER.—Ask those who heard it, what was taught among us; for you have apprehended a woman who heard it.

They then asked the woman what she had heard from Eelken.

ANSWER.—He read the four Evangelists, Paul, Peter, John's epistles, and the works [Acts] of the Apostles.

Eelken was then again examined.

QUESTION.—What do you hold concerning the Sacrament?

ANSWER.—I know nothing of your baked God.

QUESTION.—Friend, consider what you say; for these words will cost you your life. What do you hold concerning the Mother of God?

ANSWER.—Much.

(69)

QUESTION.—What say you, did not the Son of God receive flesh and blood from Mary?

ANSWER.—No. I hold that which the Son of God himself testifies thereof.

QUESTION.—What is your judgment of our holy church of Rome?

ANSWER.—I know nothing of your holy church, and I acknowledge it not. In the whole of my life, I have never been in a holy church.

QUESTION.—"You speak very bitterly; I am concerned for you;" said a gentleman of the council, "and fear your life will be forfeited. Have you not been baptized?"

ANSWER.—I have not been baptized; but I earnestly desire to be.

QUESTION.—What do you think of those false teachers who go about, and baptize people?

ANSWER.—Of false teachers I do not approve; but I have greatly longed to hear a teacher sent of God.

They said, "We have, however, heard that you were to be a teacher."

Eelken asked, "Who has made me a teacher?" and they told him they did not know. Eelken said, "Do you ask me, since you know it not? How then should I know it? I know no one who has made me a teacher; but God has given me all those things for which I have prayed to him." They said, "We have now written down all the articles that we have at this time demanded of you; if there be anything therein for which you are sorry, we will readily take it out." The ques-

tion in reply to the nobleman was, "Do you think,
then, that I would deny God?"

Eelken and his companion, Fye, both received
sentence; and as soon as they were brought together they embraced, yea, kissed each other's
hands and feet with great affection, so that all
were astonished who saw and heard it. The
capuchin friars and servants ran and said to the
magistrates, "Never did persons love each other
like these." Eelken spoke to Fye, saying, "Dear
brother, do not reproach me for having been the
occasion of your being brought into suffering."
Fye answered, "Dear brother, do not think that:
for it is the power of God."

After the sentence was pronounced, they were
kept till the third day. Eelken was executed first
by the sword. While the sentence upon Fye
was being read, he heard nothing of it by reason
of his great joy; and not knowing what was done,
or about to be done with Eelken, he sang and
leaped, praising and thanking God; and said,
"This is the only way."

They now led Fye to the ship in which Eelken
lay beheaded, and the wheel on which he should
be laid, and also the stake at which Fye was to
stand to be burned. In the ship his hands were
unbound. But though he sat still, the monks
said, "Bind him again." The executioner said,
"Do you bind him;" but the constable of the
castle ordered him to bind Fye again. A woman
who saw it greatly wept; but Fye said, "Weep
not for me, but for your sins." Turning to the

executioner, he asked, "What will you do to me?" The answer was, "That you will see." "Yes, yes," said Fye, "do what you please. I have already committed myself to the Lord's hands."

He was now attended by some of his brethren, who had accompanied many of the common people. Fye, seeing some of his acquaintances, called out, "Friends, rejoice with me over such a marriage feast as is provided for me." As he ascended towards the gallows, some of the brethren spoke to him, and greatly rejoiced with him, saying, "This the narrow way; this is the winepress of the Lord; to this belongs the crown." But when the constable of the castle heard the shout, he cried out, "Let no one touch them, on forfeiture of life and goods." The executioner having forgotten his implements, ran into the town to fetch them.

In the meantime, the constable, with the two monks, had got Fye into the confessional, annoying him with bread and wine, but they could not prevail on him to take any, for he did nothing but sing and speak, praising and thanking God. Unable to succeed, and the executioner having returned, they said to Fye, "How is it that you are so obstinate, seeing you say you are a member of Christ? Will you not then do such a work of mercy, as to receive this bread and wine as wine and bread for our sake?" He answered, "For your bread and wine I do not hunger; food is prepared for me in heaven." Finding they could not overcome his determined spirit, they said,

"Go, heretic; go." The constable said, "I have in my life seen many a heretic; but never a more obstinate one than this."

Fye standing ready to meet death, said to the executioner, "Master, have you completed your work?" He answered, "Not yet." Fye said, "Yes, here is the sheep with which you have to do." The executioner then went to him, and tore open his shirt; next he took the cap from his head, and filled it with gunpowder. Fye, standing at the post at which he was to be strangled, exclaimed, "O Lord, receive thy servant!" Whereupon he was strangled, and then burnt. Thus did he pass to his beloved Lord. The common people cried out, "That was a pious man! If he was not a Christian, there is not one in the whole world!"

HANS, OF OVERDAM

This admirable man was put to death at Ghent, in 1550. The following account of his imprisonment and pretended trial was written by himself, and cannot fail to afford both interest and instruction to every reader whose heart is under the influence of genuine piety.

Hans, of Overdam, with his fellow prisoners for the testimony of Jesus Christ, wishes to all his brethren and sisters in the Lord, grace, peace, and ardent love from God the Father, and the Lord Jesus Christ, to whom be praise, honor, and majesty, for ever and ever. Amen.

And you, the best beloved of my heart, be not cast down on my account; but praise the Lord that he is to me so good a Father, that, for the testimony of Christ, I am permitted to suffer bonds and imprisonment, and hope likewise to ascend to him from the flaming pile. The Lord strengthen me by his Holy Spirit. Amen.

My heart's wish, the deepest desire of my soul, is, O dear brethren and sisters in the Lord, that you always give increasing diligence to fulfill the vocation by which you are called by God the Father, through Jesus Christ, to the majesty and glory of the kingdom of his beloved Son, who has purchased the church with his own blood; and given himself for it, that he might sanctify and

(74)

cleanse it with the washing of water by the word ; that he might present it to himself a glorious church, not having spot or wrinkle, or any such thing, but that it should be holy and without blemish.

Therefore, O my dear friends, behold what great love the Father hath bestowed upon us, that he has not spared his only Son ; and how Christ has so willingly given himself, to suffer for us the most shameful death of the cross, and to shed his precious blood, in order to wash and cleanse us from our sins. Oh! dear brethren and sisters, let us regard this ; let us diligently watch and pray, that the saving grace of God, and the unspeakable love of the Father and of Christ, be not neglected or forgotten by us, through any temporal anxieties or perplexities of this world, its lusts and desires, which kill the soul; so that as spots or wrinkles we should be removed from the glorious Church of Christ; yea, as unfruitful branches be cast into fire. For, dearly beloved, it is not enough that we have received baptism on the confession of our faith, and by that faith have been ingrafted into Christ, unless we hold fast the beginning of our confidence steadfast unto the end. Is there, therefore, one who feels that he is become a spot or wrinkle, let him see to it, and hasten before that day overtake him, as a snare for the bird, and repent with unfeigned grief and sorrow ; and lift up the hands which hang down, and the feeble knees, and run with vigor the race set before him, that what is lame be not turned out of the way, but

rather that it become sound and strong. Let us
pass the time of our pilgrimage here in the fear of
God, and keep ourselves unspotted from this vile
and sinful world, which is full of deceit, snares,
and nets, which the devil employs to deceive the
souls of men, to entrap them by various kinds of
lust and delusions.

O Lord, defend thy pilgrims, who walk hoping in
thee, from this murderer, and expect help and comfort from thee alone. O heavenly Father, through
Jesus Christ our Lord, wilt thou fulfill the good
work which thou hast begun in us to the praise
and glory of thy holy name. O thou almighty and
eternal God, how surpassing all understanding is
thy mercy, and thy fatherly compassion towards
them that fear and love thee! O Father! who
would not fear such a God, who knoweth how to
deliver them that are his, although they seem here
for a short space to be forsaken, despised by all,
rejected and accursed in this world! Yet he forsakes not his own, but gives them comfort by his
Holy Spirit in their hearts, which makes us bold
and joyful to suffer reproach for his name's sake.
And we hope, through the goodness of God, that
our pilgrimage will speedily be ended, and we be
released from this miserable world, this vale of
tears, and the earthly house of this our tabernacle
be dissolved, that we may be at home with our
heavenly Father, and receive the crown of eternal
life which is set before us, and which we trust
shall by no creature be taken from us. May we
for this be strengthened by the almighty and eter-

nal God, the Father of mercies, through Jesus Christ our Lord. Amen.

Understand, dear friends, what happened to me before my imprisonment, and how they have dealt with us since I have been in confinement.

It happened at the time that four friends were offered up, when I wrote a hymn, and I had seen them burnt, that I heard it said that the other friends who still remained in prison had been assailed with greater subtlety and deception, by advice of the false prophets, who have always in their thoughts the devil's craft, which indeed they had boasted they would practise. Our friends who remained there were two young servants and a young girl. We were very diligent in daily prayer for them, fearing lest by some deceitful allurement they should be beguiled. We were also daily apprehensive that they would be put to death. I was much exercised in mind, on account of their youth, to go and stand in front of the scaffold where they should suffer, that in case they were in anything cast down I might be able to comfort them, and rebuke the monks who greatly distress our friends when led out to suffer death. But, alas! the poor young creatures were not advanced so far; they incautiously suffered themselves to be led into disputations with the false prophets, notwithstanding they had been sufficiently warned to avoid such discussions as they valued their souls, for every one has not the gift of disputation. Boldly to confess the truth, as it has been received from the Lord, becomes the Christian well.

7*

The poor lambs, however, having er.tered into discussion, became confused in their consciences, and in consequence fell away from the truth. The false prophets acquired great renown by this, as having won their souls, and brought them again into the "holy church." Hearing that, I was much cast down in mind and spirit on account of the loss of the poor sheep, and because the false prophets and the council gloried so much in the fall and ruin of the poor lambs and sucklings, to which they had been brought by means even of oaths, as you shall hear.

Thus cast down, I made my complaint to God, groaning over the power and violence of the devil, which he employs by the hands of his children who believe not the truth; and it came into my mind that I would write some short letters, and placard them in some public place, rebuking their vain triumph over the loss of the poor sheep whose souls they had murdered. I then began to write, and in writing my soul became so inflamed, that instead of a short piece of a hand's breadth, it grew to an address of a whole sheet. The Lord opened my understanding, so that I was surprisingly led to show the magistrates, from the Scriptures, their punishment and end, with that of the whole Romish church. I also said that I wished and desired the opportunity of a public disputation with all their learned men before a large fire, and that whoever should be vanquished should be thrown into the fire, while the poor lambs should be left in peace, and that they should lay aside the sword of the magistrate, and strive alone with the sword of the word of God.

When this writing was put in order, I allowed the brethren to see it, who were well pleased with it, and had six copies of it taken by a brother who could write better than myself. In the mean time the poor corrupted sheep were let out of prison, having recanted every thing. One young servant died the same day he was released, a mile from the town, and became an example or mirror to those who thus seek to save their lives. At the time this took place, I came from Antwerp with Hansken Keeskooper, having arranged our matters with relation to the letter, which we sent to the magistrates of the town on Saturday evening. Two copies were posted in the middle of the town, that every one might read them. We greatly praise and thank the Lord who enabled us to do this before we were apprehended, for we were all betrayed by a Judas who was amongst us, and who seemed to be the most pious brother of all who were there, so hypocritically could he carry himself, and which he had, as we now perceive, long practised, in order to betray a number of friends. This traitor was present when the letters were placarded. It was also arranged to meet the other friends on Sunday morning to speak the word of God, for I wished to take leave of the brethren, and to proceed on my journey the next day; but the Lord be praised, who had otherwise appointed.

Early in the morning Hansken went with me to

the wood where we were to assemble, but we did
not find our friends at the place where we expected.
We sought them a full half hour, and thought they
had not come, because it had rained the previous
evening exceedingly hard. We were about to
return home, when I said, "Let us go on, perhaps they are before us;" and we sang softly, that
if they were there they might hear us. I then
heard a rustling in the wood, and said to Hansken,
"Here are our friends." We then stood still, that
we might see who were approaching. Three persons then came forward with arms and staves. I
said, "Well, comrades, have you been seeking a
hare, and not caught it?" Their countenances
then became deadly pale; they came to us, and
taking me by the arm, said, "Surrender yourself
a prisoner." They apprehended us and said, "We
have arrested a great many more." We then saw
a whole wagon load of our brethren, sitting bound,
and three justices, with all their officers, guarding
them: a large number. As we approached them,
we saluted our brethren with the peace of God,
and comforted them with the word of the Lord,
encouraging them now valiantly to strive for his
name's sake. We also rebuked the justices for
being so desirous of shedding innocent blood.

They then fastened Hansken and me together
with iron bands, and also our thumbs. We thought
they were about to take us into the town; but as
it was in another lordship we were apprehended,
we were obliged to go half a mile farther. We
esteemed it a great happiness to be so long to-

gether, and that going along we were able to comfort each other with the word of the Lord before
we were separated. We were led to the castle a
mile from the town. There we were kept together
in a chamber, and remained for three days: for
that was a right of the lordship where we had
been apprehended. We thanked and praised the
Lord our God, that he, in his wisdom, had so arranged it, that we had so long a time freely to exhort one another. Many people from the town
came to see and hear us; but at last no one was
permitted any longer to come to us in the room.

We were then examined by the high bailiff of
the province of Aelst concerning our faith, which
we freely confessed to him. We thought that we
should be conducted to Aelst, but because the
bailiff of Ghent had put us into the wagon when
we were apprehended, in order to take us to
Ghent, therefore we had to be taken altogether to
Ghent. And the traitor who had betrayed us
was apprehended with us, that we might not notice
it. They purposely put us into another room,
which grieved us. He was thereby prevented
being with us, and we were ignorant that he was
our betrayer. He was likewise taken in the wagon
to the prison in Ghent, and there we first came to
know that he had betrayed us. When we were
brought out of the castle to be taken to the town,
there were many people who had come from the
town to see us. My brother's wife was at that
time apprehended, she was also a sister, because
she had spoken to me. She was placed in the

wagon, and likewise another person, a man, who wished us happiness.   We spoke freely to the people who were come to us, how they must all be made a prey who would depart from evil and follow Christ.   Many of the people would willingly have spoken to us, but they durst not on account of the wicked magistrates.

Thus were we ready, with our ten companions in bonds, standing two and two, and four youths; the two others were apprehend^d because they had spoken to us.   They bro˙.ght us, filling two wagons, to the town in broad daylight : and on the road they seized another woman, because she had said to us, " God protect you."   She was likewise placed in the wagon.   But when we came into the town, had they apprehended all who spake to us, and to whom we likewise called, speaking the word of the Lord, they could not have conveyed them in twenty wagons; for the people came running quickly from all quarters, wherever we should pass by.   Like water running down from the hills and becoming a large body, the people ran together; and this lasted from one gate of the city to the Earl's castle, which stands at the end of the town, a distance of an hour's walk. We were then led to the castle, and the magistrate of the province of Aelst delivered us over into the hands of the magistrates of the imperial council.

We were now separated from one another; some above into rooms; the women likewise remained above; but eleven of us were taken into a dark deep vault.   In the vault were built many dark cells of masonry. There we were all put, three and three; but Hansken and I were placed in the darkest of all, in which was a little dirty straw, as much as might be carried in one's lap, which was our best accommodation. I said, "Methinks we are with Jonah in the fish's belly, it is so very dark; we must, like Jonah, cry unto the Lord, that he may be our comforter and deliverer; for we are now deprived of all human comfort and succor." At this we were not cast down, but praised and thanked God that we were permitted to suffer for his name's sake. We likewise spoke to our brethren who lay in the other dungeons; for we could plainly hear each other speak.

When we had lain here three or four days, Hansken and I were both summoned before the justices, where we were examined, and questioned as to the ground of our faith, and when we were baptized. The Lord, according to his promise, then gave us a mouth to speak boldly, and we requested to answer publicly from the word of God But they replied that they would appoint learned men, who should instruct us; and thus we were again conducted below.

Shortly after, I was fetched up to another chamber, before two councillors and a clerk, who sharply demanded of me where I had been, and if I did not well know that I had been banished more than six years ago, in Martin Huereblok's time, and where we had held our assemblies? They knew all that already; for our betrayer had told them. I said, "Why do you inquire of me, who am come from foreign lands?"—-For I had purposely avoided making inquiries, that if I should be apprehended, I might not then have much to answer.—"Why do you ask so sharply? have you not shed enough innocent blood? do you still thirst for more? Inquire as vigorously as you will, it shall be inquired of you again by the righteous Judge, unless you repent."

They then asked me still more, and adjured me by my baptism that I should inform them, "for we know," said they, "that your people do not lie, therefore answer us." I said, "You knowing that we do not lie is to us a token of salvation, and to you of perdition, since ye put such to death; but your adjurations have no power against the truth." All I said was written down, and they threatened to torture me, unless I would tell them the whole. I said, that "what I did not know, I could not tell;" but they thus harassed me a long time. I was then again conducted below. They dealt in the same manner with all our friends, one after the other, alone.

On a Saturday I was again fetched up into the same chamber. There were then present four monks. The superior of the Cordeliers, with another; and the father of the Jacobins, with another. With me came a young brother who had not yet received baptism, but stood ready.

When I was seated and had asked what they desired, they said, that they were appointed by the magistrate to instruct us, and to converse with us on the ground and articles of faith. I then answered, that I was ready to be instructed from the word of God, and desired to enter into conversation on the grounds and articles of faith, and that publicly, in the presence of the judges who were to pass sentence upon us, and in the hearing of our brethren and sisters, who were prisoners with us.

ANSWER.—That they will not be willing to grant.

HANS, OF OVERDAM.—Well, they can do then as they please; but we will not dispute thus alone and in secret, that our words may not be wrested behind our backs.

ANSWER.—We will not wrest your words.

HANS.—No? We know you well.

QUESTION.—What do you know of us? What harm have we done you? Tell us what harm you know of us.

HANS.—If you *will* know it; I consider you to be false prophets and deceivers.

We then fell into a dispute about their show of spiritual sanctity, and the command of the Pope respecting the purity of the priests and monks, and why they were called spiritual, and the others secular, seeing they ought all to be spiritual persons. Then thinking that hereby no progress was made, they said, "Let us dispute concerning the articles of faith." On which I said, "Well, so I proposed." They said, they would inform the magistrates. And thus we separated, after having disputed together for two hours.

Two days after this, Hansken and myself were

8

called before the Council. The four monks were present, and proposed a discussion. I then said to the Council, " Gentlemen, I ask you in whose house we are ? In one of justice or of violence ?"

ANSWER.—In one of justice.

HANS.—God grant it may be so; but, gentlemen, of what do you accuse us, that you have apprehended and confined us as thieves and murderers ? Have we defrauded any one ? or do you lay to our charge assault or murder, or any villany ?

ANSWER.—No; we know nothing of the kind against you.

HANS.—Well, gentlemen; why then have you apprehended us ?

ANSWER.—That your accusers will tell you.

HANS.—Are you then our accusers ?

ANSWER.—No ; we are your judges.

I then said to the monks, "Are you then our adversaries ?"

ANSWER.—No.

HANS.—Well; if no one is our accuser, why are we prisoners ? Then one of the Council said, " The Emperor is your accuser."

HANS.—We have done nothing against his Imperial Majesty. We will obey him, according to the power he has received from God, and observe all his ordinances as far as in our power, consistently with the truth.

COUNCILLOR.—You have held assemblies of this new doctrine, and the Emperor has forbidden such to be holden.

HANS.—It is not given him of God to make such laws; therein he exceeds the power granted him of God. In this matter we know him not as a ruler; for the salvation of our souls is dearer to us, and we must give our obedience to God.

The monks then said, " We are your opponents herein, for your doctrine is not good. If it were, you would not preach in woods and corners, but in public."

HANSKEN then said, " Allow us a free place in the market, or in your cloisters and churches, and then see if we go into the woods. But, no; you are afraid that men would rebuke you, and therefore you have so managed that you cannot be reproved, and have driven us from town and country."

MONKS.—Alas! we have not done that; it is the Emperor.

HANSKEN.—You have urged him to it.

THE MONKS.—We have not.

The council then began to speak to us; why we were not satisfied with the faith of our parents, and with our baptism? We said, " We know of no infant baptism; but of a baptism upon faith, which God's word teacheth us." Many more words passed, in which we reproved them for wishing to be judges in matters of faith, while they understood not the Scriptures. " But if ye will be judges, be impartial, and let the business take a regular course and order, and both parties be equally dealt with; and let our brethren and sisters, who are brought as prisoners here with us, be also present, and then one of us will speak, whose mouth the Lord will open, and the other side shall listen and be silent as long as he speaks, and let our opponents do the same.

THE COUNCIL.—We will not let your people come together, we will have you dispute here alone.

We then said, " Gentlemen, it would be the most suitable way, and the discussion would proceed regularly through; otherwise you will have to begin the disputation afresh with two or three only together."

COUNCIL.—It does not signify, we will not have it so.

A councillor then said, " They wish to have the others with them, to mislead them still more; therefore it must not be permitted."

HANS, OF OVERDAM.—Gentlemen, you say that you are judges; but we consider you our opponents, for you seek to weaken us in every way, and by violence and fraud to withdraw us and our companions from our belief.

ANSWER.—Why should we not do so, in order to recover the erring to the right way ?

HANS.—Well, gentlemen, then hear! Since we see that you are no judges, but are our adversaries, and employ all force and craft where you can and may, to your own advantage and our prejudice :— first in having taken from us, by violence, and bereft us of our Testament, in which we find our comfort; next, in having us placed apart, some in deep dark cellars, the others in high chambers;

and, thirdly, in seeking now to entrap and deceive us into various discussions, and then to say to our brethren, and behind our backs, that you have vanquished us, and then the same of our brethren and sisters to us :—therefore, gentlemen, we will not dispute here alone, unless our brethren and sisters be present.

When they heard that their design did not succeed according to their mind, they became very indignant, and the monks likewise. We saw well what their object was, and that what they were driving at was all knavery; for should it be proved from the holy Scriptures that they were wrong in any point, yet they would not confess it, but excuse themselves by pleading the Emperor and his mandate; and the monks the ancient customs of the Romish church, and the great number of fathers; and when proof was brought from the Scriptures to the contrary, it was as before, to no purpose, but like speaking into the air.

We then said, "Well, gentlemen, will you not then permit us to dispute in a reasonable and orderly manner, as we have desired?" Their answer was, "No." "Well then," said we, "you know the grounds of our faith, which we have freely confessed to you; you can now do with us what you please, so far as God permits you; but consider well what you do, for there is another judge above you. May the Lord open the eyes of your understanding, that you may see how lamentably you are misled and deceived by the false prophets in fighting against God and the Lamb; it will

8*

bring upon you a heavy judgement, unless you repent."

We were then again led away, not being willing to dispute further. For we had agreed together to adopt this course when we were yet in the castle outside the town, in order that they might not take advantage of the simple in the disputation. In this way they would be prevented from making any one believe they had obtained the victory, as all well knew there would be no disputation unless the rest were there also, and then the disputation would be to the comfort and admonition of the brethren and sisters who heard it. For as we saw that their own advantage was their only object, we likewise would not neglect our own, for we knew well that it was necessary.

When they perceived that they had failed of their object, they took counsel, and adopted another plan. They placed one of the council and two monks, (a grey and a black,) in a chamber, into which each brother or sister were brought to dispute or defend the reasons of their faith with the monks. But they said that they would not dispute alone in the chamber, but in public, and with the rest before the council. Then said they, "We adjure you by your faith and baptism that you dispute here." The brother said, "My faith and baptism I know and acknowledge, but with your adjuration I have nothing to do. Let us come together, that is just our desire, in order to dispute with you publicly, but not thus in a chamber alone." They then sent for another, and so on until they had the whole before them, and not one would, in such a way, engage in disputation.

I was then called alone into a chamber where were one of the council and two monks, who likewise began to adjure me. I then said, "What would you adjure me to do? To cast roses before dogs, and pearls before swine, to be trodden under foot? No, that the Lord has forbidden me to do. No, I esteem God's word too highly to let that light shine here in vain, where no one is enlightened, but which is traduced and contemned as it is by you when the truth is spoken." They then adjured me still more solemnly. Whereupon I said, "To what purpose is so much adjuring? I do not regard it; for it is the manner of wizards who swear against the truth. But I now see plainly by what means the souls of our two brethren and our sister were seduced and murdered. Through your swearing and enchantment they were not on the guard against the devil's subtlety, and had not the gift of disputation.

Then said the superior, "You have given a challenge in your letter to hold a public disputation; wherefore are you afraid to dispute now?"

HANS, OF OVERDAM.—You monk, I desire with all my heart to defend my faith in public by God's word, before all men; but your cowl would tremble if you had to dispute with me before the flames, and the magistrate were not your protector.

THE COUNCILLOR.—No; we have no inclination to let you dispute in public; you are in our hands.

HANS.—I wished it before I knew that I should

fall into your hands; but I see plainly that we are in the eagle's talons, and whoever is there cannot escape; he must there lose either soul or body.

COUNCILLOR.—Who is the eagle? the Emperor?

HANS.—No. It is the Roman empire or power. Read the letter I wrote to you, that will give you an answer.

Many other words passed between us. The monks were wroth with me, and began to speak great swelling words. I then said that Paul had rightly prophesied of them, that they were blasphemers, fierce and puffed up. Brother Jan de Crook then became so angry, that he began to exclaim, "Simpletons! simpletons! Heretics! ye are heretics!"

HANS.—See! is not that a fine teacher? Paul says that a bishop must not strive, nor be angry. The councillor was himself ashamed of the monk, and admonished him to be silent.

At another time after, there came two secular priests, Master Willem, of Nieuwen-land, and the parish priest of St. Michael's. I asked them what they desired. They said, "We are come for your soul's good." This time I kept myself as close as possible, hoping that we might dispute publicly before the Council, they having told me they would do their best thereto. When I heard that it might not be, and they came a second time to me with a clerk, I thought we must take another course with these than we did last time. I then asked, "What then do you wish?"

ANSWER.—We wish you to allow yourself to be instructed, for we seek your soul.

HANS.—Are you then so diligent in seeking souls?

ANSWER.—Yes.

HANS.—Well, go then into the town, into every place, to drunkards, whoremasters, swearers, revilers, the covetous, the proud, idolaters, tipplers, gluttons, and murderers, to them that shed innocent blood. These are all your brethren; go and seek their souls; mine, Christ has found.

ANSWER.—We admonish them, and have delivered our souls.

HANS.—That is not enough; you should go and reprove them, and if they will not hear you, bring them before the church, and rebuke them publicly. If they then will not hear, cast them out of the church, and let them be to you as heathens and publicans, as Christ teaches, and Paul to the Corinthians. Rebuke also your judges who employ force and injustice, yea, who spill and shed innocent blood.

A priest then said, "Should we go and reprove our superiors?" I asked, if God was a respecter of persons?

ANSWER.—No.

HANS.—Will you be God's servants, and respect the persons of men?

ANSWER.—That would make an uproar in the town, and they would put us to death.

HANS.—Do you thus suffer for righteousness sake?

But methought they had no great desire to suffer in such a cause. In short, we discoursed much on excommunication; that if the words of Christ and Paul should be followed, then the Pope, prelates, emperor, and king, yea themselves and their whole company would be shut out, and the number become extremely small. I then said to them, that their house was on fire, kindled by the fire of hell, which they should first quench before they came to see if our house was in danger of fire. They then went away, and one of the priests came no more again. With Master Antonis, of Hille, I discoursed in like manner, who troubled the others; but he let me be in peace.

Herewith, I commend my dear brethren and sisters in the Lord to the hands of Almighty God the Father, through Jesus Christ the Lord. Amen.

Written in prison for the testimony of Christ.

In this dark dungeon I have lain a month. I now lie in a deep round dungeon, which is somewhat lighter, and in which I have written this letter. I hope this week to make my offering, if it please the Lord, with those whom the Lord has thereto appointed. For if it do not take place this week, it will be two months longer, as their sittings are only once in six weeks. Know that our brethren and sisters are comfortable and of good courage, through the mercy of the Lord. God be praised.

I pray you by the brotherly love you bear me, to forward this letter to Friesland, particularly to

Embdenland, this letter itself, as speedily as you can. You may copy it; but be expeditious. That I request as a friend; and let it be taken care of, so that it be not torn or soiled.

The brethren who are lying with me in the vault greet you unitedly, wishing you peace in the Lord. We pray daily for you. Do the same likewise for us. Walk in peace in the Lord; so shall it be well with you. When this letter has been read, forward it to Antwerp, that it may reach the church at Embden, and be read by every one. This I desire of you, my dear brethren, by the brotherly love which you bear towards me.

The first volume of Underhill's edition of the "*Dutch Martyrology*," contains the very long and forcible letter addressed by this excellent man to the judges and council of Ghent, the day before he was apprehended, to which reference has already been made. It is full of Scriptural truth, and manifests great holy courage in stating it, but is too long for insertion in our volume. Hans, of Overdam, and Hans Keeskooper were sentenced to death. When they were condemned, the procureur-general said, "The reason of your being condemned as heretics is this:—that various learned persons have disputed with you, and you have not suffered yourselves to be instructed."

HANS, OF OVERDAM.—Gentlemen, had we been allowed to dispute in public, it would soon have been seen what kind of learned persons those were.

THE PROCUREUR GENERAL.—It is too late now. It is too late now.

HANS, OF OVERDAM.—Yes, yes, it is now too late.

They were then both taken away, and departed with a smiling countenance.

Hans Keeskooper had agreed with Hans, of Overdam, that while he drew off his hose on the scaffold, Hans, of Overdam, should speak to the people. This was done. The executioner being about to assist Hansken, [Hans Keeskooper,] he wished to do it alone, that Hans, of Overdam, might speak the longer to the people. This being done, they were each fastened to a stake, and presented their bodies a sacrifice to God.

JAQUES DOSIE.

DURING the sixteenth century, the exact date we have not been able to ascertain, though it is highly probable that it was in 1560, Jaques Dosie, (probably a Fleming who had fled to Friesland to escape the intolerant edict of the emperor, by which a modified form of the Inquisition was established in the Netherlands,) was apprehended at Leeuwarden, the capital of Friesland, for the sake of the truth of the holy gospel. He is said to have been but fifteen years of age, but God wonderfully exhibited in him the power of his grace, and enabled him to bear a noble testimony for the Lord Jesus.

On one occasion, when the governor of Friesland and his lady, with many other gentlemen and ladies, were assembled at Leeuwarden, they had this Jaques brought before them, and spoke with him, inquiring if he was tainted with any heresy. Fully did he realize that God gave him "a mouth and wisdom which the enemies could not gainsay or resist."

After a few words, the governor of Friesland, in consequence of the people's waiting for him, took his leave; but his lady, as it appears, being deeply interested, spoke with him, and asked him wherefore he, being yet so young, was thus rigorously confined and bound.

9 (97)

Jaques answered, "This has happened only because I believe in Christ, and depend on him
alone, and will by no means forsake him."

The lady asked him, "Are you not one of the
people who rebaptize themselves, and do so much
evil in our country, exciting uproar, running together, and who say that for their faith they are
driven away, and boast of being the church of
God; but who are a dangerous set, and make
great disturbance among the people?"

JAQUES.—My lady, tumultuous people I know
none, and am in no wise of the number of such;
but we desire much rather, as the Scripture teaches
us, to assist our enemies, and if they are hungry
or thirsty to satisfy them with food and drink, and
in no wise to resist them by violence or to avenge
ourselves.

Some one said, "It would be soon seen, in case
you had the power."

JAQUES.—Oh no, my lady; believe me, if we
were free to oppose the wicked with the outward
sword, you ought to know that then seven men
could not have brought me here, and I had escaped out of your hands; for strength enough
would have been found.

LADY.—I know that there are sects, that are
very infamous, that kill people, and hold a community of goods and wives.

JAQUES.—Oh, no, madam; such wicked things are
laid to our charge without our fault, and people
seek occasion thereby to persecute us; but we must
suffer and bear all such things with patience.

LADY.—Were they not your people who disgracefully and shamefully took up the sword against the magistrates at Amsterdam and Munster?

JAQUES.—Oh, no, madam; those persons greatly erred. But we consider it a devilish doctrine to resist the magistrates by the outward sword and violence. We would much rather suffer persecution and death at their hands, and whatever is appointed us to suffer.

LADY.—It is, however, laid to your charge, and they do very ill who excite uproar; but I sincerely believe what you say hereupon.

JAQUES.—My lady; do we not read much of the same kind, how that wicked men spoke untruly of the Apostles themselves, and the whole Christian multitude, and sought by many evil charges to stir up the higher powers to vengeance against them? yet it was all falsehood.

LADY.—Do you not think that all are lost who are not baptized in your way?

JAQUES.—Oh, no, madam; judgment belongs to God alone, who will reward every man according to his works, as plainly appears in many places of the holy Scriptures. Besides, water has no power to cleanse us from sin, as Peter says; but is only a token of obedience.

LADY.—When you have been baptized, tell me, can you then still sin?

JAQUES.—Yes, indeed, madam; for that clearly appears from Paul's words; for we are encompassed still with a weak sinful body, and offend in many things. But we must. continually crucify and put the same to death, and not do or fulfill the works of the flesh, otherwise we should, by the righteousness of God, be consigned to everlasting death.

LADY.—In what then do you differ from the Inquisitor? let me hear now.

JAQUES.—Madam; in that I will in nowise receive his doctrine, except he first clearly show me that it every way agrees with God's word; otherwise he labors in vain. My faith is founded alone upon the pure word of God. Concerning the use of infant baptism, we speak with reason against it, as being no command of Almighty God; but much rather an invention of men, considering that the young children have no knowledge or discernment about whatever is required and contained in the baptismal service. But Christ, from affection to such innocents, without their seeking it themselves, graciously promised them the kingdom of God. Besides this, madam, I think the papacy chargeable with many other errors; for they seek to bring Christ into the bread, or to change the bread itself into his flesh and blood. This we can by no means believe; but consider it as a gross error and absurdity. But we believe that Christ is truly ascended into heaven, and sits at the right hand of the Father. Believing this, we neither believe nor hold any salvation to be in their meal, or their mass, or purgatory, or their prayers for the dead, or in any such inventions of men, which abound among them, none of which are known in the sacred Scriptures, but are excluded therefrom. But in opposition thereto, we invoke God, and seek our salvation in him, and not in any creature; that we may not rob God of the honor due to him, by giving the same to any of the creatures he has made.

The Provincial being now come, he began to speak, saying, "Will you not believe in the sacrament which Christ himself instituted ?"

JAQUES.—Sir, Paul says, that the bread is broken in remembrance of Him, and the cup of blessing is a communion of the blood of Christ.

Herewith the Provincial ended his discourse.

LADY.—I consider the worst in you to be, your refusal to baptize the children; for all Germany, and every kingdom, regard your conduct as heresy.

JAQUES.—Madam, such is indeed the truth, that we are everywhere contemned, and are, like the apostolic band, spoken against in all the world; but do not think that all such will therefore in the last day be lost.

LADY.—My dear child, consider; I beg you to come over to our side, and repent; you will then be freed from this trouble, and I again fully promise to procure your entire deliverance and freedom.

JAQUES.—Madam, I thank you heartily for the affection and kind disposition you have towards me; but I will not exchange my faith to please any mortal being, unless it is proved from the Scripture that I have erred. That I might be the

9*

friend of God, I have given myself over entirely to him, in whom I hope to live and die.

LADY.—My son, look at all this multitude of people. I compassionate you, and earnestly beseech you to repent of your baptism, and not to continue thus hardened. Should you, so young a child, die in consequence, it would be a heavy cross to my heart. Take the course then by which you may again be at liberty and return to your home.

JAQUES.—Madam, in my baptism I can find nothing criminal, considering that herein I have followed not my own will, but the institution of our Lord Jesus Christ. Could I have found another and better way to the kingdom of God, it would not have taken place; for I was desirous with my whole heart to seek the Lord my God.

LADY.—Could they then all err, so many learned men, who were before you? Can you dare to be thus presumptuous?

JAQUES.—Madam, in Israel there were as many as four hundred prophets against one Micaiah, who alone spoke the truth, and was fed on bread and water; but king Ahab found it to be true too late in his distress.

LADY.—I find many good qualities in you; but your greatest error I hold to be in your baptism. That I do not think to be of God.

This lady frequently required that Jaques should be brought before her; but though he was young in years, he was highly intelligent in the knowledge of the Saviour, and firmly settled on the foundation stone, Jesus Christ; so that he valiantly warded off, with the sword of the Spirit, which is the word of God, all the crafty attacks of Satan, whether by cruel threatenings, or the fair promises of the men of this world. He could by no means be brought to deny Christ; and so was condemned by rulers of the darkness of earth to pass from life to death. He witnessed a good confession in life before many witnesses, and proved the sincerity of his faith in the truth by suffering a bloody and cruel death; thus obtaining the crown of martyrdom, and by the infnite grace of God, we doubt not, the crown of eve lasting glory.

AN OLD MAN IN HOLLAND.

BRANDT, in his "*History of the Reformation in the Low Countries*," gives a fine illustration of Baptist patience and boldness in the face of death, which it would be unjust to withhold from the readers of this volume.

The scene was in Holland, the period preceded the year 1551. An old man of seventy-five was brought before the bloody tribunal; his hair was white, his body thin with age, and his manners, which sprung from a heart fearing God, were irreproachable. He had been baptized in his old age, and then had found, though late, a home in the church. Knowing well the character of those before whom he stands, he feels himself as a sheep bound for the slaughter house, and, surrounded by a number of the burghers, he calmly awaits the approach of the criminal magistrate to pronounce the sentence of death.

An officer speaks to him. "Good father, why do you continue thus obstinately in your cursed error, do you think there is such a place as hell?"

OLD MAN.—Sir, I believe in a hell, most certainly; but I know nothing of the errors you mention.

ANOTHER.—Yes, you are in an error, and in so dreadful a one, that if you die in it you will be damned for ever.

(104)

OLD MAN.—Are you sure of that?

OFFICER.—Yes, it is as sure as anything in the world.

OLD MAN.—If it is so, then are ye murderers of my soul.

There was deep silence in the multitude as the old man thus discoursed; their attention became more earnest, and the officer, half enraged, and ashamed, loudly continued,—

OFFICER.—What do you say, you impertinent fellow? Are we the murderers of your soul?

OLD MAN.—Do not be angry, sir, at the sound of truth. You yourself know that faith is the gift of God, that neither I nor any other can extort this saving gift out of God's hands; that God bestows his gifts on one man early, on another late, just as he called the husbandmen into the vineyard. Suppose now that I had not yet received this gift, as you have, ought you to punish me for this misfortune? Might not God, in case you suffered me to live, impart to me, as well as to you, this excellent gift in a week, a month, a year? If then you hinder me from sharing therein, by depriving me of this time of grace, what are you otherwise but murderers of my soul?

The officer of justice hurried him away, notwithstanding the murmurs of the people, whose hearts were moved by his courage and his words. His condemnation did not linger, neither did the sun reach his meridian till the glory of the Lamb burst upon the vision of his martyred servant. He was beheaded for his testimony to Christ.

CHAPTER II.

———❦———

BALTHAZAR HUBMEYER AND HIS WIFE

——

In the time of Zuingle lived the famous BAL-THAZAR HUBMEYER, of Friedburgh, a learned and eloquent man, who, while yet among the Catholics, had been called a Doctor of the Holy Scriptures.

He was first a reader and preacher at Ingold-stadt, and afterwards removed to Regensburg, where he preached with great power. By the illuminations of the Holy Spirit, he was so con-vinced of the abominations of Popery, that, fol-lowing the counsel of God, he separated himself from it. He afterwards rejected, with other errors, their self-invented infant baptism, and taught with all possible zeal the baptism of believers according to the command of Christ. But the dark world could not bear the light of the holy gospel, and the testimony thus given to their false faith and evil works; therefore Hubmeyer, with many others, was hated and persecuted by the world.

After many trials, banishments, and imprison-ments, he removed to Niclasburg, in Moravia, and was there, together with his wife, apprehended,

(106)

and taken to Vienna, in Austria, where, after various trials, and long imprisonment, endured with great steadfastness, he was burned to ashes, and his wife drowned; both thus confirming by their deaths, the faith they had received from God.

Some interesting particulars of the life and death of this excellent man may be given. He was one of the earliest coadjutors and intimate friends of Zuingle. He was born in Friedburg, near Augsburg, in Bavaria, not later than the year 1480, and thence often called Friedburgher, or, in its Latinized form, Pacimontanus. By the Cardinal de Sandoval, in his "Index of Prohibited Books," he is ranked by name with Luther, Zuingle, Calvin, Schwenckfeld, standing fourth on the list as a principal leader in the Reformation.

Beneath the shadow of the beautiful minster of the High school of Friedburg, Hubmeyer acquired, under the renowned controversialist and theologian, Eck, his knowledge of the ancient tongues. His first intention was to become a physician; but he soon exchanged medicine for theology. Barely supplied with the means of subsistence, he was for a time compelled to suspend his studies, and assume the office of schoolmaster at Schaff'hausen. The friendships he there formed were continued to a later period of his life, especially with an eminent physician of the name of Adelphus. In 1511, he graduated at Friedburg; and in the following year, on account of his erudition and eloquence, became professor of Divinity and principal preacher

in the Maria Kirk at Ingoldstadt, a fortified city
in Bavaria, by the appointment of that ancient
university. For three years and five months he
continued his eloquent and instructive labors;
and by his earnest and powerful preaching revived
the decayed spirit of Catholicism.

His fame reached Regensburg, the modern
Ratisbon, and one of the most ancient cities of
Germany. Early in 1516, he removed to that
city. The inhabitants flocked to the grand but
gloomy cathedral to hear his denunciations of the
vices of the times; and the soft blue colored light
which fell upon the waving mass, from windows
richly painted, helped to increase the superstitious
awe and enthusiasm which his eloquence inspired.

The Jews were the especial objects of his denunciations. He treated on the evils of Judaism, but
particularly on the damage received by the entire
German nation from the Jewish usury. The enraged senate sought from the emperor an edict of
banishment against them; and on the last day of
February the Jews were driven from the city, their
goods plundered, and their synagogue, with other
buildings, levelled to the ground.

In its stead arose a chapel dedicated to Maria
Formosa, and before the door was set up a wonder-
working stone statue of the Virgin! Pilgrim-
ages were made to it. Its fame spread on every
side. The chronicler hints that the clergy were
not sparing of incantations and magical arts to
attract the vulgar, that they might be enriched
by the liberality of the congregated multitudes.

Laborers engaged at their work, when they saw the long lines of people pass by—woodmen, tailors, and maidens—to the Virgin's fane, would shoulder their axes and reaping hooks, hasten to join the devout procession, and wildly cast themselves at the feet of the goddess of Regensburg.

To this infatuation Hubmeyer contributed, until the noise of Luther's strife with Tetzel, and of Zuingle's bold proclamation of the gospel at Enisidlin, awoke his suspicions, and led him to see the errors of that church which he had so zealously served.

While yet a Romish priest, Hubmeyer had sought to revive the ancient spirit of religion, to render the services of his church more intelligible, and to awaken the lost devotion of the common people. He appears to have gladly hailed the dawn of better days. His course, as a reformer, was begun by translating the gospels and epistles into the German tongue, and he read the mass in the language of the common people. He next altered the canon of the mass, and celebrated it under both the forms of bread and wine. He now taught the true doctrine concerning it, that Christ was not bodily present in the bread, and that after the consecration it continued to be bread. His hearers, to whom for two years he had preached, were directed to reverence the blessed Virgin and the saints no more, and the use of the "Ave Maria" was abolished. Fasts were set aside, and permission given to eat meats without distinction. He laid aside the chalice and the robes worn at mass, and sold the sacred utensils. He clothed himself in a coat made of a black camlet priest's cloak. He lifted up his voice against images in churches, broke some into pieces and burnt them, and called their worship idolatry. It was at a later period that he rejected the baptism of infants.

Thus changed in opinion, he left Regensburg, and for a time abode at Schaffhausen. About the year 1519, he received the appointment of preacher at Waldshut. There he investigated with diligence the Holy Scriptures, and led many of the people to abandon the superstitions of Rome. He also formed an intimacy with Erasmus, who then resided at Basle. In a letter to his friend, the physician, John Adelphus, of Schaffhausen, June 23, 1522, he testifies of this learned man, that he spoke boldly but wrote timidly.

Meanwhile, Hubmeyer's return to Regensburg was longed for by many of his former hearers; and in 1522, he returned for a year to minister among them as a teacher of the doctrines of the Reformation. In March, 1523, he ventured to Waldshut; and in May, visited Zuingle at Zurich, with whom he enjoyed much Christian intercourse. His mind was at this time unsettled on the subject of infant baptism, and it formed one of the topics of their conversation. Zuingle and Oecolampadius were in a similar state of doubtful opinion.

To carry on the great work of the Reformation, Hubmeyer preached the gospel, and with amazing success, in St. Gall. As the church could not hold the crowds who assembled to hear him, he preached on the place in the open air. He there contracted a friendship with the eminent Dr. Joachim Von Watt, afterwards burgomaster of St. Gall, who, at a later period, offered him a refuge from the persecutions he endured.

It was at the second great disputation, held in October of this year, that Hubmeyer appeared side by side with Zuingle and Leo Jude, as the maintainer of the word of God against the priests of Rome. The assembly was convened in the large hall of the town house of Zurich, in the presence of the members of the great council. Three hundred and fifty priests, chiefly from the cantons of Schaffhausen and St. Gall, were there, with more than nine hundred spectators. Joachim Von Watt and two others were named presidents of the assembly. The subject of the first day's discussion was the worship of images—a question then of pressing interest. But a few weeks before, a citizen of Zurich, animated with zeal, had ventured to dash into pieces a crucifix that was held in high estimation at Stadelhofen. The publication of a small pamphlet by Louis Hetzer, had deepened the feeling of intense hatred towards the use of images. In this tract, Hetzer adduced the condemnation pronounced in Scripture against idolatry, and its approval of the iconoclastic zeal of Hezekiah.

Hubmeyer, on the first day, appears to have spoken but once, and then briefly. He spoke of the Christian's duty, by command of God, to assist his brother if he should have fallen into error, and if possible to enlighten him upon those mistakes and idolatrous abuses which, in the course of centuries, had disfigured the church. In all the disputed matters the clear word of God, contained in both testaments, which God has himself sanctified, is the sole judge. That word must be made known. It testifies of Christ. Holy Scripture alone is the true light and lamp, by which every human argument and darkness must be illumined. Christ hath himself taught us to take in hand the lamp of his saving word, that when the Bridegroom cometh we may enter with him to the wedding. By this alone can errors relating to images and the mass be destroyed; and what is built thereon will last for ever, for the word of God is immortal. Thus he proclaimed the supremacy of God's word, and none was found to answer him.

The second day's disputation was on the subject of the sacrifice of the mass. It was opened by Zuingle and Leo Jude, who met with but few and feeble opponents among the assembled priests. After a pause, Hubmeyer arose. He referred to the decision of the preceding day. It was well and truly established from Scripture that images ought not to be used, and he wished that images had never come into use among Christians. The laws of Moses were clear and explicit in their condemnation. God commanded them to be burnt, and they who made them were accursed,—"*And all the people shall say, Amen.*" The hall echoed with many voices, saying, "Amen."

Hubmeyer continued:—Either images were

commanded to be honored, or they were not. If
they were commanded, let the text of Scripture be
produced,—that would settle the question. If
they were not commanded, they were unnecessary.
What God teaches, whether by word or works, is
useful and profitable. But whatever plant he hath
not planted shall be plucked up. Were they useful, God would have commanded them. It is
blasphemy to send sinners to images to pray, to
draw and invite them to exercises of devotion. For
it is Christ who calls the sinner, who invites him
to the wedding feast; he alone moves men to embrace that which is good, and God the Father dis-
ciplines those who come to Christ. Thus did this
eminent man clearly perceive, that not only were
those devices in the worship and institutions in the
church to be laid aside that were clearly forbidden
by the word of God, but those also which could
not be maintained by the direct command or
authority of Scripture.

The discussion on the mass was renewed on the
following day. After a few words from Conrad
Grebel, asserting the existence of various abuses,
Hubmeyer proceeded at some length to refer to
them, and point out how far the 'practices of
Rome had departed from the institution of
Christ. He would prefer to lay aside the term
"mass," and call the ordinance the testament of
Christ, or a memorial of his bitter death. It was
the greatest abuse of all to call it a sacrifice. His
dear brethren in Christ, Ulrich Zuingle, and Leo
Jude, had well shown its contrariety to the word

10*

of God. Thence it followed that it could be no
sacrifice for the living or the dead. As we cannot
believe for another, neither can we offer a sacrifice
or mass for another. The institution of Christ
was given to strengthen the faith of the believing.
The pure, clear word of God ought to be an-
nounced with the ordinance of which it is a sign,
and the whole service be observed in the language
of the people. The Lord's people should, moreover, communicate in both kinds; he who does
otherwise, does wrong to the directions of Christ,
which he has given in his last testament.

Hubmeyer nobly continued:—"These are my
opinions, which I have gathered from the Scriptures, upon images and the mass. If they are not
right and Christian, I pray you all, by Jesus
Christ our only Saviour—I entreat you by the last
judgment, that ye will instruct me in a brotherly
and Christian spirit from the Scriptures. For I
may err: I am a man; but a heretic I cannot be.
I wish from my heart to be instructed, and I will
promise gratefully to confess my error. Most
cheerfully I submit in all obedience to the word
of God, and will faithfully follow you as ye are followers of Christ. I have spoken; judge ye;
teach me. To Christ I will pray, that he may
grant us his grace to do his will."

A brief colloquy ensued between Zuingle and
Grebel, the latter urging the abolition of abuses,
the former admitting their existence, but referring
the subject to the mandate of the magistracy!
The disputation closed; but not without the

magistrates committing to prison, or banishing, the men whose zeal against idolatry had given rise to the discussion. The Reformation halted, and waited the pleasure of the ruling power— and Zuingle would have it so.

Hubmeyer returned to Waldshut. Early in 1524, he published eighteen propositions to his companions in office in the chapter, inviting them to a discussion, to be closed with a fraternal meal at his expense. Some of these propositions follow :—

1. Faith only justifies us before God.

4. Those works only are good which God hath commanded : those only are evil which he hath forbidden.

5. The mass is no sacrifice, but a solemn memorial of Christ's death ; for which reason it cannot be offered for the living or the dead.

8. As every Christian believes and is baptized for himself, so should every one, according to the Scriptures, for himself judge whether he is fed by the pastor of his soul.

9. As Christ alone died for our sins, and as we all are baptized into his name, so must he alone be addressed as our Intercessor and Mediator.

12. The time is at hand, indeed has already come, that no man shall be regarded as a priest who does not announce God's word.

13. The fellow-believers are bound to maintain, and properly to support, with food and clothing, those who preach to them purely and plainly the word of God.

18. He who labors not for bread with the sweat of his brow, is excommunicate.

Other propositions condemned fasting, images, and purgatory; and thus show that Hubmeyer was prepared to forsake the entire circle of Romish doctrine. The chapter met early in 1524. The truths advanced were vigorously discussed, until but one priest, a young nobleman, remained steadfast to the old communion. From this time the reformation rapidly advanced in Waldshut, under the wise guidance of the chief pastor Hubmeyer.

The governing powers of Austria now interfered. Rumors of the approaching peasant-war began also to utter their voices amid the revelry and reckless atrocities of the feudal lords. Revolution and Reformation appeared to be synonymous words, and the imperial power drove Hubmeyer from his home. His refuge was Schaffhausen, a town of Switzerland, not far north of the forest towns. Soon were found in that free city men prepared to sacrifice the exile, for political favor with the emperor; and he was again constrained to return to Waldshut. His safety was of brief duration. The men of Zurich, who in their reforming zeal had hastened to Waldshut with arms to aid the reformation so early stayed by Austria, were compelled to return; and soon after, Hubmeyer sought an asylum in the houses of some faithful men of Zurich. His appearance in that city was with very different feelings and results to his former visit. Now he was a Baptist, a proclaimed adversary of

Zuingle,—a hunted bird, that quickly fell a prey to the arts of the fowler.

Two years before, the question of infant baptism had excited much interest among the leading reformers of Switzerland; several of Zuingle's early coadjutors had already seceded from his side, opposing his indiscriminate church constitution, and its alliance with the state. Early in 1524, Hubmeyer had opened a correspondence with Zuingle on the subject, and was accustomed to affirm that he possessed an early writing of Zuingle, in which he expressed himself against the baptism of infants. The people of Waldshut were advised not to bring their babes to the font. Hubmeyer was sure that infant baptism had no authority from the word of God; but was not quite sure that it was right, in opposition to the advice of Zuingle and Oecolampadius, to abolish it altogether. The parents were therefore spoken with, and not until their entreaties were very urgent did our Reformer yield to the celebration of the rite. In December of this year he wrote this sincere and earnest note to Zuingle:—

"Write to me again, for God's sake, on baptism. And if I shall have offended thee and Leo, the fault is unawares. Pardon me. Farewell. Salute Leo. From our nest at Waldshut. Thine.

"BALTHAZAR.

"Margaret will answer the request of Leo."

From this time his views rapidly matured, and

he was soon treated as a bitter foe by his eminent correspondent. So late as November, 1524, Hubmeyer wrote of Zuingle as his " brother in Christ;" but early in 1525 he complains to Oecolampadius that Zuingle and Leo had forsaken him. Would the Reformer of Basle forsake him too? Would he not from friendship, for the sake of Christian peace, and for God, hasten to correct his errors, and to restore the wandering sheep? For openly did Balthazar teach the institutions of Christ. Who, asked he, instituted Baptism?—Christ. Where?—in the last chapter of Matthew. In what words?—" Go ye into all nations and teach them, and baptize them into the name of the Father, and the Son, and the Holy Ghost." Altogether right. Why, therefore, do we baptize children? Baptism, they say, is a mere sign. A sign truly it is, and a symbol instituted by Christ in most pregnant and august words. But it cannot be made to apply to babes; therefore is infant baptism without any authority whatever. "I believe and know," he concludes, that Christendom shall not receive its rising aright, unless baptism and the Lord's supper are brought to their original purity."

Thus simply and clearly, assuming Zuingle's views of a sacrament to be correct, did Hubmeyer reason. The answer of Oecolampadius was to th ▸ effect, that as all children are born in original sin; —since some have even in the womb been sanctified;—since also the Most Merciful will listen to the prayers of the church, seeking the salvation of the offspring of the faithful;—and as otherwise the children of Christians would be worse off than the children of the circumcision; therefore it was right to bring them to the sacred font. These, and such like arguments, did Oecolampadius now use, though, in another letter, he admitted that the New Testament gives no authority for infant baptism. Such arguments, however, failed to convince Hubmeyer, as they have many others, that infant baptism is an institution of the Saviour; and at Easter, at a retired village not far from Waldshut, in company with one hundred and ten persons, he was baptized by William Roubli, one of the earliest of the Swiss Baptists, and for some time a pastor at Basle.

The matter was now public. Hubmeyer himself baptized some three hundred persons in the few following months. Great excitement everywhere prevailed. He published a work on Baptism, which brought in the autumn a violent and virulent reply from Zuingle. Some of the Baptists were cast into prison; and so cruel were the proceedings, that even the populace complained that injustice was done to them. The public opinion was so strong that at the persuasion of the ministers, a public conference was called at Zurich, in which Zuingle took a leading part. It failed, however, to convince the Baptists of their errors, which many of them were made to atone for by imprisonment and fines.

Hubmeyer published a tract, in which he complains of Zuingle and his followers:—that they had proceeded so far as at one time to throw into a dark and miserable tower, twenty persons, both men and pregnant women, widows and young females, and to pronounce the sentence upon them —that thenceforward they should see neither sun nor moon for the remainder of their lives, and be fed till their days were ended with bread and water. And that they should remain in the dark tower together, both the living and the dead, surrounded with filth and putrefaction, until not a single survivor of the whole remained. He tells us, farther, that some of these persons would refuse to take even a mouthful of bread for three days in succession that the rest might have the more to eat. " O God !" he writes, " what a hard, severe, cruel sentence upon pious Christian people, of whom no one could speak evil, only that they had received water baptism in obedience to the command of Christ !"

About July, 1525, Hubmeyer entered Zurich, and sought a refuge at the Green Shield with a few friends and faithful followers. His coming was soon known among his fellow-believers, and soon also to the council of Zurich. He was sought out, and immured in the cells of the court house. For many days and weeks Zuingle and his old associates endeavored to shake his adhesion to the truth. At last the torture was applied. Protestant historians say that a promise of recantation was willingly given, and written with his own hand. Alas ! how willingly ! the pains of the rack were the sharp and effectual arguments.

On the 22d of December, he was led to the

minster, and placed at a desk facing that from which Zuingle long and vehemently declaimed against the heresies which his friend was there come to confess. The sermon was over, and every eye turned to the rising form of the sick Balthazar. Though not old, his trials have told on his robust frame ; and with a quivering voice he begins to read from the paper of recantation before him. As his articulation becomes distinct, he is heard to affirm that infant baptism is without the command of Christ. As the words continue to flow, and add certainty to the incredulous ears of the crowd in the thronged cathedral, murmurs float ominously in the resounding roof, increasing by degrees to audible expressions of approbation or of horror. Zuingle's voice rises above all. He quiets the coming storm, and Hubmeyer is rapidly conveyed to his cell in the Wellenburg.

Redoubled efforts were afterwards made to recall the mischief that had been done. Probably renewed tortures were applied or threatened ; for in a few months, the sufferer is said to have made a public recantation both at Zurich and at St. Gall; but with so little satisfaction to his persecutors, that although released from prison, he was kept in the town under strict surveillance. About the middle of the year 1526, by the aid of distant friends, he succeeded in escaping from Zurich, and after preaching at Constance for a short time, he journeyed to Moravia, passing through Augsburg on his way. There he freely proclaimed the gospel, and in all the region round about, baptizing many, and forming churches of Christ according to his word.

In the year 1528, he was arrested, probably at Brünn, where he was teacher of the church, at the command of king Ferdinand, and sent to Vienna. After some days he was thrown into the dungeons of the castle of Gritsenstein. At his own request he was visited by Dr. Faber, of Gran, in Hungary, who had been in former days his friend. Their interviews, at which two other learned men assisted, lasted the greater part of three days. The substance of their discussions Faber afterwards published, and hints that on several points Hubmeyer yielded to the cogency of his arguments. It is impossible, however, to gather from Faber's book what Hubmeyer's sentiments really were. A written exposition of his views was afterwards sent to king Ferdinand, by Hubmeyer himself; and it is impossible that any important change could have taken place, as he was immediately sentenced to death. The sentence was read to him in presence of many thousand men. He courageously went to the stake, on the 10th of March, 1528.

The partner of his life was also partner of his sufferings; imprisoned with him, she too was led to Vienna, and there condemned to death by drowning. This faithful woman in the river Danube found a watery grave. What a meeting must these noble martyrs of Christ have had in heaven in the presence of their Lord!

JERONIMUS SEGERSON AND HIS WIFE, LYSKEN DIRKS.

On September 2d, 1551, these excellent persons, who had fallen into the hands of their spiritual tyrants, and endured long and trying sufferings, passed through several severe examinations, and having given full evidence of their cordial attachment to Christ, nobly sealed their testimony with their blood. Jeroninus, in company with a devoted Christian, called Tall Hendrik, died at the stake, and the wife of Jeronimus was drowned in a sack in the river Scheldt.

We have before us a long and deeply interesting correspondence between these excellent persons, who were confined in different cells, as well as with other friends. The whole is much too long for insertion in this volume, but two letters shall be given at length, and a few passages selected from others. To explain a passage in the first letter, it may be remarked, that the Baptists on the continent of Europe, at that period, refused to be married by the clergy of the dominant church, but were united before the church of which they were members, similar to the practice of the society of Friends at the present day. This was made a matter of reproach and accusation by their enemies, as if they encouraged and practiced licentiousness, than which nothing could be farther

from the truth. After the Revolution, when marriage became a civil act in the Netherlands, in
1574, and 1580, the Baptists ceased to marry in
their own assemblies, and resorted to the civil authorities.

The following is the first letter we shall give.
It will be remembered that both parties were now
in prison, charged with the high crime of worshiping God in what they esteemed the New Testament way.

"FEAR GOD ALWAYS.

"In lonesome cell, guarded and strong I lie,
  Bound by Christ's love, his truth to testify;
  Though walls be thick, the door no hand unclose,
  God is my strength, my solace and repose.

"Grace, peace, gladness, joy and comfort, a
firm faith, good confidence, with ardent love to
God, I wish my most beloved wife, Lysken Dirks,
whom I married in the presence of God and his
holy church, and took thus, agreeably to the
Lord's command, to be my wife. Consolation,
joy, and gladness, my dear wife, be increased and
multiplied unto you.

"I pray the Lord very earnestly for you, that he
would comfort you, and remove what is too heavy
for you. I know well, my chosen lamb, that you
are greatly dejected on my account; but put away
all sorrow, and look to Jesus, the Leader and
Finisher of our faith, and let us henceforth walk
in all righteousness and holiness, as the children
of peace. Let us employ well the time of grace,

and think what great mercy the Saviour has shown us. Oh, my dear wife, think only what a faithful God we serve. He will not suffer us to be ashamed. Think how faithfully he led the children of Israel through the Red Sea with an outstretched hand, out of Pharaoh's house of bondage, and from the land of Egypt. Think how they had to prepare themselves before they could depart, and how they ate the paschal lamb with unleavened bread, and must eat it standing, and how they covered up in their garments the unleavened bread they had, and began to depart toward the wilderness. The angel of the Lord went before them, by day in a pillar of cloud, and by night in a pillar of fire, and thus enlightened them. But when they were afraid of Pharaoh and his host, the people began to murmur against Moses, for they had no steadfast confidence in the Lord that he would lead them forth; but the Lord told Moses what he would do, and how he would display his power on Pharaoh and his host, and he commanded Moses to take his rod and stretch forth his hand over the sea, and when Moses did so the sea dried up, and the waters were divided, and became a wall unto them on the right hand and on the left, so that they went through the sea dry-shod. But Pharaoh pursued them with his host, and was drowned with all his captains and people; while Israel passed through without loss, and praised and gave thanks to God, that he had delivered them from Pharaoh's house of bondage. But they were not yet in the promised land. They came into the terrible desert,

11*

where there was no bread. The bread which they
had brought out of Egypt was not much; it was
the unleavened dough which they had brought in
their clothes on departing from Egypt. Then
were they disheartened, because they had nothing
to eat; but the Lord fed them with bread from
heaven.

" In like manner, my most beloved wife, we
have not overcome all things when we have confessed the truth and separated ourselves from the
world, and renounced all sensual delights and desires. We must likewise wrestle with enemies,
that is, we must wrestle here in this world with
emperors, with the powers and princes of this
world. We must in this world suffer, for Paul
has said, that 'all that will live godly in Christ
Jesus, must suffer persecution.' We must com-
pletely conquer the world, sin, death, and the
devil, not with material swords and spears, but
with the sword of the Spirit, which is the word of
God, and with the shield of faith, wherewith we
must quench all sharp and fiery darts, and place
on our heads the helmet of salvation, with the
armor of righteousness, and our feet be shod with
the preparation of the gospel. Being thus strengthened with these weapons, we shall, with Israel,
get through the wilderness, oppose and overcome
all our enemies. They must be brought to shame
who fight against the truth.

" When now the children of Israel were passed
through the wilderness, that terrible and fearful
wilderness wherein were fiery serpents, and had

journeyed therein forty years, and surmounted so
many perils, and had taken so many cities and
countries on this side of Jordan, still they had
not yet entered into the promised land. They had
not yet passed over Jordan ; but the Lord showed
Moses the promised country from afar.

"O my dear wife, I have likewise seen from afar
the promised land. I hope soon to enter the
beautiful city so richly adorned, that John describes. Its foundations are twelve precious stones,
its walls and streets of pure and transparent gold.
The city has twelve gates, each gate of pearl, and
there is no night there, for the Lord God en-
lightens it. And the Lord told Moses that he
should not bring that people into the promised
land, but Joshua brought them in, and the Lord
led them dry-shod through the Jordan. He commanded them, that they should keep his laws but
failing the Lord gave them over into the hands
of their foes, so that they were slain by their
enemies. Even when they had passed over Jordan, they were not yet in full possession of the
land of promise, which flowed with milk and
honey; they had to take possession thereof by
mere force, and to slay all their enemies, and to
burn their cities with fire. In like manner must
we also enter the promised land by force, for
Christ saith that 'the kingdom of heaven suffereth
violence.' I now for the first time know what warfare is; no one knows it better than he who has
experienced it, so craftily do they approach in
order to seduce us.

"Know that I received your letter by my mother, which I read with tears. I thank you that you therein so heartily comfort me, and I rejoice in hearing that you are so well contented.

"Understand, my beloved wife, Lysken, that I have been before the Margrave, who had there with him two Dominican friars, and two justices, and the recording clerk. He asked me if I had not yet thought better of it, saying, that he had allowed the two good gentlemen to save [absolve] my soul if I would repent. I replied, that I would not renounce my faith, for it was the truth. They then asked me what my faith was? I said to the monks, 'Ask the Margrave; to him I have confessed my faith; ask it of him.' They harassed me sorely; but I would say nothing at all to them. They asked me how I knew that it was the truth? If God had spoken to me by word of mouth?

"As they could get nothing more from me, my confession was read, namely, that I did not approve of the sacrament. I said, 'No, it was only a bread-god.' The priests were wroth that I so contemned their god. They were desirous of talking with me. I said, 'I will not hear you, nor speak to you; but let my brother come here with me, I will then speak with you, and we will make confession of our faith.' They then asked me if I was not sufficiently established in my faith, that I thus relied upon my brother? I said, 'Yes, my faith is strong enough, but that you should not wrest our words.' They said, 'We shall not wrest your words.' I said, 'I know you too well, and am perfectly acquainted with your craftiness.'

"The Margrave said, 'It shall be granted you.'* I thought he said that he would bring a Bible with him. The priests said, 'When the little children are baptized, they then obtain faith.' At this I laughed, and asked, 'Why then did they not go to Turkey, to baptize the Turks; if men thereby became possessed of faith, as you say, they too would become believers?' They said, 'Although men should baptize the Turks, they would nevertheless remain Turks still.'

"They pressed me sore that I would recant, and become a good member of the Romish church. The Margrave and the justices were so unrighteously moved with compassion towards me, that they said, 'If your life were spared, and you repented, and became a good member of the Romish church, I should have good hope of you; for you are brought here young and for no crime, and I know by whom. [The Margrave referred to Jelis Van Aken, a Mennonite minister, by whom he had been baptized.] You are also descended from very worthy parents, and your mother is almost dying from grief.' I said, 'Even if the door stood open, and you should say, Go, only say I am sorry, I would not go; for I am sure I have

* The priests often misrepresented the martyrs as having made a recantation in these solitary interviews, partly to increase their own influence, and partly to induce others to follow their supposed example, and thus injure the cause of truth. To prevent this, the martyrs were anxious to have present some of their own friends.

the truth.' The Margrave then said, 'If you will
not listen, I will have you burned alive.' Thereat
I smiled, and said, 'Whatever you do to me, on
account of my faith, I will willingly suffer.' He
added, ' His wife is the greatest heretic there is in
the town.'

" I cannot sufficiently thank the Lord for all the
strength and vigor he gives me in this trial. I
find indeed in the present season that the Lord is
with us, for he helps us so faithfully in all our
need. He is such a faithful leader; he gives his
servants such courage; strengthens them so that
they do not fear. They neither fear nor tremble,
through the great love they have to their heavenly
Father. For St. Paul says, 'Who shall separate
us from the love of God? Tribulation, or distress, persecution, or hunger, or nakedness, or
peril, or sword? as it is written, For thy sake we
are killed all the day long: we are accounted as
sheep for the slaughter. Nay, in all these things
we are more than conquerors through him that
loved us. For I am persuaded, that neither death,
nor life, nor angels, nor principalities, nor do-
minion, nor powers, nor things present, nor things
to come, nor height, nor depth, nor any other creature, shall separate us from the love that is in
Christ Jesus our Lord.'

" Therefore, my most beloved wife, Lysken, submit yourself to present circumstances; be patient
in tribulation, and instant in prayer, and look
at all times to the precious promises everywhere
given us, if we continue steadfast to the end. Let

us guard the precious treasure, for we have this
treasure in earthen vessels, and cannot hide it. It
everywhere discovers itself, and is much too precious to be concealed. We are so joyful, having
this treasure, which is our faith, hope, and love.
These will never leave us barren of comfort should
we even be placed in a dark hole, separated from
each other. The treasure is of such a nature that
it cannot be hidden. The one calls to the other,
and pours out his treasure, so that it may be seen.
We are so happy! everlasting praise and thanks
to the Lord! We call upon him, we sing together,
we experience great joy in comforting and strengthening each other.

"The Lord gives us such strength and might,
that we cannot thank him enough for the great
mercy he displays towards us. Therefore we are
not weary; for although our outward man decay-
eth, yet the inward man is nevertheless renewed
day by day; for our affliction, which is but temporary and light, worketh a far more exceeding and
eternal weight of glory for us who look not at the
things that are seen, but at the things that are
not seen.

"Thus, my dear wife, cease not to serve the
Lord your God with all your heart, and to follow his
footsteps. 'For we know that if this earthly house
of our tabernacle were dissolved, we have a building of God, a house not made with hands, eternal
in the heavens. For this we greatly long—for our
dwelling which is in heaven; earnestly desiring
therewith to be clothed upon; for me, I would rather

be clothed than be found naked; for as long as we are at home in the body, we are on pilgrimage, and are absent from the Lord.

"Therefore, my dear wife, look diligently that you pass the time of your pilgrimage here with fear and trembling; not, however, with such fear and trembling that we should fear the world, or be afraid or tremble before the world because they are so furious against us. But we must fear and tremble before the Lord, so that we may keep his commandments and statutes, and thus finish the period of our pilgrimage in the fear of the Lord, and attain the end of our faith, namely, the salvation of our souls. Then we shall ever rejoice with the Lord, and meet him at the resurrection of the dead. Therefore, fear not the world; for the hairs of your head are all numbered. They have no power, except it be given them from above. Christ saith, 'Fear not them who kill the body, but fear him who is able, after he hath killed the body, to cast the soul into hell; there shall be weeping of eyes, and gnashing of teeth, and their worm shall not die, they shall rest neither day nor night.'

"May the almighty and eternal God, so strengthen and comfort you with his blessed word, that you may abide faithful to the end. Then shall you likewise be found under the altar with all God's dear children, where all tears shall be wiped away from our eyes. There shall all tribulations have an end. Then shall our despised body be glorified, and fashioned after the likeness of his glory. Then shall our weeping be

turned into laughter, and our sorrow into joy.
Then shall we, who for a short space are despised
and contemned, yea, persecuted and cast out, and
in great reproach, pain, and contempt are brought
to death for the testimony of Jesus Christ, enjoy
an everlasting triumph, and dwell for ever with
the Lord. We shall be clothed with white robes,
as John testifies in his Revelation concerning the
souls of those who were slain for the word of God
and for the witness they bare. They lay under
the altar, and cried with a loud voice, saying, ' O
Lord, holy and true, how long dost thou not judge
and avenge our blood on them that dwell on the
earth ?' And to each of them was given a white
robe ; and it was said unto them, that they should
rest yet for a little season, until the number of
their fellow-servants also, and their brethren, that
should be killed as they were, should be fulfilled.

" Oh ! what a glorious company shall we be,
when united with the great multitude that Esdras
describes; and of which John in his Revelations
speaks. He saw ' a great multitude which no
man could number, of all nations, and kindreds,
and people, and tongues, standing before the
throne, and before the Lamb, clothed with white
robes, and palm-branches in their hands; and
they cried with a loud voice, saying, Salvation
to him who sitteth upon the throne of our God,
and unto the Lamb. These are they who came
out of great tribulation, and have washed their
robes, and made them white in the blood of the
Lamb. Therefore are they before the throne of

12

God, and serve him day and night in his temple: and he that sitteth upon the throne shall dwell among them. They shall hunger no more, neither thirst any more; neither shall the sun light on them, nor any heat; for the Lamb which is on the throne shall feed them, and shall lead them unto fountains of living waters; and God shall wipe away all tears from their eyes.' And Esdras testifies concerning the same multitude, and says, 'that they stood in the midst of the hill of Zion, and were clothed with white raiment; and in the midst of them stood one taller than all the rest; and to each of them he gave palm-branches in their hands, and upon every one of their heads he set crowns.' And John says, that he 'saw a sea of glass mingled with fire, and them who had gotten the victory over the beast, and over his image, and over his mark, and over the number of his name, standing on the sea of glass, having the harps of God. And they sang the song of Moses the servant of God, and the song of the Lamb.' See then, my dear wife, what glorious promises we everywhere find, which God will bestow, and give to all his dear and sincere children who here abide faithfully by him, and have ended their lives to the honor of their Lord, and washed their robes and made them white in the blood of the Lamb.

"Oh! my wife, from my inmost heart beloved, I cannot sufficiently thank the Lord for all the great kindness which he shows to me-ward. He gives me such strength and power, that I cannot express it. Ah! I now find that the Lord is a

powerful helper in time of need. He forsaketh
not them that put their trust in him. For he who
trusteth in the Lord, shall not be put to shame.
He will keep us as the apple of his eye. He will
deliver us from all the assaults of the devil, and
from the tyranny of this world; yea, he will preserve us, that we shall not descend to hell; provided that we faithfully abide by him unto the
end; for Christ saith, 'He that endureth steadfast
to the end, shall be saved.'

"Oh! my heartily beloved wife, abide faithful
to the Lord even unto death; for the crown is not
at the beginning, nor at the middle, but at the
end. If you abide faithful to the Lord, he will
not forsake you, he will give you the crown of
everlasting life, and lead you into his kingdom;
he will crown you with praise and honor; he will
wipe away all tears from your eyes. My dear
Lysken, will he wipe away all tears? then here
must first be weeping. He will heal our sufferings; therefore we must in this world first suffer.
Yea, we must fight and strive against the roaring
lions, dragons, and bears; yea, against the evil and
wicked generation of vipers and serpent rulers, and
against the subtle serpents of this world, and the
wicked seed of Cain. For Paul saith that 'we
wrestle not against flesh and blood, but against
the rulers of darkness, and against the princes and
powers of this world; yea, against the spirits that
hover in the air,' which is the old serpent and
Satan, that, as Peter says, 'goeth about as a roaring lion seeking whom he may devour.' There-

fore, be diligent in the conflict with prayer and supplication to the Lord. Cleave fast to the doctrine of Jesus Christ our Saviour, that you may attain to the end of your faith, namely, the salvation of your soul. And fight, with Paul, the good fight of faith.

"Herewith, my heartily beloved wife and sister, I commend you to the omnipotent and eternal God, and to the word of his rich grace, that you may remain steadfast against all the gates of hell. Amen."

As it would extend our narrative of this excellent husband and wife beyond all proper bounds to give even half the correspondence which passed between them, we shall transcribe only one letter from Lysken to her husband, in which will be seen considerable talent, a great acquaintance with the Scriptures, and the same spirit of piety which he himself showed. Be it again remembered that both of them were now confined, though separately, in prison :—

"Grace and peace be with us both from God the Father. The love of the Son, and the fellowship of the Holy Ghost be with us, to the perfect strengthening, comfort, joy, and salvation of our souls.

"My beloved husband in the Lord, understand that at first the time seemed exceedingly long to me, because I was not accustomed to imprisonment, and I heard nothing but temptations to forsake the Lord. They said, What reason had I to meddle with the Scripture, I had better mind my sewing, 'It seems,' said they, 'that you will follow

the apostles; what are the signs that you show?
They spake with divers tongues, after they had
received the Holy Ghost. Where is the tongue
that you have received from the Holy Spirit?'
But it is enough for us that we have become believers through their words. John relates that
Christ thus spake:—'I pray not alone for them,
but for those also which shall believe on me
through their word.' Herewith I commend you
to the Lord. The grace of God be with us always.

"Praised be God the Father, who hath had, and
hath shewn such love to us, that he hath given his
dear Son for us. He will bestow upon us such
love, such joy, such wisdom, and such a steadfast
mind, through Christ, and by the might of the
Holy Ghost, that we may stand firm against all
devouring beasts; against dragons and serpents,
against all the gates of hell, now so subtle to catch
and deceive, destroy, and seduce our souls. We
ought, therefore, humbly to pray the Lord, day and
night, without ceasing; for the devourer goeth
round about us, seeking whom he may devour;
and we are not ignorant of his devices. But,
although they are very subtle, the Lord's hand is
not shortened towards those that love him and do
his will; 'for the eyes of the Lord are upon those
who love him, and his ears are open unto their
prayer; but the face of the Lord is against them
that do evil.' Therefore let each one see well to
himself, that the face of the Lord be not against
him; for the soul of him that sinneth shall die,
unless he repent before the Lord come. And it

12*

is not made known to us when the Lord shall come, for he will come as a thief in the night.

"Therefore should we pray to the Lord for each other, that our flight be not on the Sabbath day, when we are unprepared; nor in the winter, when we have no fruit on our trees; 'for every tree that bringeth not forth good fruit, shall be hewn down, and cast into the fire.' But that which bears good fruit, he will purge, that it may bring forth more abundant fruit. And further, it is made known to us by the mouth of the Lord, that to him that sins wilfully, 'there remaineth no more sacrifice for sin; but a certain looking for of judgment and fiery indignation which shall devour the adversaries.' Moses' law was so strict that he who transgressed it, 'died without mercy under two or three witnesses; how much sorer punishment shall he receive, who treads under foot the Son of God!' It is likewise said by the Holy Ghost, 'If we suffer with him, we shall also reign with him. If we be dead with him, we shall also live with him; if we deny him, he also will deny us; if we believe him not, yet he abideth faithful; for he cannot deny himself. Being then encompassed with so great a cloud of witnesses, let us lay aside every weight, and the sin that doth so cleave to us, and let us run with patience the race that is set before us, and look to Jesus, the finisher of our faith, who for the joy that was set before him endured the cross, despising the shame;' not threatening when he suffered for our sins, and the salvation of our souls.

"Thus may we suffer, my best beloved in' the Lord, to the praise of God, and the comfort of all dear friends. I desire that Christ crucified may be our everlasting joy and strength. I confide in the Lord, who only is wise, and who has given his wisdom to those alone who are simple-hearted, guileless, and outcasts from the world, that he will comfort us until the time of our travail arrive.

" My dear husband in the Lord, whom I married before God and his people, but with whom they say I have lived in adultery, because I was not married in Baal; the Lord saith, 'rejoice when men shall say all manner of evil against you; rejoice, and be exceeding glad, for great shall be your reward in heaven.'

"Understand, that I wept much because you were dejected on my account; and because you had heard that I repeatedly wished you to depart from Assuerus, and that you had not done so. Be at rest concerning it, my dearly beloved in the Lord. Had it not been the Lord's pleasure, it would not have taken place; the will of the Lord must be done, to the salvation of both our souls. He suffers us not to be tempted above what we are able to bear. Therefore be comforted, my dearly beloved in the Lord; rejoice yourself in the Lord, even as before, praising and thanking him that he hath chosen us, and counted us worthy to lie so long in bonds for his name's sake. He knows what he hath purposed by this. Although the children of Israel continued long in the wilderness, yet, had they been obedient to the voice of the Lord, they would have entered into the promised land with Caleb and Joshua. So we are now here in the wilderness, among these ravenous beasts, that spread out their nets daily to take us therein; but the Lord is very mighty, who forsaketh not his own that put their trust in him. He preserves them from all evil; yea, as the apple of his eye. Let us then be at rest in him, and take up our cross with joy and patience, and expect with firm assurance the fulfilment of the promises he has given us, nothing doubting, for he is faithful that promised, that we shall be crowned on the hill of Zion, and adorned with palms, and follow the Lamb. I pray you, my beloved in the Lord, be of good cheer in the Lord, with all dear friends, and pray to the Lord for me. Amen."

In a letter written subsequently to this, the eminently pious Lysken says to her husband:—"I beseech the Lord night and day, that he will give us such an ardent love that we may not regard whatever torments they may inflict upon us; yea, that we may say with the prophet David, 'I fear not whatever men may do unto me.' This our suffering, which is light and temporary, is not to be compared with the glory which shall be revealed in us. Since then the will of the Lord is, that with Daniel I should lie long in the lion's den, and await howling and ravenous wolves and lions, and the old serpent that was from the beginning, and shall be to the end; I entreat all my dear brethren and sisters, that they forget me not

in their prayers. I will likewise cheerfully remember them according to my abil'ty. O my
dear friends, how can I sufficiently thank my
heavenly Father, that he hath thought it meet for
me, a poor sheep, to lie so long in bonds for his
name's sake! Night and day do I pray the Lord,
that this my trial may prove my soul's salvation,
to the praise of the Lord, and to the edification of
my brethrén and sisters. Amen."

She goes on to say:—" Nicolaes, from the sugar-
refining house, brought two priests here to instruct me, whom, by the grace of God, I answered.
They told me that they were much grieved because
I held such opinions, for they could not consider it
to be faith, but only opinion, seeing that we did
not hold what the Christian congregation or church
directs. But I told them in reply,—' We desire
to do and to believe only what the church of Christ
directs. But we will have nothing to do with
Baal's temple, or other temples that are made
with hands, after the doctrines and commandments of men, and not after Christ. With these
we will have nothing to do, for Stephen saith that
' the Most High dwelleth not in temples made
with hands,' for he said that he saw 'heaven
opened, and Christ seated on the right hand of his
Father.' And Paul saith that 'we are the temple
of the living God;' if we do his will, 'he will
dwell in us, and walk in us.' They said that they
were the sent, and were those who sit in Moses'
seat. I then answered them, that to them then
belonged the woe recorded in the twenty-third of

Matthew. They asked me, if I meant to say that he who had taught me these things was sent of God? I said, 'Yes, indeed; I know assuredly that he is sent of God.' They then asked me if I knew what a teacher must be? I replied, 'A teacher must be the husband of one wife, blameless, having obedient children, no drunkard, not given to wine, not incontinent.' They then answered, 'If we do wrong, it will fall upon our own heads; the Lord is merciful.' I then asked them if they would sin because of the mercy of God, and said that it was written that we should not add sin to sin, and that we should not say [in such a connexion] the Lord is merciful.

"We spoke much more, which it would be too long to write. I told them that they were ever learning, and never able to come to the knowledge of the truth. They said, that Christ hath spoken to his apostles, 'To you it is given to understand, but to others in parables.' I said that they who rightly understand, to them it is also now given. At last they crossed themselves most zealously, and said that I should know it well when I stood before the judgment seat. 'That will be so indeed,' I said, 'we shall sit there as judges, to judge this disobedient, adulterous generation.' With this they went away. I told them that they came from Satan to torment and destroy my soul.

"Once more I wish, for my dear husband in the Lord, and for myself, Christ crucified, our unfading joy, and a love that passeth not away.

"Know, my dear husband in the Lord, when I

read that you were so happy in the Lord, I could not finish the letter. I was constrained to entreat the Lord that he would give me also the same joy, and preserve it to the end, that we might present the sacrifice of our bodies with rejoicing, to the glory of our Father who is in heaven, and the edification of all dear brethren and sisters. Know that I thank you heartily for the letter which you wrote to me. The grace of the Lord be with us always."

Shortly after Jeroninus had received this letter from his wife, he wrote to her another, breathing the same spirit of piety and of joy in the promises and presence of Christ, showing also that the rage of the enemies of the holy cause had not lessened. Among many other things, he says, "I likewise inform you, beloved, that they taught me severely * * * but the Lord, who kept my mouth, was mightier than all their torments. To the Lord be endless praise and honor, who forsakes not his own. They got no names from me, but one or two which they read to me out of a letter. I told them these, to hear what they would say. But they asked if I were mocking them, and urged me still more, and said that I should name the women, and others too, or they would torture me till the next morning, and would stretch me a foot longer than I was. They told Gileyn that he should rack me. This man did it, while Gileyn poured water into my mouth till I was full. They also had me laid naked, all but my shirt, upon the bench, and bound me to it with four cords, that I thought **my**

head and legs were gone. But they obtained nothing more, praised and adored be the Lord. When
they loosed me, they had, two or three together,
to raise me from the bench to dress me; indeed it
had not been possible to have borne the pain without help from the Lord. They told me that I
must consider of it, and become a good member
of the Roman church, and say all I knew, or they
would know still better how to deal with me. But
I replied thereto, that I had not erred, and would
much rather die than renounce my faith. They
then said that they should come again. But they
can do no more than the Lord permits them.

"Eternal honor to the Lord, who hath thus far
made us meet, and will yet make us meet, to
be children of his kingdom. My beloved wife, I
commend you to the Lord, and to the word of his
grace."

It is with reluctance that we are compelled to
omit several letters to the brethren and sisters
with whom Jeronimus was associated; but the
reader will readily suppose what their character
was from the specimens of those addressed to his
wife, which he has already read. We shall, however, give the closing paragraphs of the last letter
he addressed to her, in the immediate prospect of
death :—

"With this I commend you to the Lord, and to
the word of his grace. Herewith I take leave of
you in this world, for I expect to see your face no
more, but hope shortly to see you again under the
altar of Christ. Therefore, my beloved wife in the

Lord, notwithstanding the world counts us deceivers, and separates us bodily from each other,
yet the compassionate Father will in a little time
bring us together again under his altar, with our
brother. I doubt not of this, but steadfastly confide in him. I have committed all three of us into
his hands, that he may accomplish his divine will
in us, whereby his name may be most praised and
glorified, to the salvation of our souls, and the edification and succor of all those who fear the Lord,
and serve and love his name. This he will do I
doubt not, for he forsakes not his own who put
their trust in him. Therefore I go with a cheerful
mind to present myself a sacrifice to the glory of
God.

"Had it been in my power I would have come
to you, but Joachim would not permit it. But
Christ will soon bring us together under his altar;
that, men will not be able to prevent.

"With this I bid you adieu, till we be again
united under the altar.

"Remain herewith commended to the Lord.

"Tall Henry salutes you much in the Lord.

"Behold, my dear wife in the Lord, the hour is
now come that we must part. I go before you
with great joy and gladness to my heavenly Father, and to yours. I most humbly beseech you
that you be not therefore cast down, but rejoice
with me. Yet I am somewhat sorry that I leave
you amongst these wolves; but I have commended
you, and the fruit of our union, to the Lord, and
am fully persuaded that he will preserve you to

13

the end. In this persuasion I rest myself in peace. Abide devoutly in the Lord."

Such was the cheerful devoted spirit with which Jeronimus Segerson and his companion, Tall Hendrick, went to the stake at Antwerp, September 2, 1551.

Turn we now to Lysken, who had recently given birth to a child, referred to in the farewell letter of her husband, from which we have already quoted. We prefer to give now the beautifully simple and touching account, written at the time, and on the spot, rather than anything of our own :—

"Lysken, our sister, having lain long in bonds, has at last finished the period of her pilgrimage, remaining perfectly steadfast in the word of the Lord unto the end; the Lord be for ever praised. She very boldly and undisguisedly confessed her faith at the tribunal, before the magistrates and the multitude. They first asked her concerning baptism. She said, 'I acknowledge but one baptism, even that which was used by Christ and his disciples, and left to us.' 'What do you hold concerning infant baptism?' asked the sheriff. To this Lysken answered, 'Nothing but a mere infant's baptism, and a human institution.' On this the bench stood up, and consulted together, while Lysken, in the meantime, confessed, and explained clearly to the people the ground of her belief. They then pronounced sentence upon her. Lysken spoke in the following manner to the bench :—'Ye are now judges; but the time will come when ye will

wish that ye had'been keepers of sheep, for there
is a Judge and Lord who is above all ; he shall in
his own time judge you. But we have not to
wrestle against flesh and blood, but against the
principalities, powers, and rulers of the darkness
of this world.' The bench said, ' Take her away
from the tribunal.'

"The people then ran earnestly to see her, and
Lysken spoke piously to them ;—'Know that I do
not suffer for robbery, murder, or any kind of
wickedness, but solely for the incorruptible word
of God.' When they came to the Barg church,
she said, 'O thou den of murderers, how many
souls are murdered in thee !' Proceeding forward,
between the officers, unconfined, the officers said,
'Stand by; make room.' Lysken said, ' They
do not hinder me; they are welcome to see me,
and to take an example by me, even all who love
the word of the Lord;' and while continuing to
speak, she re-entered the prison.

"The people were hereby greatly moved. The
friends were cheerful. Some of them went in the
afternoon to the prison, to visit her, and many
others with them. Our friends conversed a little
with her, and said, ' It is well that you suffer only
for well-doing, and not for any wicked works;'
but she was constrained not to notice them on account of the other people that were there in the
prison. Lysken spoke boldly and piously to the
people, and sang a beautiful hymn, so that they
were astonished. Two monks then came to tempt
her, and they three were shut up together in a

room. Lysken would in no wise listen to them.
The chamber door, at which many persons were
standing, being once opened, Lysken came to the
door, saying to the monks, 'Go till you are sent
for; I will give no ear to you. Had I been satisfied with your leaven I should not have come
here.' She was then again shut up with them in
the room. Thus these wandering spirits, or stars,
came with their false and poisonous venom; but
Lysken, God be praised, was not affrighted. In
good spirits, she sang a hymn in the presence of
the monks. One of the friends who was present,
said, 'Sister, strive manfully!' When they heard
that, they were quite enraged, and said, 'There
is another of her people encouraging her, who deserves burning more than she.' They then departed in wrath, for their voice was strange, and
was not heard there.

"Lysken was now shut up in the chamber alone,
fronting the street where she was accustomed to
sit. No one was permitted to come to her, but
those who had the keys. When the monks came
into the street to go away, some of the friends who
were there asked the monks, 'Will she not turn?'
They replied, 'No: for there was one of her people there whom she preferred hearing.'

"As it now began to draw towards evening, the
Lord graciously ordered it that one of the friends
came to the place where Lysken sat, and spoke a
long time with her. The people in the street beginning to hear, they all locked towards the place
where the friend was. Some who were near him

were troubled, and called to him to go away. He
then said, 'I must first take leave of her,' and
thereupon said to her, 'Stand up, sister; show
yourself; look through the window.' This she
immediately did, and as she looked out upon the
people standing in the street, there were among
them some friends who called out, saying, 'Dear
sister, strive piously, for the crown of life is
set before you.' She then said to the people,
'Drunkards, whoremongers, adulterers, are all
borne with, who will read and talk of the Scriptures; but they who live according to the will of
God, and walk consistently therewith, must be
harassed, oppressed, persecuted, and killed.' She
then raised her voice and began to sing a hymn, but
before she had finished it, the magistrates, with the
officers, came to the prison. Some of the friends
said, 'Sing out, Lysken;' but before she had
finished the hymn they drew her from the window,
and the evening coming on she was no more seen.

"On Saturday morning we rose early, some before day, some with the daylight, to see the nup-
tials which we thought would then be celebrated;
but the crafty murderers outran us. We had slept
too long, for they had finished their murderous
work between three and four o'clock. They had
taken that sheep to the river Scheldt, and had put
her into a sack, and drowned her before the people
arrived, so that few persons saw it. A few, however, did see it, and they testified that she went
courageously to death, and spoke boldly, 'Father,
into thy hands I commend my spirit.' Thus she

13*

was delivered up, and it came to pass to the honor of the Lord that, by the grace of God, many were moved thereby.

"When the people assembled, and heard that she was already dead, it occasioned a great commotion among them, for it grieved them as much as if she had been publicly executed. For the people said, 'Thieves and murderers they bring publicly before all men; but their treachery is thus more manifest.' Some simple-hearted people asked, 'Why must these persons die; for many bear a good testimony concerning them?' Some of the friends were present, and spoke openly to the people, 'The reason is, that they are more obedient to God's commands than to the emperor's or men's; because they have heartily turned to the Lord their God, from lies to the truth, from darkness to light, from unrighteousness to righteousness, from unbelief to the true faith, and have accordingly amended their lives, and been baptized, seeing they were real believers, according to the command of Christ and the practice of the apostles.' They further showed the people, from the word of God, that the papists are they of whom the apostle Paul prophesied, namely, the seducing spirits who teach the doctrines of devils; and moreover, that the righteous have had to suffer from the beginning, from the time of Abel to the present; that Christ also suffered and entered into the glory of his Father, and left us an example that we should follow in his footsteps. 'For all who will live godly in Christ Jesus must suffer persecution.'"

JOHN DESWARTE AND FAMILY.

BRANDT, in his "*History of the Reformation,*" in the sixteenth century, at Halwin, in Flanders, states that John Deswarte, whom he calls an Anabaptist, and his family, who had been betrayed by the professedly Christian pastor of that town, were carried away by the dean of Rousen, to Lisle.

Deswarte was taken with his wife and four sons. The two youngest of his children not being at home when the inquisitor broke into the house, were warned by the neighbors to escape; but one of them said to the other, "Let us not seek to save ourselves, but rather die with our father and mother." In the meantime they carried the father out, who seeing his sons, said to them, "Will ye also go to the New Jerusalem?" One of them, who was scarcely sixteen, cried out, "Yes, we will, father;" and they at once surrendered themselves. These, with two other persons of the same faith, who happened to be in the house, as also two married couples, and a man who had endeavored to comfort them, were, at several times, all burnt at Lisle.

(151)

CHAPTER III.

RICHST HEYNES.

ABOUT the year 1547, there lived in Friesland, in the Ylst, not far from Sneek, a very pious woman, a Baptist, of the name of Richst Heynes, so called after her husband, according to the manner of that country. She had taken upon her the easy yoke of Jesus, hearing and following his blessed voice, and avoiding all who were strangers to Christ and his church. Her holy conduct being observed by the enemies of religion, they resolved either to compel her to abandon her religion, or to put her to death. To this end they employed several cruel emissaries, who, like devouring wolves, soon got into their power this meek and harmless follower of the Son of God.

Her husband becoming acquainted with their designs, escaped with great peril and danger of his life; but they succeeded in imprisoning his wife, cruelly binding her, and treating her with great severity, though not far from confinement, the midwife being with her. In this trying condition they led her away from her home, regardless of the screams and tears of her little children,

(152)

to the prison at Leuwarden, where, after three weeks' imprisonment, she gave birth to a son. This child bore the marks which its mother had received from these inhuman persons, more especially in its arms, which excited much attention and surprise among all who saw her.

These enemies of Christ, after this, inflicted still greater sufferings on this pious disciple, and tortured her to such a degree that she could not raise her hands to her head. Thus was she inhumanly put to the rack, because she would not give evidence against her Christian associates; for these awfully cruel men still thirsted for innocent blood. The great Redeemer she served, always a faithful Refuge in time of need, and a shield to those who trust him, guarded her lips, so that no one suffered through her.

After all means had failed to shake her religion and her constancy, and to induce her to forsake Christ, she was condemned to death; and, as though she were but a brute beast, was placed in a sack, tied up, and thrown into the water until life was extinct.

All this cruelty did this amiable woman endure patiently and unmoved, remaining faithful to her Saviour until death; and thus was she removed from suffering to enjoy her crown of everlasting life.

ELIZABETH.

On the fifteenth of January, in the year 1549, Elizabeth, a tender maiden who had formerly been a Beguin nun, was apprehended for her attachment to Christ and his people.

When the officers came to the house where she lived, they found a Latin New Testament. Having apprehended this holy woman, they said, "We have the right person,—we have now the teacher;" and asked "Where is your husband? Where is Menno Simon?" etc. They conveyed her to the council-house, and the next day two white Capuchin friars conducted her to another place, where she was brought before the council. She was asked by them, on oath, whether she had a husband. Her reply was, "It is not permitted us to swear; but our words must be yea, yea; and nay, nay. I have no husband.

Council.—We say that you are a teacher, who mislead many, and this we have been told concerning you by others. We wish to know who are your friends.

Elizabeth.—My God has commanded me to love the Lord my God, and therefore to honor my parents. I will not therefore tell you who are my parents; for to suffer for Christ's name is, [in the esteem of the public,] to the dishonor of my friends.

(154)

COUNCIL.—On this we will not further press you, but we would know what people you have taught.

ELIZABETH.—Oh no, gentlemen, excuse me herein, and ask me concerning my faith; *that* I will most readily confess.

COUNCIL.—We shall use such severe means as will make you confess.

ELIZABETH.—I trust, through the grace of God, that he will keep my tongue, so that I shall not become a traitor, and deliver my brother to death.

COUNCIL.—What persons were present when you were baptized?

ELIZABETH.—Christ said, "Ask those that were present, or that heard it."

COUNCIL.—Now we see that you are a teacher; for you wish to make yourself like Christ.

ELIZABETH.—No, gentlemen, God forbid I should; for I esteem myself no better than the sweepings of the house of the Lord.

COUNCIL.—What then do you hold concerning the house of God? Do you not consider our church to be the house of God?

ELIZABETH.—No, indeed, gentlemen; for it is written, "Ye are the temple of the living God;" as God says, "I will dwell in them, and walk in them."

COUNCIL.—What do you think of our mass?

ELIZABETH.—I do not approve of your mass; but whatever agrees with God's word, that I highly esteem.

Council.—What do you think of the most holy sacrament?

Elizabeth.—I have never in my life read in holy Scripture of a holy sacrament; but I have read of the Supper of the Lord. [Here she repeated the Scriptures which referred to this ordinance.]

Council.—Be silent; for the devil speaks by your mouth.

Elizabeth.—This indeed, gentlemen, is but a small matter; for the servant is no better than his Lord.

Council.—You speak with a proud spirit.

Elizabeth.—No, gentlemen; I speak with freedom of spirit.

Council.—What did the Lord say when he gave the Supper to his disciples?

Elizabeth.—What did he give them, flesh or bread?

Council.—He gave them bread.

Elizabeth.—Did not the Lord then continue sitting there? Who then could eat the Lord's flesh?

Council.—What do you hold concerning infant baptism, that you should have had yourself baptized again?

Elizabeth.—No, gentlemen; I have not been baptized again; I was baptized once on my confession of faith; for it is written that baptism belongs to believers.

Council.—Are our children then lost, because they have been baptized?

ELIZABETH.—No, gentlemen; far be it from me that I should condemn the children.

COUNCIL.—Do you not expect salvation from baptism?

ELIZABETH.—No, gentlemen. All the waters in the sea cannot save me; but salvation is in Christ; and he has commanded me to love the Lord my God above all things, and my neighbor as myself.

COUNCIL.—Have the priests power to forgive sins?

ELIZABETH.—No, gentlemen; how can I believe that? I say that Christ is the only priest through whom is the forgiveness of sins.

COUNCIL.—You say that you believe all that agrees with the holy Scripture: do you then agree with the words of James?

ELIZABETH.—Yes, truly, gentlemen. How could I not agree with them?

COUNCIL.—Has he not said, "Go to the elder of the *church*, that he may anoint you, and pray for you?

ELIZABETH.—Yes, gentlemen. Do you then mean to say that you are of *such* a church?

COUNCIL.—The Holy Ghost has already saved *you;* you need neither confession nor sacrament?

ELIZABETH.—No, gentlemen. I acknowledge indeed that I have transgressed the command of the pope, which has been confirmed by the emperor's proclamation. But show me any article in which I have transgressed against the Lord my God, and I will say, "Woe is me, poor miserable creature!"

14

This is recorded as the first confession. She was afterwards brought again before the council, and led into the torture tower, the executioner, Hans, being present. The council then said, "We have thus far proceeded with mildness, and if you will not confess, we will treat you with severity. The procureur-general spoke :—"Master Hans, lay hold of her." Hans answered, "Oh no, gentlemen, she will confess voluntarily." And as she would not make a voluntary confession he put thumb-screws on both her thumbs and fore-fingers,

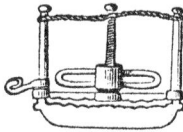

THUMB-SCREW.

so that the blood sprang out of her nails. Elizabeth exclaimed, "Oh, I cannot longer bear it!" The council said, "Confess, and we will ease your pain." But she cried to the Lord her God, "Help, O my God, thy poor handmaid: for thou art a helper in time of need." The council cried out, "Confess, and we will ease your pain; for we spoke to you of confessing, and not of calling on God the Lord." But she continued steadfastly calling upon the Lord her God, as we have already related. And the Lord relieved her pain, so that she said to the council, "Ask me, and I will answer you; for I feel no longer any pain in my body as before."

COUNCIL.—Will you not yet confess?

ELIZABETH.—No, gentlemen.

They then put on two iron screws, one on each ankle. She said, "Oh, gentlemen, put me not to shan.e." The procureur-general said, "No, Miss Elizabeth, we shall not treat you improperly." She then fainted; and they said one to another, "Perhaps she is dead." Coming to herself, she said, "I am alive, and not dead." They then loosened all the iron screws, and spoke to her with entreaties.

ELIZABETH.—Why do you thus entreat me? They deal so with children.

Thus they could not draw from her a word to the injury of her associates in the Lord, or of any individual.

COUNCIL.—Will you recant all the things you have before confessed?

ELIZABETH.—No, indeed, gentlemen; but I will seal them with my blood.

COUNCIL.—We will no longer distress you, if you will now freely tell us who it was that baptized you.

ELIZABETH.—Oh no, gentlemen; I have already told you that I will not confess that to you.

After this, the sentence was pronounced upon her, March 27, 1549, and she was condemned to death by being drowned in a sack. Thus she willingly offered her body a living sacrifice unto God. Her enemies showed the extent of their hatred; happily, however, their real power was but small, for though her body was committed to the river, her happy spirit was soon filled with the triumphant joys of the upper world.

In one of the Mennonite hymn-books is to be read a hymn descriptive of the cloister life, which is said to have been composed by Elizabeth, and handed down from one generation to another, till printed in 1618. It consists of forty-eight verses, with the following refrain or chorus:—

> " In thanks to God will I delight,
> And love and praise with all my might,
> Honor and fear him day and night."

MARIA, OF MONJOU.

It has been always true, that they who will live godly in Christ Jesus shall suffer persecution. So was it with this eminently pious woman.

Having, according to the requirement of Scripture, on a profession of faith in Jesus, been baptized, and become a member of the body of Christ, and having for a long time conducted herself with holy consistency in the church and towards society in general, the hatred of the ungodly displayed itself. The magistrate of Monjou had a great dislike to this poor widow, and at length cast her into prison. There she lay confined for more than a year; and though she had to pass through many sufferings, she cheerfully bore them. Constantly did she exhort the pious to walk in love, and abide firmly by the covenant of Jesus Christ. She was herself always diligent to present her body a living sacrifice, holy and acceptable unto God, that her soul might be built up as a spiritual house, well adorned inwardly with the word of God.

The magistrate, in every possible way, tempted her for three days, but could not induce her to renounce her faith. She firmly resolved to abide in Christ. The magistrate entreated her to go to what she considered the erroneous church; he even promised that if she would do so, he would

14*   (161)

release her, and give her support for a year.
However, she would not consent to his proposal,
but said that she would abide with Christ, and
was willing to resign her life for him. She was
therefore condemned to be drowned.

When she went towards the water, she sang with
a cheerful heart, and rejoiced that so happy an
hour had arrived. Thus, like her Lord, she went
as a sheep to the slaughter. She remembered the
testimony of Scripture, "They shall kill you, and
think they do God service." Going along the
road she said, "I have been the bride of an earthly
bridegroom, but to-day I hope to be the bride of
Christ, and with him to inherit his kingdom."

When they approached the water, one of the
dissemblers said, "O Maria, repent, or it will not
be well with you." They kept her by the side of
the water nearly three hours, hoping they might
persuade her to recant, and to follow them; but
her only reply was, "I abide by my God; proceed in the business for which you are come here.
The corn is in the straw, and it must be threshed.
In like manner the word of God has begun to
work, and it must be perfected." She then par-
tially uncovered herself, and went cheerfully to
death, saying, "O heavenly Father, into thy hands
I commend my spirit." She was then driven into
the water, where she died, witnessing to the truth
of the gospel with her last breath, and greatly encouraging the believers in Christ who witnessed
the affecting scene.

Baptist Martyrs.

A YOUNG LADY OF FOURTEEN, AND OTHERS.

ANOTHER illustration of the doctrine that the followers of Christ must suffer persecution, was given in the city of Rotterdam, in the year 1544. A number of the followers of Jesus were assembled together in his name, to speak to each other for mutual edification, and their establishment in the truth of the gospel which they had received. Here they felt the spirit and the power of prayer and praise, and rejoiced in the performance of these holy exercises. But such engagements have always excited the highest displeasure of the Catholics, who have sought to put an end to them by every means in their power.

This assembly of devoted Christians was betrayed into the hands of its enemies, by a woman who came to the house where they had met, professedly to borrow a kettle. Being thus thrown into the power of wolves, these unresisting sheep were treated by them most cruelly; in order, if possible, to draw them away from the truth. They, however, patiently endured persecution for the name of Jesus, in the certain hope of his eternal kingdom. As no torments could induce them to recant, they were sentenced to suffer death. The men were beheaded by the sword in the city itself, and the women were most tyrannically thrown

(163)

into a boat, and thrust under the ice till they were drowned.

Among those thus sacrificed was a young female only fourteen years old. She composed a favorite hymn in the old Dutch hymn books, beginning:—

> "To the wide world Immanuel came,
> His Father's kingdom left," etc.

Well may Brandt, in his "*History of the Reformation*," call this "a dreadful butchery of a religious assembly of Anabaptists at Rotterdam."

How striking the contrast between this church of the Lord, and the synagogue of Satan; and how different the spirit they breathed! The followers of Christ, like lambs, manifest no spirit of revenge, but freely resign their lives for the cause of their Lord; but their enemies "breathe out threatenings and slaughter," and delight in the attempt to destroy the church of the Redeemer. How strikingly different too, will be their treatment by the all-seeing and omnipotent Judge at the last great day!

CHAPTER IV.

———◦——

GERARD, AND HIS FRIENDS.

———

ABOUT the year 1160 appeared at Oxford, in England, about thirty men and women, called *Publicans*, a corruption, no doubt, of PAULICIANS. They came from Gascony, and soon attracted the attention of the government by the singularity of their religious opinions and practices. They were thorough Baptists, and judging from the testimony of their enemies, as well as that of their friends, they were eminently a spiritual people.

William, of Newbury, a monkish historian, tells us that these persons, whom he calls vagabonds, emigrated from Gascony, and spread their doctrine into many regions. "In the broadest provinces of France, and Spain, and Italy, and Germany, so many are said to have been infested with this pest, that according to the prophet they seemed to have been multiplied beyond the sand of the sea." He adds "they are mere rustics and men of inferior condition, hence they are dull in the comprehension of argument; yet if they are once thoroughly tainted with that pest, they will rigidly hold out against all discipline. Hence, it very

(165)

rarely happens that any of them, whenever they are betrayed and dragged out of their lurking places, is [are] ever converted to piety."

These poor peasants of Teutonic race, and speaking that language, could not accomplish much in the way of converting others. Their enemies tell us that one woman professed to have been converted by them; though she seems to have returned back to the errors of popery, and was, probably, the person who betrayed them into the hands of their enemies. Their pastor, named Gerard, was, it is said, the only person of any learning among them, and "to him," says the historian, "they all looked up, as their prince and preceptor."

When the matter was made known to king Henry II., whose love of justice had induced him to revive in England trial by jury, he would not allow them to be punished without a hearing, and ordered a council of popish bishops to be assembled in Oxford to try them. The imagination paints before us this proud array of lordly ecclesiastics in all the pomp and splendor in which popery delights, sitting in high state, assuming powers which belong not to mortal man; they call before them a little body of poor simple peasants, foreigners, without a friend, without an advocate to plead for them, without a witness to prove the innocence of their lives, or liberty to appeal to the word of God in defence of their doctrines. How forlorn and desolate appeared these poor prisoners!

Gerard, who was quite equal to the task, spoke

for the whole. His answer to his examiners was
—that they were Christians, and that they ven-
erated the doctrines of the Apostles. On a more
particular enquiry, it was found that they denied
several of the leading doctrines of the Romish
church, such as purgatory, prayers for the dead,
the invocation of saints, the baptism of infants,
and transubstantiation. They would admit nothing
contrary to the word of God, and while acknow-
ledging themselves unable to argue all the points
brought forward by their cunning adversaries, they
positively refused to surrender the faith which they
held, or to join in the idolatrous services of the
papal church. They were then threatened with
the severest sufferings, which threats they laughed
to scorn, and answered in the words, " Blessed are
they who suffer persecution for righteousness'
sake; for theirs is the kingdom of heaven."

These Publicans being found so firm in their
rejection of false doctrine, the bishops reported
them to the king as obstinate heretics, worthy of
death; and he, under priestly influence, sentenced
them all to be branded with a red hot iron on their
foreheads, as heretics; that then they should be
publicly whipped through the streets of Oxford,
and be afterwards delivered to the secular power
for further punishment, or, in other words, should
be put to death. To the proclamation was added
a command that none of the people should show
them sympathy or comfort under the severest
penalties.

The sentence was fully carried into execution.

Gerard, to distinguish him from the rest, had a mark burnt on his chin as well as on his forehead; their clothes were all cut short by the girdles, and in the depth of winter, when the hedges and the fields were covered with snow, every man, woman, and child was cast into the fields, and the whole of them perished with cold and hunger. The historian exults that having been beaten "with loudly sounding stripes," they were driven out of the city. "No one," says William, "showing them the slightest degree of mercy, they miserably perished." But the historian is wrong. Misery was no part of their lot. He himself tells us that they went forth to endure death, "not with lingering steps, but actually rejoicing with much joy; while their master preceded them, and sang, 'Blessed are ye when all men shall hate you.'"

Thus they died, but the truths they maintained, and which so fully sustained them in the hour of martyrdom, are immortal!

RICHARD WOODMAN.

As true religion is always the same, so are its
effects. The soldiers of Christ have always endured hardness, whatever post they might occupy
in his army. The mechanic as well as the clergyman has brought honor to his Redeemer, by his
bold utterance of the truth, and by his readiness
to "die for the Lord Jesus." Thus has it been
seen that the faith of Christ raises a man above
the world, and that he will, when brought before
rulers, take a stand for the truth to which nothing
else could lead him. RICHARD WOODMAN, burnt
at the stake, in the days of cruel Mary of England,
furnished a glorious instance of attachment to the
truths and ordinances of the Gospel.

This extraordinary man was a simple mechanic,
—a worker in iron; his residence was at Warble-
ton, in the county of Sussex; and his apprehension
by the so-called officers of justice took place when
he was about thirty years of age. The curate or
minister of the parish, named Fairbanke, was,
during the reign of Edward VI., a preacher of the
truth, and zealously entreated the people never to
give heed to "another gospel." He was "the
husband of one wife," and discharged his duties
with much satisfaction to his congregation. As
soon, however, as Mary came to the throne, he
veered round, embraced the creed of popery, and

taught the people the very opposite doctrines to those which they had been accustomed to hear from him.

When Richard Woodman heard these things from his lips, he could not forbear to admonish his pastor, and for doing this he was immediately apprehended, and committed to the Queen's Bench prison, where he remained a year and a half. At the end of this period he was transferred, by the notorious Dr. Story, to Bishop Bonner's coal-house, a place but too well known, with all its miseries, to many of the holy martyrs of that period. Here he remained about a month, after which he underwent twenty-six examinations, and was expecting to be led to the stake, when, to the surprise of himself and his friends, on the very day on which the noble martyr Philpot was burned, Woodman, with four others, was suddenly restored to liberty.

It must not be supposed that this happy event silenced his tongue as to the movements around him, especially as to the death of Philpot. His notice of this event was in language equally severe and just; and strongly expressive of the indignation and abhorrence excited in the minds of all good men by the murder of that excellent martyr. After saying that Bonner sent for him and his companions and discharged them, only requiring them very earnestly to speak well of him, Woodman goes on, "And no doubt he was very worthy to be praised, because he had been so faithful an aid in his master, the devil's business; for he had burnt good master Philpot the same morning, with whose blood his heart was so drunken, as I supposed, that he could not tell what he did, as it appeared to us both before and after. For but two days before he promised us that we should be condemned that same day that we were delivered; yea, and the morrow after he had delivered us, he sought for some of us again, yea, and that earnestly. He waxed dry [thirsty] after his great drunkenness, whereby he is likely to have blood to drink in hell, as he is worthy, if he repent it not with speed. The Lord turn all their hearts, if it be his will."

Woodman carefully wrote down all his earlier examinations; but the bishop of Chichester obtained possession of them, and either concealed or destroyed them. The persecutors then proclaimed that he had recanted; but this he disproved, by travelling about from parish to parish, and talking so openly, even to the principal people, that it was resolved again to confine him in prison. That they might do this under the color of law, they invented a charge against him of usurping the office of the ministry in baptizing and marrying persons; from which he so fully cleared himself, that they could not execute upon him the warrants already drawn up. However, they soon issued others, and the Queen's chamberlain sent three of his men to take him while ploughing his land. As these men were professedly friends of Woodman, he had no suspicion of them, and so was easily arrested; but going home to change his apparel, it occurred to him to demand a sight of their warrant, when they

confessed that they had none with them. He then
pleaded the right of an Englishman, and refused
to go with them unless they produced one. They
locked him in his house, and guarded the door,
while one of them went to obtain a warrant; and
he, taking advantage of the opportunity, made his
escape from the back part of the dwelling.

Of course, a strict search was instantly commenced, which Woodman eluded by taking up
his abode under the trees in a thick plantation,
within a bowshot of his own house. Here, with
his Bible, pen, and ink, he contentedly stayed for
six or seven weeks, his wife daily bringing him
food. The simple and fervent man wrote, " I
thought myself blessed of God, that I was thought
worthy to lie in the woods for the name of Christ."
Meanwhile the sea-coast, from Portsmouth to
Dover, was guarded, to prevent the poor man's
escape. But failing in their search, they abandoned it, concluding that he had left the country,
which he did when they had ceased to look for
him.

Abroad, however, he could not long stay. He
ardently desired again to see his native land. " I
thought," said he, " every day seven years, or ever
I were at home again." So in three weeks he returned, and notwithstanding the zeal with which
his enemies hunted him, he often abode a month
or five weeks openly in his own house, following
his accustomed occupation. His enemies, as he
himself said, could lay no hands on him till their
hour was fully come. It arrived at last, and by

the treachery of his own father and brother he was led into their grasp.

The circumstances were these:—Richard had entrusted property, of the value of fifty pounds a year, to his father and brother, wherewith to pay his debts, and to maintain his wife and children. They wickedly reported that it was not sufficient for the first of these purposes, whereas it was more by two hundred pounds, than all his debts amounted to; and Woodman, anxious to do justice, applied to them to restore the money and writings, and to settle the account with him. A day was appointed, on which a full account should be sent in to him with the balance; but to avoid this restitution, the wretched brother went and apprised his enemies, that at such a time they might certainly seize him in his own house. The sheriff accordingly sent a strong party of men, who concealed themselves a whole night in bushes near the dwelling. A workman in Woodman's employ, and two of his little children, falling in with them, were detained, lest they should give the alarm; and in the afternoon, while the poor man was reclining on a bed, making shoe-thongs, his little girl, who saw them approaching, ran into the room, crying out, " Mother, mother, there come twenty men." Woodman started up, and thought to have slipped out of the door, but they were too near, and his wife instantly shut and bolted it, while he made the attempt to escape by another door; the house, however, was immediately sur-

15*

rounded, and the officers called out to have the door opened, or they would break in.

Woodman's house had been searched at least twenty times, by night and by day; sometimes nearly twenty men would be at the same time examining it. There was, however, one place which they were never able to discover, being formed for concealment; and into this he went; while his wife, knowing him to be now safe, opened the door, and telling the men he was not there, excused herself for having barred it on the ground of having been often frightened by the men who were sent to search, and also supposing that the displeasure against her husband extended to her and her children. They demanded a candle, saying there were many secret places in the house; and after a most minute search they ceased from their task, some of the party going down to the churchyard, where they stood talking with the unnatural father of the persecuted man.

The conductor of these officers was a next door neighbor, who had been persuaded by the wicked brother thus to betray him. He knew of the hiding-place, which his friend had often mentioned to him in confidence; but it happened that he had never shewn him the way to it, only that the entrance was over a window in the hall. On receiving this information, they renewed the search, and one of them perceived a little loft with three or four chests in it, between two of which the entrance really was; but as they could not discover it, they insisted on his wife pointing it out. She led them to another quarter, and then gave her husband a token to escape, from which he supposed there was no farther hope of his remaining concealed. He could not descend into the house without coming into the midst of them; and his only chance was to break through some boarding, which he did by setting his shoulder against it; but unhappily the noise thus occasioned, attracted their attention, and as he attempted to jump from a window they saw him. He had not had time to put on his shoes, when the alarm was first given him by his child; and he had now to run along a lane strewn over with sharp cinders, while a shout was raised, and a pursuit commenced with cries of " Strike him, strike him!" He looked back, and saw but one man within a hundred yards of him; and had he been shod, he might have easily got away, being strong, swift, and courageous; but just then one of his naked feet fell upon a hard-pointed cinder, and starting from it, he incautiously stept into a hole full of mire, which threw him down. Before he could recover himself, the pursuer, a very powerful man, came upon him, and he was taken. On this he remarks, " It was not God's will; for if it had been, I should have escaped from them all, if there had been ten thou sand of them."

While they were conducting him to his home, to put on his shoes, and complete his dress, one of them sneeringly said, " Now your master has deceived you; you said you were an angel; and if so, why did you not flee away from us." He asked who had ever heard him say he was an angel? "It is not," he added, "the first lie by a thousand that they have made for me. Angels are never of mortal birth; but if they had said they heard me say that I do trust I am a saint, they had not said amiss." "What! do you think to be a saint?" asked the other. "Yea, that I do, and am already in God's sight, I trust in God; for he who is not a saint in God's sight already, is a devil. Therefore he who scorneth to be a saint, let him be a devil."

At his own door he met his father, who desired him to remember himself; meaning that he should consider the consequences of persisting in his religious faith; to which he answered, "I praise God that I am well remembered whereabout I go. This way was appointed of God for me to be delivered into the hands of mine enemies; but woe to him by whom I am betrayed! It would be good for that man that he had never been born, if he repent not with speed. The Scriptures are now fulfilled on me; 'For the father shall be against the son; and the brother shall deliver the brother to death,' as it is this day come to pass." One of the men sneeringly remarked, "that he was a good child to accuse his father;" he answered, "I accuse him not, but say my mind; for there was no man knew me to be at home but my father, my brother, and one more; the which I dare say would not hurt me for all the good in this town." After some further talk, and cruelly refusing him even to enter the door of his house, at which he was obliged to put on his shoes and the rest of his clothes, they bound him by putting a hound's slip over his arms; which he said, rejoiced his heart, that he was counted worthy to be bound for the name of God. He then took leave of his poor wife, his children, and his wretched father, and was led away.

In the following April the sheriffs sent Woodman to London, where, after two days, he was brought before his Ordinary, the bishop of Chichester, to whom he had appealed; Story, Cook, and others assisted in the examination. The bishop told him he was sorry for him, as were all the gentlemen of his county, where he had a good report, both among rich and poor. On this account he wished him to consider himself, with his family and friends, and not to suppose that he was wiser than all in the realm, but to receive instruction. The good man disclaimed any wish to seem wiser than others, being willing to learn of any man who could or would teach him the truth. "For my wife and children," said he, "God doth know how I love them in him, and my life also. My life, my wife, and my children are all in God's hands, and I have them all as though I had them not, I trust, according to St. Paul's words. But if I had ten thousand pounds of gold, I had rather lose it all than them, if I might choose, and not displease God."

He then told the bishop of Chichester that he had appealed to him, that if any fault was found in him, he might be reformed by him; and also, that if his blood was shed unrighteously, it might be required at his hands, who had undertaken to be the spiritual physician of that part of the country.   On his saying this, Story broke out as usual, "Is not this a perverse fellow, to lay to your charge that his blood shall be required at your hands?"   And turning to Woodman, he said, "Thinkest thou that thou shalt be put to death unjustly, that thy blood shall be required? No, if he should condemn a hundred such heretics as thou art. I helped to rid a good number of you; and I promise thee I will help to rid thee too, the best that I can."

Woodman would have replied, but Chichester enjoined them both to be silent; and then kindly addressing Woodman, calling him neighbor, told him that he, as his spiritual pastor, was **ab**out to give him spiritual counsel; therefore **he** must listen to him.   Woodman begged first to ask him a question, which was, whether he was sure that he had the Spirit of God. The bishop said "No;" swearing by St. Mary that he dare not be so bold as to say so. The prisoner then told him that he was like the waves of the sea, unstable; and threatened him with the doom of the Laodicean church; this put Story into a great rage, who, with great violence told him that he had the devil within him, and was mad; and that he was worse than Satan; with many other similar things. Chichester remarked, that the man was sent to him to learn, but presumed to teach him.

The poor man, on seeing their blindness, burst

into tears, and said, "The Jews told Christ he had a devil, and was mad, as ye have said that I am; and I know that the servant is not above his master. And God forbid that I should learn of him who confesseth that he hath not the Spirit of God." "Why," said the bishop, "do you think that you have the Spirit of God?" "I believe, verily, that I have the Spirit of God," was the reply. Chichester said, "You boast more than ever Paul did, or any of the apostles; the which is great presumption." Woodman answered, "I boast not in myself, but in the gift of God, as Paul did; for he said that he believed verily that he had the Spirit of God; making no doubt, as in 1. Cor. vii." "It is not so," said the bishop, "you belie the text." "It it be not so, let me be burned to-morrow," replied Woodman. "Thou shalt not be burned to-morrow," said Story, "but thou shalt be burned within these six days, I promise thee."

Chichester next qualified his denial of the quotation, by saying that if it was so, it was wrongly translated; as it was, he said, in a thousand other places. They then consulted the Latin and Greek passages, and he told him that in both Paul said he supposed he had the Spirit of God, but was not sure; the bishop adding, "Even so I hope and suppose I have the Spirit of God, but I am not sure."

Woodman then went on to say, that if men had wrongly translated the Bible, woe unto such translators! However, he warned them to beware that they did not slander the translators, whom he be-

lieved to have had the fear of God before their
eyes. He offered to prove, by places enough, besides the one quoted, that Paul had the Spirit of
God; as he himself, and all the elect, had. This
he did by citing, "No man can believe that Jesus
is the Lord, but by the Holy Ghost;" and went
on, "I do believe that Jesus Christ is my Redeemer, and that I shall be saved from all my
sins by his death and blood-shedding, as Paul and
all the apostles did, and as all faithful people
ought to do, which no man can do without the
Spirit of God; and as there is no condemnation to
them who are in Christ Jesus, so there is no salvation to them who are not in Christ Jesus. For he
who hath not the Spirit of Christ is none of his,
but is a cast-away." And again, " 'We have not
received the spirit of bondage to fear any one;
but we have received 'the Spirit of adoption,
whereby we cry Abba Father.' The same Spirit
certifieth our spirits that we are the sons of God.
Besides all this, John saith, 'He that believeth in
God dwelleth in God, and God in him.' So it is
impossible to believe in God unless God dwell in
us. Oh, great God! what more injury can be
done unto thee than to mistrust that we have received thy Holy Spirit by thy gift? Thus may all
men see their blindness, and whose servants they
be, as they declare themselves both by their words
and deeds!"

By this time Dr. Story had become greatly excited, and cried out, "Oh, my lord, what a heretic
is this same! Why do you hear him? Send him

to prison to his fellows in the Marshalsea, and they shall be dispatched within these twelve days." "When I heard him say so," says Woodman, from whose recital of his last examinations this account is taken, "I rejoiced greatly in my heart, desiring God, if it were his will, to keep him in that mind; for I looked surely to have gone to the Bishop of London's coal-house, or to Lollard's tower; but it pleased God to put it in their hearts to send me to the Marshalsea, amongst our brethren, and my old prison fellows: so mercifully hath God dealt with me, in easing me of my burden that I looked for."

They observed his satisfaction, and the bishop said, "Methinks he is not afraid of the prison;" to which Woodman replied, "No, I thank the living God." This again raised Story's savage temper, and he said, "This is a heretic indeed: he hath the exact terms of all heretics, ' The *living* God!' I pray you are there dead Gods, that you say the *living* God?" Woodman mildly asked in reply, "Be you angry with me because I speak the words which are written in the Bible?" "Bibble-babble, bibble-babble," said the dignified divine, adding, "there is no such word written in all the Bible." "Then I am much to blame if it be not so written," said Woodman, and quoted texts in support of his assertion. Chichester confessed that it was so written, and that it was the truth; but added that such was the language of all heretics. He was supported by Story, who sagely said, "My lord, I will tell you a heretic by his words, because I have been more used to them

16

than you have been; that is they will say 'the Lord,' and 'We praise God,' and 'The living God.' By these words you shall know a heretic." "All these words," replied Woodman, "are written for our learning, and we are commanded by the prophet to use them daily, as thus, 'The Lord's name be praised, from the rising up of the sun, even to the going down of the same,' Also, as many as fear the Lord say always, 'The Lord be praised.'"

After a little more railing, Dr. Story went off to mass; and then the bishop said to Woodman, "I would not have you use such speeches as you do, as 'the Lord be praised,' and 'the living God,' with such like words. Can you not say as well, our Lord, or our God, as otherwise?" Woodman, after declaring that he could not see how he could deserve to be censured for using the plain language of Scripture, added "It seemeth to me that you mistrust that I believe not as you do." "Yes, that is my meaning, indeed," said the bishop. "I believe in the living God," repeated Woodman; "if you do not so, then our belief is not alike, indeed. But if it please you to examine me on any particular matter now, I will make you answer thereto by God's help."

The bishop then proceeded to charge Woodman and his friends with erring from the church; and in proof of it showed him a great bundle of writings; which, as soon as Woodman saw, he acknowledged to be his own, which had been privately stolen from his house by the sheriff's men. They contained his examinations and discussions

during his former imprisonment. He expressed
his gladness that the bishop might now see, under
his own hand, a full statement both of what had
been said and what had been done against him,
referring him to the parties named there for a confirmation of its truth.

Then followed a very long conversation, in
which the bishop manifested a spirit so different
from that of his brethren in general, that if he was
sincere in it, his mind must have been ill at ease
under the burden of such companionship in evil.
Gently, kindly, and candidly he both spoke and
listened, as one who was far from desiring to turn
away his ears from the truth; and even admitted,
with evident satisfaction, Woodman's refutation
of all the false charges against him. Having
cleared himself, the martyr thus spoke,—" Wherefore look ye to it, for I am now in your hands, and
you ought to be a house of defence against mine
enemies; for if you suffer them to kill me, my
blood shall be required at your hands. If you can
find in me any just cause of death by God's word,
you may condemn me yourself, and not offend
God. Wherefore look to it; the matter is weighty;
deliver me not into their hands, and look to be so
discharged." Chichester told him that he was not
yet fully invested with the authority of his office,
but he would do what he could for him.

They then entered on the question, whether or
no St. Paul was married, and Woodman proved
that he was not; speaking very fully on the subject, in a way which seemed to please the bishop,

who said he was very glad to have heard him so speak, and warmly repeated his assurance of a sincere wish to serve him. Woodman told him that he was willing to renounce anything that he held, which could be proved contrary to God's word. "And the truth is," continued he, I have talked with a dozen priests at the least, since I was delivered out of prison, of certain matters, and they have not been able to certify me in anything that I have asked them; and therefore they have complained of me to the sheriff and justices, making tales and lies to turn me to displeasure, as much as in them lieth. I promise [assure] you that there are as many unlearned priests in your diocese as in any one diocese in England, so I think; the more is it to be lamented." The bishop's answer was much to his honor,—"I promise [assure] you I do much lament it myself, for I hear no less; but it is true as you say. I would I could remedy it, but I cannot; but I will do the best that I can when I come into the country; and I will be glad to talk with you some other time, when I shall be somewhat better at ease. You see, I am very tender [out of health] now, as I have been this half year and more. Come to dinner; our dinner is ready. I counsel you not to tarry for any great cheer that you shall have; nor would I that you should think I go about to win you with my meat; but you are welcome with all my heart; come, sit down."

After enjoying a plentiful dinner with the bishop, in company with a merchant and one of

the sheriff's officers who guarded him, he was told
by the bishop that he must deliver him to Story's
man, but that he would soon send for him again,
and prayed God he might do him good. Woodman begged that he might have nothing to do
with Story, requesting the bishop to examine him
himself. They then began to discuss the subject
of the sacraments, of which Woodman would acknowledge but two; and the bishop engaging to
convince him by God's word that there were seven,
kindly bid him farewell.

Thus does the bold and faithful Baptist conclude
this part of his narrative :—" And so I was brought
me to the Marshalsea, where I now am merry—
God be praised therefor—looking for judgment of
my flesh, for they intend to dispatch me shortly,
if God will give them leave; but He hath their
hearts in his hand, and they can do nothing to me
but as he will give them leave. Wherefore I commit my cause to God only, and I am sure there
shall not one hair of my head perish without my
heavenly Father's will, though I bide [endure]
never so much trouble. Job perished not for all
his trouble, though God gave the devil leave to
trouble him in divers and many ways, as God hath
suffered his members to trouble and try me divers
and many ways, I praise God. They shall as little
prevail against my faith, I have no mistrust, as the
devil prevailed against Job, whatsoever they do
with my goods, body, or life. For he who kept
Job in all his trouble neither slumbereth nor sleep-
eth, but keepeth me and all his elect, that whether

we live or die it shall be to the praise and glory of
God.   For if we live, we live at the Lord's will;
and if we die, we die at the Lord's will; so whether
we live or die we are the Lord's—blessed be his
name.

" Wherefore, dear brethren and sisters, to whom
this my writing shall come, be of good cheer, and
fear not what man can do unto you, for they can
but kill the body; but fear him who hath power
to kill both body and soul.   And yet once again I
bid you be of good cheer, for the sheriff, with divers other gentlemen and priests, when I was at
the sheriff's house, said to me, that all the heretics
in the country hung on me, as the people did in
times past upon St. Augustine, or St. Ambrose, or
such like.   Wherefore, said they, look well on it;
you have a great thing to answer for.   To the which
I answered, I pray God to lay nothing more to my
charge than he will do for heresy, as I am sure he
will not; for He hath set my sins as far from me
as it is from the east to the west, so that I am sure
they shall never come near me any more.   Yea,
and by that they call heresy we serve God.   And
I am sure that there is no man or woman that
hangeth on me, but on God.

" But such are *their* imaginations and thoughts,
that if they might win me to them, they should
win a great many likewise.   And thinking to kill
me if they cannot win me, as I trust in God, and
am sure they never shall, by God's grace, if it were
possible for them to kill me ten times; for I am so
linked to Christ in a chain by faith, that it is im-

possible for men to loose us asunder, neither for
life nor death, I praise my Lord God therefor. No
doubt their full intent and purpose is to kill me,
thinking thereby to make others afraid; which
death of my body were best of all for me, if God
was so pleased. But if I may live for the comfort
of others, his name be praised. I know what he
can do, but what he *will* do I know not. But if
death be offered me, so that I cannot refuse it
without displeasing God, I trust in God I shall not
offend my brethren in receiving death, but shall
rather be an occasion of strengthening their faith,
by choosing and receiving it, and that with joy.
For as Christ hath given his life for us, so ought
we to give our lives for the defence of the gospel,
and comfort of our brethren. And whereas the
bishop saith he will prove seven sacraments, be
you out of doubt he shall never be able to do it,
no more than he hath proved other arguments
with me already. Thus fare ye well. From the
Marshalsea, where I now am, as a sheep appointed
to be slain. God be praised therefor."

Of all the English army of martyrs, Richard
Woodman seems to have the most resembled Martin Luther in the cast of his natural character, and
the peculiarity of his spiritual gifts. As we proceed in our narrative we shall find him applying
the hammer of God's word to the hardened iron
which formed the sinews of the necks of his enemies, with as much force and as little ceremony as
he was wont to exercise when working the metal
in his worldly calling. In archdeacon Philpot,

this boldness of speech, and energy of thought, appeared under the polish of rank, education, learning, and ecclesiastical dignity; in Woodman it stands forth rough and unmitigated, save by the subduing influence of true piety. Even this, however, in his case, added emphasis to the impulse of holy indignation, when he looked upon those whose hearts were really, as he has before expressed it, made drunk by the blood of the saints and martyrs of Jesus; the blood of men by whom he had been taught the way of salvation, whose dungeons he had shared, whose sufferings he had witnessed, and the smoke of whose cruel burnings had hardly ceased to darken and infect the air. Strong must have been the power of that grace which withheld from bitter revilings the tongue of one whose natural courage shrunk from nothing; and who was so keenly sensible of the wrongs inflicted on his murdered pastors, and the blasphemous dishonor heaped upon the name of his God!

Richard Woodman, the humble ironmonger of Sussex, made more than one mitred head cower beneath his righteous rebukes; and forced them to wince under the scornful irony which touched the idolatrous priests of Baal from the inspired lips of Elijah. We do not intend to soften down any part of the recital; but to give it, with as few curtailments as our limits will allow, in the very words of our martyr.

Woodman's second examination was in the house of the bishop of Chichester, where Story had sent him. He returned the bishop's courteous greeting with the most respectful salutation he could render; at the same time thanking him for his former kindness. Chichester requested that he would be brief in his discourse, as the length of their former conversation had impaired his health.

The seven sacraments were proposed for discussion; and on Woodman denying five of them, and requiring the bishop to prove them from Scripture, he became greatly excited, swearing in a very coarse and shocking manner; for which his prisoner reminded him that he was not setting a good example to his flock. Chichester seems to have been exposed to evil influence since their last meeting; for when Woodman justified his rebuke by quoting the command to reprove an offending brother, he and the priests pronounced him past cure; and the bishop desired Dr. Story to be called, as he would talk no more with him; adding that the company of his fellows in the Marshalsea had made him worse than he was; for before he went there he had some hope of him. After some more hard speeches, the bishop a little moderated his displeasure, and consented to proceed in the matter of the sacraments.

The subject on which they began was that of *matrimony*, where the bishop fortified himself with the word *sacramentum* used in the Latin version; and Woodman holding to the English rendering, "a great mystery," as typifying the union of Christ with his church, showed, very beautifully, that the "mystery," or unseen thing, was the union of heart, invisible to the eye ; whereas a sacrament was a visible sign.   He asked the bishop, "My lord, I pray you what is a sacrament ?"   "It is the sign of a holy thing," replied the bishop, who had parried the last argument by insisting that the ceremony being seen, and the man and woman also seen, it was not an invisible mystery. Woodman, then, on this new ground of the bishop's choosing, disproved his assertion, saying, "There need not be a sign of a holy thing where the holy thing itself is.   Matrimony is a holy thing in itself, and is ended outwardly, and needs no more signs but themselves ; wherefore it cannot be a sacrament as others are."   To this the bishop returned a singularly ridiculous answer :—"Lo, now you speak against yourself; and for an example, I came by an hosier's, and there hangeth a pair of hose, that are to sell within."   At this the priests chuckled, and Woodman answered indignantly, he wondered they were not ashamed of themselves. When taunted by the priests for being angry, he replied, "I am not angry, but I am earnest, I tell you, to see your blindness and folly.   I talked of the Scriptures that are written, and they are God's word, to prove my matter true by ; and you will prove your matter true by a pair of hose.   And as well can you prove it by that, as by God's word."   "Why," said a priest, " is there nothing true but what is written in the Bible ?"   Woodman replied, " St. Paul saith to the Galatians, "If an angel came from heaven, and holdeth any other doctrine, than may be proved by God's word, hold him accursed; and so do I tell you plainly."

The priest resumed, "Here is a Testament in my hand; if I hurl it in the fire, do I burn God's word or not? I will buy a new one for sixteen pence." Woodman answered, "I say you have burned God's word; he that would burn a Testament willingly, would burn God himself if he could; for he and his word are as one." They made a great jest of this; and he continued, "Laugh on. Your laughing will be turned to weeping, and all such joy will be turned to mourning, if you repent not with speed." Chichester, to cover the folly of his priests, said, "Why, if my counting-house were full of books, and if my house were by chance on fire, and so burned, is God's word burned?" "No, my lord, because they were burned against your will; but yet if you should burn them willingly, or think it well, or not be sorry for it, you burn God's word as well as he. For he that is not sorry for a shrewd turn, [an evil thing,] doth allow it to be good."

Chichester remarking that he had little learning, then asked him what St. Paul meant by the passage, "We have an altar whereof you may not eat." He answered, "There is no man so foolish as to eat stones, I trow." This greatly annoyed the bishop, who said it was a plain mockery; but Woodman reminded him that he had just accused him of having no knowledge or learning, or understanding, wherefore he ought to make things more plain to him, and not ask him such dark

questions, and blame him too. The bishop declared that the greatest fool in his house would
understand his meaning, and calling by his name
a servant who stood a little way off, " Come hither;
I say to thee, thou shalt not eat of this table.
What do I mean thereby?" " Forsooth, my lord,
you would not have me to eat of this table," lay-
ing his hand upon it, answered the man. This
made all the party laugh; including Woodman,
who said, " He hath expounded the matter almost
as well as I." " He meaneth well enough," said
the bishop, " if you would understand him.
Answer me again, to make it more plain. I say,
thou shalt not eat of this table. What mean I
thereby?" " Forsooth, you would not have me
eat this table." At this they laughed again; and
the bishop, almost angry, said, " He meaneth that
I would not have him eat of the meat that is set
upon the table. How sayest thou, dost thou not
mean so?" The man replied, " Yes, forsooth, my
lord, that was my meaning indeed;" and Woodman observed that he had answered according to
the prompting; showing that he could have replied to the first question.

They then passed on to the sacrament of the
altar. Chichester asked Woodman what he said
to it. He replied, " You mean the sacrament of
the body and blood of Jesus Christ?" " I mean
the sacrament of the altar, and so I say." " You
mean Christ to be the altar, do you not?" asked
Woodman. " I mean the sacrament of the altar
in the church. What! is it so strange to you?"

"It is strange to me, indeed, if you mean the altar of stone," returned Woodman. "It is that altar which I mean," said the bishop. Woodman remarked that he understood not the altar so; and craving permission to show his belief, brought some Scriptures to prove that Christ, in the midst of his assembled people, is the true altar, where Christians, at peace with each other and all the world, should come and offer their prayers to God.

After hearing him to the end, Chichester said, "Do you understand the offering and the altar so? I never heard any man understand it so; no, not Luther, the great heretic, who was condemned by a general council, and his picture burnt." To which Woodman shrewdly replied, "If he were an heretic, I think he understood it not so indeed; but I am sure all Christians ought to understand it so." The bishop maintained his own view, which was quite a Jewish one; and when Woodman showed him so, he said, "Who shall be judge betwixt us in this matter?" Woodman replied, "The twelfth of John declareth who shall be judge in the last day." "You mean," said Chichester, "The word shall judge the word. How can that be?" Woodman replied, "St. Peter saith the Scripture hath no private interpretation; but one Scripture must be understood by another." He also said "the true church of God is able to discuss all doubts; to whom I refer it." The bishop, of course, took this as an admission in favor of his false church.

Woodman asked what he offered up on his altar? he said, "We offer up in the blessed sacrament of the altar, the body of Christ to pacify the wrath of God the Father." At that they all took off their caps in honor of the idol. Woodman proved from Paul's epistle to the Hebrews, that the one offering of Christ was sufficient; and added, "as far as I can see, you are priests after the order of Aaron, who offered up sacrifice for their own sins, and the sins of the people?" The bishop said, "No; they were priests after the order of Melchizedek, who offered bread and wine in remembrance, to signify the giving of Christ's body in bread and wine, which he, at the last supper, gave to his disciples, and ordered to be used to the end of the world." Woodman liked this exposition. He said the bishop had made it very plain to him, that as Christ was the end of all sacrifice, so was he the beginning of the sacraments, willing them to be used in remembrance of him to the world's end. The bishop, however, insisted on more than a remembrance; on transubstantiation; but he desired Woodman to be brief.

The martyr then said, "My lord, if you will answer me to one sacrament, I will answer you to another. If you say the words of baptism over the water, and there be no child there, is it true baptism?" "No; there must be the water, the word, and the child; and then it is a baptism." "Very well," rejoined Woodman; "then if a child be baptized in the name of the Father and of the

Son, it is not truly baptized?" "No; the child must be baptiz?d in the name of the Father, and of the Son, and of the Holy Ghost, or else it is not truly baptized." "Then," said Woodman, "there may be nothing added, or taken away from the sacraments, may there?" "No," replied the bishop. "Now, my lord, I will answer to you, if it please you." "Well," asked the bishop, "how say you? 'Take, eat, this is my body,' is it not Christ's body as soon as the words are said?" "My lord," replied Woodman, "I will answer you by your own words, that you answered me. The water, the word, and the child, you say, all these together make baptism: the bread, the wine and the word make the sacrament; and the eater, eating it in true faith, maketh it his body. Here I prove it is not Christ's body but to the faithful receiver. For he saith, 'Take, eat, this is my body.' He called it not his body before eating, but after eating. St. Augustine said, 'Believe, and thou hast eaten.' And St. John said, 'He that believeth in God, dwelleth in God, and God in him;' wherefore it is impossible to dwell in God, and to eat his body, without a true faith."

One of the priests said, "Then the faith of the receiver maketh it his body, and not his word, by your saying. I pray you, what did Judas eat." Woodman replied, "Judas did eat the sacrament of Christ, and the devil withal." "He did eat the body of Christ unworthily, as St. Paul saith," returned the priest. "Nay," said Woodman, "St.

Paul saith no such thing. He spoke not of eating his body unworthily, but of the sacrament unworthily. For he saith, 'Whoso eateth this bread, and drinketh this cup unworthily, eateth and drinketh his own damnation, because he maketh no difference [discernment] of the Lord's body;' and not because he eateth the Lord's body. If Judas did eat Christ's body, it must needs follow that Judas is saved; for Christ saith in the sixth of John, 'Whosoever eateth my flesh, and drinketh my blood, hath eternal life; and I will raise him up at the last day.'"

On this the priests and bishop agreed that it was lost labor to talk any more with him; so the bishop demanded a final answer as to his belief in the matter, and received this reply:—"I do believe that if I come to receive the sacrament of the body and blood of Christ truly ministered, believing that Christ was born for me, and that he suffered death for me, and that I shall be saved from my sins by his blood-shedding; and so receive the sacrament in that remembrance, then I do believe that I receive wholly Christ, God and man, mystically by faith. This is my belief." Chichester observed, "Why then, it is no body without faith; God's word is of no force, as you count it." "My lord," he replied, "I have told you my mind without dissimulation; and more you get not of me, without you will talk with me by the Scriptures; and if you will do so, I will begin anew with you, and prove it more plainly; three or four manner of ways, that you shall not say nay to that I have said yourself."

When he said this they began to laugh heartily, saying to each other, "This is an heretic indeed; it is time he were burned." Their ridicule and malignity moved him to give them a very severe rebuke; "Judge not lest ye be judged; for as you judge me, you shall be judged yourselves. For what you call heresy, I serve God truly with, as you all shall well know, when you shall be in hell, and shall be compelled to say, from pain, 'This was the man that we jested on, and whose talk we called foolishness, and his end to be without honor; but we now see how he is counted among the saints of God, and we are punished.' These words shall you say, being in hell, if you repent not with speed, if you consent to the shedding of my blood. Wherefore look to it; I give you counsel." A priest taxed him with being angry; and began to repeat some words which he had spoken against their idols, and in answer to bishop Stephen Gardiner. He answered, "That I said, I said; and where you said I was angry, I take God to my record that I am not, but am zealous for the truth, and speak out of the Spirit of God with cheerfulness." The priest, with marks of contempt, mockingly repeated, "The Spirit of God! think you that you have the Spirit of God?" "I believe surely," answered the martyr, "that I have the Spirit of God, I praise God therefor; and you are deceivers, mockers, and scorners before God, and are the children of Satan, all of you, as far as I can

17*

see." Here Story came in, and after railing as
usual, advised the bishop to have nothing more to
do with him, and ordered him back to the prison
without farther question. When they had all left
to receive a party, who were come to dine with
the bishop, a priest began to flatter Woodman,
urging him to recant; but he met with no success;
and after a few minutes, he was conducted again
to the Marshalsea prison.

Soon after this, the marshal came to the prison,
and questioned Woodman as to his having been
abroad, speaking seditious words, both of which
he so clearly disproved, that the officer owned that
it must be a false report; and then took him away
for another examination, to lord Montague's house,
in Southwark, where Dr. Langdale, the bishop's
chaplain, was waiting for him. A very long conversation ensued; which Langdale began, by
charging him with forsaking the faith of his
fathers, and so forth. Woodman answered wisely
and scripturally, and the doctor, after blaming
him for quoting the Bible too much, tried by the
assurance of much good will, to induce him to
speak his mind freely. The martyr, in a strain of
admirable prudence, mingled with his natural
frankness, told him that he knew not how to trust
his fair words, when he could not trust his own
father and brother, and others who had been his
familiar friends;—that Christ had bade him to be
wise as a serpent, and as innocent as the dove,—
and also to take heed of men, for they would betray. He added, that the doctor's dislike to his

quoting Scripture made him suspect him; therefore he must not be angry if he found him circum-
spect in his answer; "For," said he, "it shall not be
said, by God's help, that I run wilfully into mine
enemies' hands; and yet, I praise God, that my life
is not dear unto myself, but is dear with God;
wherefore I will do to the uttermost I can to keep it."
Langdale then made a misstatement of what had
taken place before Woodman's last apprehension,
which he very calmly and soberly answered, fully
showing in what he had been wrongfully charged.

Woodman was next charged with baptizing his
child, and in the same breath with leaving it un-
baptized. He indignantly proved the falsehood
of this strange contradiction; and referring to a
part of Langdale's speech, where he had said that
if the child died before baptism it must have
been eternally lost, he asked him, "How think
you? are all condemned who receive not the outward sign of baptism?" "Yea," said the doctor,
"that they be." Woodman asked, "How prove you
that?" Langdale replied by repeating our Lord's
words which command baptism, assuring eternal
life to such as believe and are baptized, and condemnation to them who believe not. "Then,"
observed Woodman, "by your saying that baptism bringeth faith; and all that are baptized in
water shall be saved, shall they?" "Yea, that
they shall," replied the doctor; "if they die before they come to discretion, they should be saved
every one of them; and all that be not baptized,
shall be damned, every one of them."

This greatly roused Woodman, who exclaimed, "How dare you speak such blasphemy against God and his, as you do ?   How dare you for your life take upon you to preach, and teach the people, and understand not what you say ?   For I protest before God that you understand not the Scriptures, but as far as natural reason can comprehend; for if you did, you would be ashamed to speak as you do."   Langdale told him to take heed, for he had a toy in his head that would make him despair; and asked why he reproved him as he did. Woodman answered, "Because you blaspheme God;" and then challenged him to prove his doctrine by Scripture, which made the other turn pale and tremble.

Woodman then proceeded to show that the perdition threatened was not to them who are not baptized, but to such as believe not; quoting the words of John, "He that believeth not is condemned already, because he believeth not."   He went on, "I dare not say, for all the good things under heaven, that all they who receive no material baptism by water, shall be condemned, as you have said; yet I would not that you should gather from these words that I deny baptism, as you were about to lay to my charge, before I had half told out my tale.   But I would not have you nor any man, so rash in judgment, to condemn the thing that they are not able to prove by the word; and to make it seem to the simple that the outward washing of the water were the cause of faith."   "Why, is it not so ?" asked Langdale; "will you deny it ? **how** say you, will you deny it? I say the child hath no faith before it is baptized; and therefore the baptism bringeth the faith. How say you to it? Make me a plain answer to the question."

"Now," said Woodman, "I see you go about nothing else but to take advantage of my words. But, by God's help, I will answer you so that you shall well see your sayings untrue. And yet I will not speak mine own words, but the words of the Holy Ghost, out of the mouth of the prophets and apostles; and then ask them whether they will deny it." He then asked where Jacob was baptized before he had faith; alleging the passage which speaks of his election before his birth; but Langdale parried this, as it was before the institution of baptism. He demanded an answer to his former question, observing, that Woodman denied original sin, and free will; "for," said he, "if children can be saved without baptism, it must needs follow that children have no original sin; the which is put away in the baptizing. But I think that you know not what original sin is, or free will either." Woodman then told him that he thanked God, that he thought he could tell him better than he could; and then asked him, "what free will hath man to do good of himself?" Langdale answered, "I say that man hath as much free will as Adam had before the fall." "I pray you, how prove you that?" "Thus I prove it," saith the doctor, "that as sin entered into the world, and by the nature of one that sinned all became sinners, the which was by Adam; so by

the obedience of one man, righteousness came
upon all men that had sinned, and set them as free
as they were before their fall; the which was by
Jesus Christ. See the fifth of the epistle to the
Romans."

Woodman exclaimed, " Oh, what an overthrow
have you given yourself here in original sin, and
yet you cannot see it! For, in proving that we
have free will, you have quite denied original sin.
For here you have declared that we are set as free
by the death of Christ as Adam was before his
fall; and I am sure that Adam had no original
sin before his fall. If we are as free now, as he
was then, I marvel wherefore Paul prayed thrice
to God to take away the sting of it; God making
him answer, and saying, ' My grace is sufficient
for thee.' These words, with divers others, prove
original sin in us; but not that it shall hurt God's
elect people, for his grace is sufficient for all of
them. But you say in one place that it is not
without baptism; and in another place you put it
away quite by the death of Christ; and in very
deed you have spoken truer in the matter than
you are aware of. For all who believe in Christ
are baptized in the blood of Christ, that he shed
on the cross; and in the water that he sweat for
pain, and putting away of our sins at his death.
And yet I say with David, 'In sin was I born, and
in sin did my mother conceive me;' but in no
such sin as shall be imputed, because I am born
of God by faith, as John saith in the third chapter
of his first epistle. Therefore I am blessed, as

saith the thirty-second psalm, because the Lord imputeth not my sin, and not because I have no sin; but because God hath not imputed my sins. Not of our own deserving, but of his free mercy, he hath saved us. Where is now your free will that you speak of? If we have free will, then our salvation cometh of our own selves, and not of God; the which is great blasphemy against God and his word." He quoted the apostles James, John, and Paul, and went on to apply these Scriptures. "Seeing then that every good and perfect gift cometh from above, and lighteneth upon whom it pleaseth God, and that he worketh in us both the will and the deed, methinks all the rest of our own will is little worth, or nothing at all unless it be wickedness."

Woodman then craved leave to answer to the matter of Jacob's faith, which Langdale had put aside as having nothing to do with baptism. The doctor consented, probably, as Woodman suspected, hoping to lay hold on some of his words; and he proceeded, "First you may be reminded, you said that if my child had died without baptism, if I had been the cause that it had not been baptized, the child should have been damned, and I too. How say you?" "Yea, that you should," answered the doctor. Woodman replied, "That is most untrue; for the prophet saith, the father shall not bear the child's offences; nor the child the father's offences; but the soul that sinneth shall die. What could the child have done withal, if it had died without baptism? the child could not be blamed.

How say you to this? And I am sure that what I brought in, in the old law, to prove that faith is before baptism is not disagreeable unto the word. For circumcision was a figure of baptism; and that I may bring to prove baptism by, as well as St. Peter did; for he brought in Noah's flood, which was a long time before Jacob and Esau, to prove baptism; saying, 'While the ark was a preparing, wherein few, that is eight souls, were saved by water, like as baptism now saveth us; not in putting away the filth of the flesh, but there is a good conscience consenting to God.' Here Peter proveth that water had not saved Noah and the other seven, no more than it saved all the rest, if it had not been for their faith; which faith now saveth us; not in putting away the filthy soil of the flesh by the washing of water, but a good conscience consenting unto God.

"But you say, that if they are baptized with the water, if they die before they come to the years of discretion, they are all saved; the which St. Peter is clean against, unless you grant that children have faith before they are baptized. Now I ask you, what consent of conscience the children have, being infants? For you say they believe not before they are baptized; therefore, then, they consent not to be baptized, because they believe not. And by this it followeth that none shall be saved, although they are baptized. I would fain see how you can answer this." Langdale replied, "You are the most perverse man that ever I knew. You know not what you say. The children are baptized in their godfathers' and godmothers' faith, and that is the good conscience which St. Peter speaks of; and the christening is the keeping of the law which St. Paul speaketh of, saying, 'Neither is circumcision anything, nor uncircumcision, but the keeping of the law.' Like as circumcision was the keeping of the old law, so is baptism the keeping of the new law."

To all this Woodman replied, " Ah! methought if you talked with me, you would be compelled to bring in the old law to maintain your sayings by; though you refused it when I brought it in. But yet it serveth not your purpose so much as you think for. For here you have confessed that neither circumcision availeth, nor uncircumcision; the which you have coupled with baptism, proving that none of them availeth, but keeping the law is the whole thing. The which law is kept, you say, by the outward signs; which is not so; for 'Abraham believed God, and that was counted to him for righteousness,' and this was before he was circumcised."

After saying a little more on this point, Woodman asked, "Where you said the children are baptized in their godfathers' and godmothers' faith, being all unbelievers, in what faith is the child baptized then? In none at all, by your own saying." This greatly excited the doctor, who exclaimed, "What! then you would count that there are very few believers, if there be not one of three that believeth. You enter into judgment against the people. Belike you think there are

18

none that believe well, unless they are of your mind. Indeed, then Christ's flock were a very little flock!" Woodman replied, " Indeed, these are Christ's own words, in Luke the twefth, ' Fear not little flock,' the which we may see to be very true. Yea, you said that if there were not one amongst three, that were very few. But there is not amongst three hundred for anything that I can see; for if there were, there would not be so many that would seek their neighbors' goods and lives as there are." Langdale cunningly asked him how many he thought there were of that little flock; but he got not the information he wanted, for Woodman told him it would be making himself equal with God to answer it; he then quoted many passages of Scripture, to show that the great mass of mankind are in error, and Christ's believing people a small number, ending by an offer to furnish farther evidence; and also to show that the doctor and his party were not in that small number.

Langdale then began to stamp the floor, to show his rage, railing at him for a long time. When he had finished this, Woodman asked him, wherefore he was so angry at his answering the questions proposed? Langdale said he had not answered him as to original sin, and that he denied original sin.

Before the martyr could reply, a Mr. Gage, who had been kind to Woodman, came into the room. He acted as a peacemaker, and persuaded the angry doctor to resume the examination, suggest-

ing that he should question him on the sacrament
of the altar ; and here the former discussion with
Chichester and the priest was, in substance, repeated. It ended, of course, by remanding the
prisoner to the Marshalsea.

It may be proper to remark here, that Woodman seems to have had rather singular views of the
meaning of some figurative passages of Scripture.
As, for instance, his supposing the symbol, " lively
stones," to refer to flint stones, out of which fire
might be struck to enlighten the darkness of
others. A beautiful idea, though singular, and
not the meaning of the text. Salvation by grace,
however, was the main point which the holy martyrs of that day were anxious to guard against the
system of salvation by works, which was taught
by the persecuting church.

Woodman's next examination took place at St.
George's church, in Southwark, before the bishops
of Winchester and Rochester, with others. Winchester commenced by giving a long history of
his former imprisonment and release, his alleged
offences since, and his capture. In this he made
just as many mistakes as he made statements ; and
at the end Woodman showed him the utter falsehood of what he had said. The whole time was
occupied in reporting stories of Woodman's reported sayings and actions, contrary to the laws,
not one of which charges could they maintain; and
he was sent to prison, when there seemed a greater
probability of their being compelled to release

him. But what can the lamb's innocence avail, when the hungry wolf has it under his paw?

Three weeks afterwards, he was brought to St. Mary's, in Southwark, where sat the bishop of Winchester, Harpsfield, Langdale, and other commissioners, in the presence of more than three hundred people. Winchester began by rebuking him for defending himself so strongly on the last occasion, when Woodman had maintained that he was not sent to prison for any heresy, but for the breach of a statute in speaking to a priest in the pulpit. The bishop now tried to disprove this; but Woodman told him he had bought a statute book since he was imprisoned, and had made out the whole case, confirming what he had before asserted, and proving the bishop's charge to be false. Finding this would not answer, Winchester then produced the account, in the prisoner's own writing, of the former examinations before the commissioners, and proceeded to question him as to his belief in the sacrament of the altar. Woodman, seeing that the bishop only wanted to make him utter, in his discourse, something that he might catch hold of, to assume the character of his ordinary, replied, "I will answer you to no such thing, for I am not of your diocese; therefore I will not answer to you." Winchester said, "Thou art within my diocese, and thou hast offended within my diocese; and therefore I will have to do with thee." "Have to do with me if you will," replied the martyr, "but I will have nothing to do with you, I tell you plainly. For

though I be now in your diocese, I have not offended in your diocese, if I have, show me wherein." He was told of his own handwriting, there
present, which stated his heretical opinions. He
owned it as his, but said that, being merely a relation of the talk between him and the commissioners, it was no offence, nor had they anything
to do with it. The bishop then ordered him to
be sworn, that he might question him as to where
he wrote it, and whether he still held the same
doctrines; but Woodman refused to be sworn by
him, not being his ordinary; and also protested
he wrote no word of the paper in that diocese.
Langdale then asserted that it was written in the
King's Bench prison. Woodman declared that
he did not write it there. A fat proud priest next
demanded where he wrote it. He answered, that
he owed him not so much service as to tell him;
they must find it out how they could, for they only
sought his life. Winchester then went on to read
from his paper the replies that he had formerly
given to the commissioners, and several times
sought to entrap him into some expression of his
opinion there; but Woodman was too wary to be
caught.

When the bishop, after reading his remarks on
the publication of false doctrine in pulpits and
churches, asked him, where it took place, he replied, "In the synagogue of Satan, where God is
dishonored by false doctrine." "I pray you, where
is one of them?" asked Winchester; "Nay," he
replied, "that judge yourself; I came not here to
18*

be a judge." Having, in like manner, baffled all attempts to make him commit himself, he answered the bishop very severely as to some of his railing speeches, quoting the book of Revelation, and also the apocryphal one called the Book of Wisdom. When he named this Winchester cried out, " Wisdom! what speakest thou of wisdom? thou never hadst it; for thou art as very a fool as ever I heard speak." Woodman answered, "Do you not know that the foolish things of the world must confound the wise things? wherefore, it grieveth me not to be called a fool at your hands." " Nay, thou art none of those fools," returned the bishop; thou art an obstinate fool and a heretic. Lay hand on the book, and answer to such things as I will lay against thee." Woodman refused, repeating that he was not of that diocese. Winchester exlaimed, " This man is without law; he careth not for the king or queen, I dare say, for he will not obey their laws. Let me see the king's commission. I will see whether he will obey that or not." The martyr remarked, " I would you loved the king and queen's majesty no less than I do, if it pleased God; you would not do then as you do now." " Hold him a book," repeated the angry bishop, " he is a rank heretic. Thou shalt answer to such things as I will demand of thee."

Woodman then said, " I take heaven and earth to witness that I am no heretic; neither can I tell wherefore I am brought to prison, no more than any man here can tell." He looked round upon the people, and then continued, addressing the bishop, "If you have any just cause against me worthy of death, lay it against me, and let me have it; for I refuse not to die, I praise God, for the truth's sake, if I had ten lives. If you have no cause, let me go home, I pray you, to my wife and children, to see them maintained; and other poor folk that I would set to work, by the help of God. I have set to work a hundred persons ere this, all the year together, and was unjustly taken from them; but God forgive them who did it, if it be his will!" The inhuman bishop now said, "Do you see how he looketh about for help? But I would see any man show thee a cheerful countenance, and especially you that be of my diocese. If any of you bid God strengthen him, or take him by the hand, or embrace him, or show him a cheerful countenance, you shall be excommunicated, and shall not be received again till you have done open penance; and therefore beware of it." The martyr replied, "I look for no help from man, for God is on my side, I praise him therefor; and therefore I need not to care who are against me; neither do I care." The judges called out, "Away with him, and bring us another." So he was carried back to prison.

The sixth and last examination of this bold champion took place, also, at St. Mary Overy's, two days after the preceding one; where were present the bishops of Winchester and Chichester, Harpsfield, Langdale, Roper, and the same priests who had formerly assisted them. Winchester told him that he had affirmed certain heresies the last

time before them ; and asked if he held them
still, or would revoke them.　He answered that he
held no heresies, as the Lord knew.　"No !" said
the bishop, " did you not affirm that Judas received
bread ? which is a heresy, unless you tell what
more than bread."　Woodman replied, " Is it
heresy to say that Judas received no more than
bread ?　I said he received more than bare bread,
for he received the same sacrament that was prepared to show forth the Lord's death ; and because he presumed to eat without faith, he ate
the devil with all, as the words of Christ declare ;
after he ate the sop, the devil entered into him, as
you cannot deny."　"Hold him a book," said the
bishop, "I will have you answer directly whether
Judas did eat the body or no."　But Woodman
refused to be sworn, maintaining that the bishop
of Winchester had no jurisdiction over him in the
cause ; and to this he inflexibly stood.　He also
pleaded that the bishop of London had discharged
him of all the matters laid against him ; and that
it was unlawful as well as unjust, to imprison and
try him over again on the same charges.

Winchester said, that if he was again suspected
of being a heretic, they had a right to call him
before him and examine him of his faith, upon
suspicion.　"Indeed," said Woodman, " St. Peter
willeth me to render account of my hope that I
have in God ; and I am contented so to do, if it
please my bishop to hear me."　"Yes, I pray
you, let us hear it," said the bishop of Chichester.
"I do believe in God the Father, Almighty, Maker

of heaven and earth, and of all things visible and invisible; and in one Lord Jesus Christ, my Saviour, very God and very man. I believe in God the Holy Ghost, the Comforter of all God's elect people, and that he is equal with the Father and the Son. I believe in the true Catholic church, and all the sacraments that belong thereto. Thus have I rendered account of my hope that I have of my salvation."

Winchester asked, "And how believe you in the blessed sacrament of the altar?" And at that word they all took off their caps in honor of the idol. Woodman replied, "I pray you be contented, for I will not answer to any more questions; for I perceive you go about to shed my blood." "No!" said the bishop, "hold him a book. If he refuse to swear, he is an Anabaptist, and shall be excommunicated." Woodman firmly repeated, "I will not swear for you, excommunicate me if you will. For you are not fit to receive an oath; for you laid heresies to my charge in yonder pulpit, the which you are not able to prove; wherefore you are not meet to take an oath of any man. And as for me, I am not of your diocese, nor will have anything to do with you." Winchester repeated that he would have to do with him: and that he was a strong heretic. Woodman remarked, that all truth was heresy with them; but offered to show them his belief concerning the sacrament, and then repeated what he had before declared, as to his coming in faith that Christ suffered for his sins, and that he should be saved by his blood-shedding; and so receiving a whole Christ, mystically, by faith. On his uttering the last words they all cried out; and the fat priest, calling him a fool, demanded what he meant by "mystically." He replied, "I take mystically to be the faith that is in us; that the world seeth not, but God only."

Here Winchester remarked that he knew not what he said; and demanded once more a direct answer, as to the real presence in the sacrament. Woodman replied, "I have said as much as I will say; excommunicate me if you will. I am not of your diocese. The bishop of Chichester is mine ordinary. Let him do it if you will needs have my blood, that it may be required at his hands." Chichester said, "I am not consecrated yet; I told you so when you were with me." The martyr seems to have penetrated the true character of this man, whose name was Christopherson, and who, after his consecration, became as violent a persecutor as any of his brethren. Woodman, on recollecting that a bull from Rome must arrive before he could receive consecration, quaintly remarked, "No, indeed, your kine bringeth forth nothing but cow-calves, as it chanceth now." This put the pope's clergy in a rage; and they all railed at him together, telling him that he was out of his wits. "So Festus said to Paul when he spake the words of soberness and truth, as taught by the Spirit of God, as I do," said Woodman. "But as you have judged, you shall be judged yourselves. You will go to hell, and all like you, if you condemn me, and repent not of it speedily."

After some commotion, Winchester and Harps-field said, "We go not about to condemn thee, but go about to save thy soul, if thou wilt be ruled, and do as we would have thee." "To save my soul!" repeated the martyr, "Nay, you cannot save my soul. My soul is saved already; I praise God therefor. There can no one save my soul but Jesus Christ; and he it is who has saved my soul before the foundation of the world was laid." On this a priest cried out, "What a heresy is that, my lords! He saith his soul was saved before the foundations of the world were laid." Then turning to Woodman, "Thou canst not tell what thou sayest. Was thy soul saved before it existed?" "Yes, I praise God I can tell what I say, and I say the truth. Look at the first chapter of the Ephesians, and there you shall find it, where Paul saith, 'Blessed be God, the Father of our Lord Jesus Christ, who hath blessed us with all spiritual blessings in heavenly places in Christ, according as he hath chosen us in him before the foundation of the world, that we should be holy and without blame before him in love; having predestinated us unto the adoption of children.' These are the words of Paul, and I believe they are most true. And therefore it is my faith in and by Jesus Christ that saveth; and not you or any man else."

"What!" said the priest, "faith without works? St. James saith, 'faith without works is dead;' and we have free will to do good works." Woodman replied, "I would not that any of you should think that I disallow good works. For a good faith cannot be without good works. Yet not of ourselves, for it is the gift of God; as St. Paul saith to the Philippians, 'It is God that worketh in us both to will and to do, of his good pleasure.'"

Winchester, not enduring to hear so much sound doctrine, now interposed, saying, "Make an end; answer to me. Here is your ordinary, the archdeacon of Canterbury; he is made your ordinary by my lord cardinal, and he hath authority to examine you of your faith upon a book, to answer to such articles as he will lay to you. And I pray you refuse it not, for the danger is great if you do. Wherefore we desire you to show yourself a subject in this matter." Then the rest, having by this time discovered that nothing was to be done with this resolute victim by harshness, all joined, saying, "Lo, my lord desireth you gently to answer him, and so do we all. For if you refuse to take an oath, he may excommunicate you. For my lord cardinal may put whom he will in the bishop's office, until he is consecrated." But Woodman was not to be so led. He answered, "I know not so much. If you will give me time to learn the truth of it, and if I can find it to be as you say, I will tell you my mind in anything he shall ask of me without any flattering." The priest said, "My lord and we all tell thee it is true, and therefore answer to him." "I will believe none of you all," replied Woodman, "for you are turncoats and changelings, and are wavering-minded, as St. James says; you are neither hot nor cold, as saith St. John, therefore God will cast you out of his mouth. Wherefore I can believe none of you all; I tell you the truth." "What!" said Winchester, "are we turncoats and changelings? What meanest thou by that?" "I mean," answered the plain-spoken prisoner, "that in king Edward's days you taught the doctrine that was set forth then, every one of you; and now you teach the contrary; therefore I call you turncoats and changelings, as I may well enough." These words made them quake, and Winchester said, "Nay, not all, as it chanced." "No! I pray you, where were you then?" asked Woodman. The bishop replied, "I was in the tower, as the lieutenant will bear me record." "If you were in the tower," said Woodman, "it was not therefor, I dare say; it was for some other matter." Then the others took heart, and said, "My lord, he cometh to examine you, we think; if he will not answer to the articles, it were best for you to excommunicate him." The bishop replied, "He is the naughtiest, and most impudent heretic I ever knew; I will read the sentence against him." After some more angry speaking, and being told again by Woodman that if he condemned him he would be punished everlastingly; with the assurance that he himself was not afraid to die for God's sake, if he had a hundred lives; the bishop repeated, "For God's sake? nay, for the devil's sake. Thou sayest thou art not afraid to die; no more was Judas, who hanged himself, as thou wilt

19

kill thyself wilfully, because thou wilt not be ruled." Woodman said, "Nay, I defy the devil, Judas, and all their members. And the flesh of Judas was not afraid, but his spirit and conscience were afraid, and therefore he despaired and hung himself. But, I praise God, I feel no unwillingness in my flesh to die, but a joyful conscience and willing mind thereto. Wherefore my flesh is subdued to it, I praise God; and therefore I am not afraid of death."

The bishop of Chichester then said, "Woodman, for God's sake be ruled. You know what you said at my house. I could say more if I would." "Say what you can," said the undaunted martyr; "the most fault that you found in me was, because I praised the living God; and because I said, 'I praise God and the Lord;' which you ought to be ashamed of, if you have any grace; for I told you where the words were written." Winchester spoke next:—"Well, how say you? Will you confess that Judas received the body of Christ unworthily? tell me plainly." "My lord," he replied, "if you, or any of you all, can prove before all this audience, in all the Bible, that any man ever ate the body of Christ unworthily, then I will be with you in all things that you will demand of me; of the which matter I desire all these people to be witness." "Will you so?" said the priest, "then we shall agree well enough. St. Paul saith so." Woodman asked, "I pray you where saith he so? Rehearse the words." The priest answered "in the eleventh chapter of the first epistle to the Corinthians, he saith, 'Whoso eateth of this blood, and drinketh of this cup, unworthily, eateth and drinketh his own damnation, because he maketh no difference of the Lord's body.'" Woodman then asked, "Do these words prove that Judas ate the body of Christ unworthily? I pray you let me see them." They gave him the book, and he went on:— "These are the words, even that you said; good people hearken well to them. 'Whoso eateth of this bread, and drinketh unworthily;' he saith not Whoso eateth of this body unworthily, or drinketh of this blood unworthily; but he saith, "Whosoever eateth of this bread, and drinketh of this cup unworthily, (which is the sacrament,) eateth and drinketh his own damnation,' because he maketh no difference between the sacrament which representeth the Lord's body, and other bread and drink. Here, good people, you may all see that they are not able to prove their sayings true. Wherefore, I cannot believe them in anything that they do."

Winchester then exclaimed, "Thou art a rank heretic indeed! Art thou an expounder? Now I will read sentence against thee." "Judge not, lest you be judged," said the martyr again; "for as you have judged me, you are yourself." Winchester commenced reading, and he asked, "Why will you read the sentence against me, and cannot tell wherefore?" "Thou art a heretic," answered the wicked prelate, "and therefore thou shalt be excommunicated." "I am no heretic, I take heaven and earth to witness, I defy all heretics; and if you condemn me, you will be condemned eternally, if you repent not. But God give you grace to repent it, if it be his will."

"And so," writes Woodman, in closing his story, "he read forth the sentence in Latin, but what he said God knoweth, and not I. God be judge between them and me. When he had done, I would have talked my mind to them, but they cried out, 'Away, away with him!' So I was carried to the Marshalsea again; where I now am; and shall be, as long as it shall please God. And I praise God most heartily that ever he hath elected, and predestinated me to come to so high a dignity, as to bear rebuke for his name's sake; his name be praised therefor, for ever and ever. Amen."

Woodman was not burned alone. He was one of ten who were consumed in the same pile. George Stevens had been some time in the prison also for the truth; but the remaining eight had been only apprehended two, or at most three days before they received sentence at the mouths of these persecuting ministers, professedly servants of the meek and lowly Jesus. W. Maynard, and A. Hosman, his servant; J. Morris, with his aged mother, Margery Morris; Thomasine Wood, Mr. Maynard's maid-servant; Dennis Burgess; and two married women, named Ashdowne and Grove, were all at large, some say the very day before they were committed to the flames. No time was allowed for a writ to come down from London, to

Lewes, in the county of Sussex, where they suffered.   Such legal proceedings were then scarcely
thought of.   The process of the murderers was
like that of the Babylonian tyrant on the plains of
Dura.   Whosoever would not worship the idols,
was seized, bound, and cast into the fire.

JAN PETERS AND HIS FRIENDS.

THERE is an important sense in which it may be said that the developments of history are progressive. History has of late been more carefully studied; fiction has been sifted from fact; private documents have been brought forward to substantiate or correct public statements; and we are less disposed than formerly to be terrified by mere names. We have become fully satisfied that *Anabaptist* may be a nickname for a truly eminent Christian.

The good men and women of whom we are now writing had fled to London from the Low Countries, to escape the sufferings to which Baptist principles exposed them. "We had to forsake our friends," says one of the sufferers, "our country, our possessions, on account of tyranny, and fled as lambs from a wolf; only because of the pure evangelical truth of Christ, and not for uproars' or factions' sake, like those of Munster, whose views are an abomination of which we have been slanderously accused."

The English are often boasting of their good Queen Elizabeth, but the following, among many other similar facts, shows that she had little in which they can honorably glory. In her day, the fierceness of ecclesiastical intolerance was severely felt.

As early as 1568, the Baptists had engaged the attention of the bishops, who obtained a proclamation from the queen directing a severe visitation to be made throughout London, and ordering all persons "that have conceived any manner of such heretical opinions, as the Anabaptists do hold, and meaneth not by charitable teaching to be reconciled, to depart out of this realm within twenty days, upon pain of forfeiture of all their goods, and to be imprisoned and further punished." This proclamation does not appear to have had its intended effect, for the sectaries rapidly increased. A short time prior to the death of Archbishop Parker, a congregation of them was discovered in Aldgate, London, twenty-seven of whom were committed to prison.

These persons had fled from the slaughterings and devastations caused by the Duke of Alva in Flanders, and in the expectation that in now Protestant England they would be free from the persecutions to which they had been exposed. But their peace and security did not last long. Popery had passed away only in name, and its spirit still lived in full vigor in the queen and the government; and these simple-hearted Christian people soon felt its power.

The morning of the Sabbath, April 3d, 1575, had dawned. It was deemed by the dominant party a holy season—Easter day, the grand feast in commemoration of the resurrection of Jesus Christ from the dead. Thirty disciples of the Lord, men and women, had assembled in an upper room for worship near the *Aldgate*, one of the entrances of the city of London. How pure, how tender, but how unearthly the devotion of such a meeting! Outcasts and strangers, they sought a heavenly citizenship, and in this sojourn met to comfort each other, and to unite their prayers at a throne of grace. What a power of principle did they unfold! All the dignity of Christian manhood was there seen! They knew the power of suffering; they were prepared again to brave its fury, if necessary, for the advancement of the truth. Imagination realizes more than this, as by an effort it aims to identify itself with this little band of Christian disciples.

Their meeting, though conducted in quietude, was detected by their neighbors, and a constable was soon on the spot with an assistant or two from whom they might all have easily escaped. Addressing them as devils, this professed officer of justice demanded which was their teacher. Seven and twenty of their names were at his command recorded, and taking the promise of the rest to remain, he proceeded with seven of them to a magistrate. He soon after returned, and with opprobrious and cruel words drove the rest before him to the jail. Two escaped on the way; the rest were led "as sheep to the slaughter." On the third day they were released,—heavy bail being taken for their appearance, whenever and wherever it should please the authorities to determine.

Information of the capture was conveyed to the

queen's council; and at the suggestion of arch-bishop Parker, a commission was issued on the 27th of April, to Sandys, the bishop of London, assisted by several civilians and judges, to "confer with the accused, and to proceed judicially, if the case so required." In a very few days the summonses were issued, and these poor people stood criminally arraigned for worshiping God according to their convictions. The court assembled in the consistory of St. Paul's, because it was a case of heresy. Their reconciliation to the Dutch church was the avowed end of this imposing procedure. The episcopal smile was first tried, and then came the terrible frown. These sturdy confessors were assured that their recantation would have the most healthful influence upon the state of their souls, and be hailed as a special token of God's great goodness to the whole church; whilst the alternative in this world would be banishment or death, and in the future hopeless misery.

The following graphic account is from the pen of Von Byler, one of the prisoners; it will show us the nature of the charge upon which these holy men were tried, and throw a gleam of light upon the mode of their proceedings:—

"When we came before the bishop, there were present, *Master Joris,* [the minister of the Dutch church,] James de Koninck, John de Kodemaker, two members of the council, and a French clergyman. We were placed before those lords, and their servants, who propounded four questions to

us, to which we were to give an affirmative or a
negative.

"'1. Whether Christ did not assume his flesh
from the body of Mary?'

" We replied, 'That he is the Son of the living
God.'

"'2. Whether infants should not be baptized?'

"'We cannot understand matters so, for we
read nothing of it in the Scriptures.'

"'3. Whether it was lawful for a Christian to
attend to, or discharge the duties of a magistrate's
office?'

"We replied, 'That our conscience would not
suffer us to do so; but we considered the magistrate as a minister of God, for the protection of
the servants of God?'

"'4. Whether a Christian was allowed to take
an oath?'

"We again replied, our conscience would not
allow us to do so, for Christ said, 'Let your com-
munication be yea, yea, nay, nay.' We then kept
silent. The bishop said that our misdeeds were
very gross, and we could not inherit the kingdom
of God. O Lord, avenge not!

"The bishop then remanded us to prison. A
young brother who was first interrogated, boldly
confessed the truth; and was on that account
sorely accused, and led to Westminister, where he
was imprisoned by himself. This caused us much
grief."

Some additional information may be collected
from an interesting letter written by a countryman

of these persecuted saints to his mother, then resident at Ghent. She was a woman of great piety,
and had requested her son to supply her with all
the information he could procure. His name was
Somers, a resident in London, a member of the
Dutch church there, and subsequently, on his return to his native land, was raised to the highest
honors of the State.

"It is probable," he says, "that I am better
acquainted with the circumstances than the gene-
rality of people, inasmuch as I have had frequent
intercourse with them, and have received information from all of them: so that I cannot forbear
giving such an account of it as accords with the
extent of my information in reference to the matter. In connection with which I send you a copy
of their confession; on account of which some
died and others are retained in prison."

On their return from their examination to their
place of confinement, Mr. Somers says, " That ten
or twelve of them made their escape, as they were
aware of the danger to which they were exposed,
and perceived the fine opportunity of escape that
presented itself; the guard consisted of but two
or three individuals. The whole of them, however,
in the course of two or thee days, returned to the
prison, partly in order to acquit their bail, who
was bound in the sum of £100, and partly because
the bishop, as a man of honor, promised with an
oath, that he would set them all free in the course
of five or six days if they would return ; but if not,
the rest should remain in prison till Candlemas."

The dreary solitude of their prison-house was
soon disturbed by their officious opponents. Again
and again they were visited by many Netherlanders, and twice they were summoned into the
august presence of the London pontiff. To one
of these visits the following extract refers:—
" When we were all lodged in prison, came Master Joris, and said, if we would join the church he
would set us at liberty—for these are the bishop's
orders. But we contended valiantly for the truth
in Christ Jesus,—for he is our Captain, and none
else ; upon him we put all our confidence." These
means of proselyting, sooner or later to some extent, were successful. For soon " after this, five
of the men were converted (through much disputation with these Netherlanders which belonged to
the church) before they were condemned as heretics ; nevertheless, they were placed before a ros-
trum in St. Paul's church-yard, in a large assembly of some thousands of Englishmen, and a bundle
of fagots was laid upon each one's shoulder, as a
sign that they deserved to be burnt.* In addition

* The form of abjuration made by these men is a curious document, as it proves to what lengths the prelatists wished persons
professing these sentiments to go. It was taken before Dr. De
Laune, in the Dutch church Austin Friars, of which the Doctor
was minister. It is as follows:—" Whereas, we being seduced by
the devil, the spirit of error, and by false teachers, have fallen
into the most damnable errors; that Christ took not flesh of the
substance of the Virgin Mary, that the infants of the faithful ought
not to be baptized, that a Christian may not be a magistrate, or
bear the sword and office of authority, and that it is not lawful for
a Christian man to take an oath. Now, by the grace of God, and

to which they inflicted many other injuries and ignominy upon them, though the bishop had promised that he would set them at liberty without any incumbrances if they would only sign the four articles; but the event proved the contrary. This ·transpired the 25th of May, A. D. 1575."

For the fourth time these worthy Christians were called before the priestly tribunal. "It was," says Von Byler, "On Whitsuntide morning we were chained two and two, and led before the lords. When we were brought before them, they presented the same four questions, urging us to 'subscribe to them;' but we told them we would abide by the Word of the Lord. We were then remanded to the prison and fettered as before; the women were confined at Newgate, together with a young brother; but they were released and transported. The young man, however, was tied to a cart and scourged, and afterwards whipped out of town."

The statement of Mr. Somers is rather fuller,

the assistance of good and learned ministers of Christ's church, we understand the same to be most damnable and detestable heresies; and do ask God, before his church, mercy for the said former errors; and do forsake, recant, and renounce them; and we abjure them from the bottom of our hearts, protesting we certainly believe the contrary. And further, we confess that the whole doctrine established and published in the Church of England, and also that which is received by the Dutch church in London, is found true according to God's word. Whereunto in all things we submit ourselves, and will be most gladly members of the said Dutch church; from henceforth utterly abandoning and forsaking all and every Anabaptistical error."

20

and gives us an occasional glimpse of the tender-
ness with which episcopal hands dealt with their
erring brethren. "In the course of a few days,
the bishop perceiving that the rest would not apostatize from their faith, sentenced them all to death
in the ecclesiastical court room, St. Paul's church,
(as was customary with the Papistic bishops, during
Queen Mary's reign, who were wont to condemn
the Christians to death,) and delivered them into
the hands of the civil judge; then they bound
the women hand to hand, and conducted them
to Newgate—the prison for capital convicts,—
together with one of the men which was considered the youngest and most innocent among
them ; but the rest of the men were conducted to
their old episcopal prison, for which reason it was
supposed that the women would be executed first,
even as persons came daily to threaten them, and
to present death to them unless they would apostatize. Hence they suffered great anguish and
temptation for five or six days, supposing every
day they would be burnt; nay, on the very day
that sentence of their banishment came from the
court,—for the bailiff came with the servant at ten
o'clock in the evening into the prison, to take an
inventory of all their property, informing them, in
addition, that they should prepare for death the
next day. This he did, in order to see whether
any of them would apostatize through fear; but
perceiving that they all remained steadfast, he informed them that it was the queen's pleasure to
be gracious to them, and merely banish them from

the country, and have the young man whipped behind a cart. Accordingly, in the course of five or six days, about fourteen women were conveyed from the prison, which is situated in the space between St. Martin's church and St. Catharine's, to the ship, by the apparitors; but the young man was whipped behind a cart which moved on before him. Thus they were all banished from the country, on pain of imprisonment, and reside for the present in Holland and Zealand!

" A few days after, the five men that remained in the bishop's prison were likewise sentenced to death by the bishop, and conveyed to Newgate, *where one of them died of wretchedness and a load of chains;* and the rest were apprehensive that they would inflict extreme punishment upon the women. They were also informed that the queen and her whole council were so highly offended at them that no person would venture to present a petition for them, since an evil report arose, that they denied God and Christ, and rejected all government and all respect for the magistrate and civil power, as ungodly and unchristian."

Efforts were made to obtain the lives and freedom of these Christians. A petition and confession of their faith were presented to her majesty; but the cruel and haughty sovereign refused to listen to it, and indigantly reprimanded those through whose influence it had been laid before her. Failing in this, they laid them before the bishop, through a noble lord. He graciously condescended to tell them how distressed he was on their account; but there was no hope of favor unless they would sign the four articles and abjure their heresy.

It is to the immortal honor of John Foxe, the Martyrologist, whom Elizabeth, notwithstanding his Puritanism, used to call "my father Foxe," that he now interposed on behalf of these despised and hated sectaries. He addressed an eloquent letter to the queen, in which he pleads for their lives in a strain of earnest and impassioned supplication. "To roast the living bodies of unhappy men," he says, "who err rather through blindness of judgment than perverseness of will, in fire and flames, raging with pitch and brimstone, is a hardhearted thing, and more agreeable to the practice of the Romanists, than to the custom of the gospellers. I do not speak these things because I am pleased with their wickedness, or favor thus the errors of any men; but seeing I myself am a man, I must favor the life of man; not that he should err, but that he might repent. Wherefore, if I may be so bold, I humbly beg of your royal highness, for the sake of Christ, who was consecrated to suffer for the lives of many, this favor at my request, which even the divine clemency would engage you to, that if it may be, (and what cannot your authority do in such cases?) these unhappy men may be spared. There are excommunications and imprisonments; there are bonds; there is perpetual banishment; burning of the hand; whipping; or even slavery.

"This one thing I most earnestly beg; that the

piles and flames of Smithfield, so long ago extin-
guished by your happy government, may not be
revived. But if I may not obtain this, I pray with
the greatest earnestness, that out of your great
pity, you would grant us a month or two, in which
we may try whether the Lord will grant that they
may turn from their dangerous errors, lest with
the destruction of their bodies, their souls be in
danger of eternal ruin."   But the queen was inexorable, and they must die.

From the Confession of Faith, to which we
have referred, as sent by these persons to the
queen, we select a few sentences, that our readers
may see what it was his lordship of London condemned as heresy, and for the defence of which
the writers were burnt at the stake :

" We, poor and despised strangers, who are persecuted for the testimony of Jesus, desire that God
may grant all mankind peace, so that they may
live together in all godliness to the praise of the
Lord, and the advancement of their soul's salva-
vation.   Since so many, both by writing and ver-
bal statement, do us great injustice, accusing and
charging lies upon us, we are constrained to present
our belief very summarily.   They do not speak to
us, and do not, in a mild manner, inquire of us
what our religious views are, as the Scriptures
teach ; but they speak all manner of evil of us, so
that they increase our miseries and sufferings ;
and, besides, they have no compassion either on
our distressed wives or helpless children.

" We seek no salvation in our works, as it is re-
20*

ported we do, but we hope to be saved alone through the merits of our Lord Jesus Christ. Nor do we boast that we are without sin, but we always confess ourselves sinners before God. But we have to refrain from voluntary sins if we would be saved; such as adultery, fornication, sorcery, sedition, bloodshed, cursing and swearing, lying, and cheating, pride, drunkenness, envy; these are the sins that the Scriptures declare, who do them shall not inherit the kingdom ol God.

"They also say, we refuse to hear the Word of God, because we do not go to hear the preachers of the church. To this charge we would say, that we do not hear the preachers, because the word of God constrains us not to do so; because they are a people not fit to attend to the sacred calling of a Gospel preacher. For Paul teaches Timothy, and says, 'The things that thou hast heard of me, among many witnesses, the same commit thou to faithful men,' etc. Now if the preachers were such as the apostles required, we would cheerfully hear them,—we would be the first and last in the church. . . . .

"We are also accused of not being subject to the magistracy, because we do not baptize infants. To this we reply, we desire to submit to the magistracy in all things not contrary to the word of God. That we do not suffer our children to be baptized by the priests, is not done out of temerity, but we do it out of fear to God, because Christ commands believers to be baptized; for Christ's apostles did

not baptize infants, but adults only, and those on
their faith and confession of their sins.   .   .   .
If it had been the will of God that infants should
be baptized, he would have commanded it to be
done.   Christ would have been baptized in his in-
fancy as well as circumcised; but as it is not the
will of God, therefore did he teach them differently, and received baptism differently himself."

Fourteen women and a youth finally received,
as we have already seen, the milder sentence of
banishment.   They were led by the sheriffs to
the water-side, and put on board a ship at St.
Catherine's.   The youth followed, tied to a cart's
tail, and was whipped to the place of embarkation.
Thus the ties of nature were severed: some of the
poor exiles had to mourn in anguish over husbands
and fathers, left in the hands of their persecutors,
for whom yet more cruel severities were reserved.

The next day, June 2d, the five men, who remained of this company, were again led bound
into the consistory.   The terrors of the stake were
vividly set before them; their only escape was
subscription to the articles.   They were urged,
they were threatened; it was unavailing.   "It is
a small matter thus to die," said Jan Peters, with
a courageous mind.   The bishop sharply inquired,
"What does he say?"   Peters replied as before.
The bishop listened with some moderation, and
then stoutly said, "We must shave such heretics,
and cut them off as an evil thing from the church."
Said Hendrik Terwoort, "How canst thou cut us
off from your church, since we are not of it?"

The bishop said, " It was all the same ; there were none in England who were not members of the church of God." And now were these friends of Christ unjustly condemned, and led away to New-gate to await the day of death.

Here they were strongly secured, heavily ironed, and thrown into a deep and noisome den, swarm-ing with foul and disgusting vermin. " Then we thought ourselves," says Byler, " within one or two days of the end, after which we earnestly longed, for the prison was grievous ; but it was not yet the Lord's will. After eight days, one of our brethren was released by death, trusting in God; his dying testimony filled us with joy." Even the society of thieves and malefactors was deemed too pure for them, both the bishop and a preacher saying, that care must he taken, lest the criminals should be corrupted by the association. Great indeed must have been the horror their opinions had inspired, when an English preacher occasionally visiting their dungeons, would lay his hands upon them, and falling upon his knees, cry aloud, " Sirs, be ye con-verted;" and then, exorcising the devil within them, exclaim, " Hence, depart, thou evil fiend!"

A month's reprieve from death was all that the clemency of the queen allowed. As Mr. Underhill has said, " The month expired, without any altera-tion in the resolution of these servants of God, or in their fidelity to the truths they had received. Early in the month of July, it was intimated to two of them, that they must die. Incarcerated in separate cells, they were not permitted to enjoy

each other's society, and words of love. On the
15th, the queen signed, at Gorhambury, the warrant and writ for the execution to proceed. Jan
Peters and Hendrik Terwoort were the two selected.

"Jan Peters was an aged man, and poor, with
nine children. His first wife, some years before,
had been burnt for her religion, at Ghent, in Flanders ; and his second wife had lost her first husband
by martyrdom for the truth. They had fled to
England, hoping there to worship without danger.
His circumstances were laid before the bishop, and
he had earnestly entreated permission to leave the
country with his wife and children, but the bishop
was inexorable.

"Hendrik Terwoort was a man of good estate,
five or six-and-twenty years of age, and a gold-
smith by trade. He had been married about eight
or ten weeks before his imprisonment. But neither
domestic affection, nor the solicitations of his
friends, nor the dread of death, weakened his resolution.

"On Sunday, the 17th, tidings were brought
them, that within three days they would be burnt,
unless they desired delay. To this Terwoort replied, 'Since this your design must come to pass.
so we wish you to speed the more quickly with
the matter, for we would indeed rather die than
live, to be released from this frightful den.' He,
however, asked till Friday. We again quote the
affecting narrative of their companion in tribulation. 'Upon Tuesday, a stake was set up in

Smithfield, but the execution was not that day. On Wednesday many people were gathered together to witness the death of our two friends, but it was again deferred. This was done to terrify, and draw our friends and us from the faith. But on Friday our two friends, Hendrik Terwoort and Jan Peters, being brought out from their prison, were led to the sacrifice. As they went forth, Jan Peters said, 'The holy prophets, and Christ, our Saviour, have gone this way before us, even from the beginning, from Abel until now.'

"It was early morning when they reached the scene of their triumph. They were fastened to one stake, neither strangling nor gunpowder being used to diminish their torture. As defenceless sheep of Christ, following the footsteps of their Master, resolutely, for the name of Christ they went to die. An English preacher was present, to embitter, if possible, by his cruel mockings, the closing moments of their martyr-life, and martyr-death. Before all the people he exclaimed, 'These men believe not on God.' Saith Jan Peters, 'We believe in one God, our heavenly Father Almighty, and in Jesus Christ his Son.' While standing bound at the stake, the articles were again, for the last time, presented to them, and pardon promised on subscription. Peters again spake, 'You have labored hard to drive us to you, but now, when placed at the stake, it is labor in vain.' One of the preachers attempted an excuse : 'That all such matters were determined by the council, and that it was the queen's intention they should die.'

'But,' said Peters, 'You are the teachers of the queen, whom it behoves you to instruct better, therefore shall our blood be required at your hands.'

"And now with courage they entered on the conflict, and fought through the trial, in the midst of the burning flame; an oblation to the Lord, which they living offered unto him—'accepting not of deliverance.' For the truth's sake, they counted not their lives dear unto them, that they might finish their course with joy.

> "'For what were thy terrors, O death ?
> And where was thy triumph, O grave ?
> When the vest of pure white and the conquering wreath
> Were the prize of the scorner and slave ?'

"We are saved comment on this painful scene. All writers, of every party, are agreed in condemnation of its folly and criminality. 'How utterly absurd and unchristian,' saith our Dutch martyrologist, 'do all such cruel proceedings and sentences as are here seen, appear, when contrasted with the Spirit of Christ! The Christian host is described as sheep and lambs, sent forth among cruel and devouring wolves : who will be able with a good conscience to believe, that these English preachers were the true sheep of Christ, since in this matter they brought forth so notably the fruit of wolves ?' "

EDWARD WIGHTMAN.

In the early part of the reign of James I. the Baptists of England considerably increased; so that they were emboldened, with a view of lessening the public prejudice and of extending the truths of divine revelation, to publish a confession of their faith. But, alas, this rather increased the evil than lessened it; for bishops were still found who determined to persecute the Baptists even unto death.

In 1611, the very year of the publication of the commonly received version of the Bible, Bartholomew Legate, charged with Arianism, was burnt in Smithfield, and on April 11, 1612, Edward Wightman, of Burton on Trent, Staffordshire, was called to the fire of martyrdom at Lichfield. Among other charges brought against him were these:— "That the baptizing of infants is an abominable custom; that the Lord's supper and baptism are not to be clebrated as they are now practised in the church of England; and that Christianity is not wholly professed and preached in the church of England, but only in part." Who would have thought that a person would have been burnt by Protestants for such opinions! Thank God, we trust that this day of bigotry has passed for ever.

It has been thought by Ivimey and others, that William Sawtry, a Lollard priest, who was the first

(240)

man burnt in England for religion, was a Baptist. Certainly, Edward Wightman, a Baptist, was the last man who was burnt in that country *professedly* for his religious views, though we have yet to give a painful narrative of some who were sacrificed on the altars of persecution for their efforts to obtain religious freedom. In the days of James a strong public opinion had begun to extend itself against these *religious burnings*, so that it was found un-safe to persevere in the practice. Besides which, very soon after this, indeed as early as 1614, Christians in England and Wales began to emi-grate to this country.

It will show the spirit of the rulers of those times to place before the reader the warrant issued from the "Dread Sovereign" to the sheriff of Lichfield to act out the wishes of the bishop who had con-demned poor Wightman, authorizing the said sheriff to put him to death. The document here follows:—

"The King to the sheriff of our city of Lichfield, greeting:—

"Whereas the reverend father in Christ, Richard, by divine providence, of Coventry and Lichfield, bishop, hath signified unto us, that he, judicially proceeding, according to the exigence of the eccle-siastical canons, and of the laws and customs of this our kingdom of England, against one Edward Wightman, of the parish of Burton upon Trent, in the diocese of Coventry and Lichfield, and upon the wicked heresies of Ebion, Cerinthus, Valentinian, Arius, Macedonius, Simon Magus,

Manus, Manichees, Photinus, and of the Anabaptists and other arch heretics; and moreover, of other cursed opinions, by the instinct of Satan exicogitated, and heretofore unheard of; the aforesaid Edward Wightman appearing before the aforesaid reverend father, and other divines learned in the law, assisting him in judgment, the aforesaid wicked crimes, heresies, and other detestable blasphemies and errors, stubbornly and pertinaciously, knowingly, maliciously, and with an hardened heart published, defended and dispersed; by definitive sentence of the said reverend father, with the consent of divines learned in the law aforesaid, justly, lawfully, and canonically, against the said Edward Wightman, in that part brought, stands adjudged and pronounced a heretic; and therefore, as a diseased sheep out of the flock of the Lord, lest our subjects he do infect by his contagion, he hath decreed to be cast out and cut off.

"Whereas therefore the holy mother Church, hath not further in this part what it ought more to do and prosecute, the same reverend father, the same Edward Wightman, as a blasphemous and condemned heretic, hath left to our secular power to be punished with condign punishment; as by the letters patent of the aforesaid reverend father, the bishop of Coventry and Lichfield, in this behalf thereupon made, is certified unto us in our Chancery.

"We, therefore, as a Zealot of Justice, and a Defender of the Catholic faith, and willing that the holy church, and the rights and liberties of the same, and the Catholic faith to maintain and defend, and such like heresies and errors everywhere, so much as in us lies, to root out and extirpate, and heretics so convicted to punish with condign punishment, holding that such an heretic in the aforesaid forms convict and condemned, according to the laws and customs of this our kingdom of England, in this part accustomed, *ought to be burned with fire.*

"We command thee, that thou cause the said Edward Wightman, being in thy custody, to be committed to the fire in some public and open place, below the city aforesaid, for the cause aforesaid, before the people; and the same Edward Wightman, in the same fire, cause really to be burned, in the detestation of the said crime, and for manifest example of other Christians, that they may not fall into the same crime. And this no ways omit, under the peril that shall follow thereon.

"Witness, etc."

If from charges so various and so vague, we can gather anything with certainty, Wightman was unsound in his views of the Person of Christ. While this must seriously diminish our regard for him *as a martyr* in the proper sense of that term— still in the absence of clearer evidence we cannot wholly deny him that honor.

BENJAMIN AND WILLIAM HEWLING.

It is well known that towards the close of the seventeenth century, England was ruled by the cruel tyrant James II., who was at length driven from the throne by his incensed people, and succeeded by William III. Previous to the revolution, the Duke of Monmouth and his party struggled hard, but unsuccessfully, for freedom, civil and religious. Very many of the best Christian men of that day, of all sections of the church, united with the duke, and no more stigma can attach to them, than would have been connected with the Prince of Orange and his friends had they been equally unsuccessful.

Among those whose lives were sacrificed in this cause were two young men, grandsons of the venerable William Kiffin. These young men were brothers, and their character and tragical end made a very great impression on the minds of the people of England. Noble, in his History of the Protectoral house of Cromwell, thus speaks of them:—"These two amiable but unfortunate gentlemen were the only sons of Mr. Benjamin Hewling, a Turkey merchant of great fortune in London, who, happily for himself, died before them. After their father's death they were most carefully brought up by a tender mother, and their maternal grandfather, Mr. William Kiffin, who, though very

(244)

much advanced in years, as well as his wife, sur-
vived them both."

The excellent Mr. Kiffin, to whom reference has
thus been made, was one of the wealthiest men
and one the most eminent preachers among the
Baptists of that day. He left a manuscript account of his life, written when in his seventy-
seventh year, for the use of his descendants, and
which was, a few years since, printed in London.
He gives the following account:—

"Not long after the king died, and James II.
coming to the crown, the summer after his coming
the duke of Monmouth with a party came over
with a few armed men that landed at Lyme, and
I having a young grandson, William Hewling, at
board and school in Holland, he came over with
him, although unknown to me or any of his
friends, he being about the age of nineteen years.
And his eldest brother, Benjamin Hewling, conversing with those who were under great dissatis-
faction, seeing popery encouraged, and religion
and liberty likely to be invaded, did furnish himself with arms, and went to the said duke, and in
the first fight, being afterwards both taken prisoners, were brought to Newgate, which to me
was no small affliction. And it being given out
that the king would make only some few that
were taken examples, and the rest would leave to
his officers to compound for their lives; I endeavored with his mother to treat with a *great
man*, and agreed to give three thousand pounds
for their lives.

21*

"But the face of things was soon altered, so that nothing but severity could be expected, and indeed we missed the right door; for the Lord Chief Justice [Jeffries] finding agreements made with others, and so little to himself, was the more provoked to use all manner of cruelty to the poor prisoners, so that few escaped. Amongst the rest these two young men were executed. But how graciously the Lord showed himself to them, both in their behaviour before their trial and at their deaths, the consideration thereof to such as please to peruse it; I think it may be of use to leave to you and to your children, and to such as may read the same, which is as followeth.

"The gracious dealings of God manifested to some in dying hours have been of great advantage to those living that have heard the same, giving them occasion thereby to reflect on their own state, and to look after the things of their peace before they be hid from their eyes; also a great encouragement to strengthen the faith of those that have experienced the grace of God to them.

"To that end it is thought necessary, by parents especially, to preserve to their children that remain, those blessed experiences that such have had which God hath taken to himself.

"Here then is presented a true account of the admirable appearances of God towards two young men; Mr. Benjamin Hewling, who died when he was about twenty-two years of age, and Mr. William Hewling, who died before he arrived to twenty years. They engaged with the Duke of

Monmouth, as their own words were, for the English liberties, and the Protestant religion, and for
which Mr. William Hewling was executed at
Lyme, the 12th of September, 1685; and Mr.
Benjamin Hewling at Taunton, the 30th of the
same month; and however severe men were to
them, yet the blessed dispensation of God to them
was such, as hath made good his word, that 'out
of the mouth of babes he hath ordained strength,
that he may still the enemy and avenger.'

"After the dispersing of the duke's army they
fled and put to sea, but were driven back again,
and with the hazard of their lives got ashore, over
dangerous rocks, where they saw the country filled
with soldiers, and they being unwilling to fall into
the hands of the rabble, and no way of defence or
escape remaining to them, they surrendered themselves prisoners to a gentleman whose house was
near the place where they landed, and were from
thence sent to Exeter jail, the 12th of July, where
remaining sometime, their behaviour was such,
that, being visited by many, caused great respect
towards them, even of those that were enemies to
the cause they engaged in. And being on the
27th of July put on board the Swan frigate, in
order to their bringing up to London, their carriage [conduct] was such as obtained great kindness from their commander, and all other officers
in the ship. Being brought into the river, [Thames]
captain Richardson came and took them into custody, and carried them to Newgate, putting great
irons upon them. He put them apart from each

other, without giving liberty for the nearest relation to see them, notwithstanding all endeavors and entreaties used to obtain it, though in the presence of a keeper; which though it did greatly increase the grief of relations, God, who wisely orders all things for good to those he intends grace and mercy to, made this very restraint, and hard usage a blessed advantage to their souls; as may appear by their own words, when after great importunity and charge, some of their near relations had leave to speak a few words to them before the keeper, to which they replied, they were contented with the will of God, whatever it should be.

"Having been in Newgate three weeks, there was an order given to carry them down into the west, in order to their trial; which being told them, they answered, they were glad of it; and as they went out of Newgate, several that beheld them, seeing them so cheerful, said, surely they had received their pardon, else they could never carry it with that courage and cheerfulness. Although this must be observed, that from first to last whatever hopes they might have received from their friends, they still thought the contrary, never being much affected with the hopes of it, nor cast down, nor the least discouraged at the worst that man could do. In their journey to Dorchester, the keepers that went with them have given this account, 'that their carriage was so grave, serious, and Christian, that made them admire to see and hear what they did from such young men.'

" A near relation [a sister] that went into the west to see the issue of things, and to perform whatsoever should be necessary for them, gives the following account:—' At Salisbury, the 30th of August, I had the first opportunity of conversing with them.   I found them in a very excellent composure of mind, declaring their experience of the grace and goodness of God to them in all their sufferings, in supporting and strengthening them, and providing for them, turning the hearts of all in whose hands they had been, both at Exeter and on shipboard, to show pity and to favor them; although since they came to Newgate they were hardly used, and now in their journey loaded with heavy irons and more inhumanly dealt with. They with great cheerfulness professed that they were better and in a more happy condition than ever in their lives, from the sense they had of the pardoning love of God in Jesus Christ to their souls; wholly referring themselves to their wise and gracious God to choose for them life or death, expressing themselves — Anything what pleaseth God, what he sees best, so be it. We know he is able to deliver; but if not, blessed be his name; death is not terrible now, but desirable.   Mr. Benjamin Hewling particularly added, As for the world, there is nothing in it to make it worth while to live, except we may be serviceable to God therein. He afterwards said, Oh! God is a strong refuge: I have found him so indeed !

" ' The next opportunity I had was at Dorchester, whither they were both carried, and remained together four days. By reason of their strait confinement, our conversation was much interrupted; but this appeared, that they had still the same presence and support from God, no way discouraged at the approach of their trial, nor at the event of it, whatever it should be. The 6th of September, Mr. Benjamin Hewling was ordered to Taunton, to be tried there. Taking my leave of him, he said, Oh, blessed be God for afflictions. I would not have been without them for all this world.

"'I remained still at Dorchester to wait the issue of Mr. William Hewling, to whom, after trial, I had free access, and whose discourse was much filled with the admirings of the grace of God which had been manifested towards him in calling him out of his natural state. He said, God by his Holy Spirit did suddenly seize upon his heart when he thought not of it, in his retired abode in Holland, as it were secretly whispering in his heart, Seek ye my face, enabling him to answer his gracious call and to reflect upon his own soul, shewing him the evil of sin and the necessity of Christ, from that time carrying him on to a sensible adherence to Christ for justification and eternal life. Hence he found a spring of joy and sweetness beyond the comforts of the whole earth. He also said that he could not but admire the wonderful goodness of God in so preparing him for what he was bringing him to, which then he thought not of; giving him hope of eternal life before he called him to look death in the face, so

that he did cheerfully resign his life to God before
he came, having sought his guidance in it; and
that both then and now, the cause did appear to him
very glorious, notwithstanding all he had suffered
in it, or what he farther might suffer; although
for our sins, God had withheld these good things
from us.   But he said, God carried on his blessed
work on his own soul in and by all his sufferings;
and whatever the will of God were, life or death,
he knew it would be best for him.

"'After he had received his sentence, when he
returned to prison, he said, Methinks I find my
spiritual comforts increasing ever since my sentence.   There is no condemation to them who are
in Christ Jesus.   It is God that justifieth; who
shall condemn?   When I came to him the next
morning, when he had received news that he must
die the next day, and in order to it was to be carried to Lyme that day, I found him in a more excellent, raised, and spiritual frame than before.
He was satisfied, he said, that God had chosen
best for him.   He knows what the temptations of
life might have been.   I might have lived and
forgotten God; but now I am going where I shall
sin no more.   Oh, it is a blessed thing to be freed
from sin, and to be with Christ!   Oh, how great
were the sufferings of Christ for me, beyond all I
can undergo!   How great is that glory to which I
am going; it will soon swallow up all our sufferings here!

"'While he was at dinner, just before his going
to Lyme, he dropped many abrupt expressions of

his inward joy, such as these;—Oh, the grace of
God; the love of Christ! Oh, that blessed supper
of the Lamb; to be for ever with the Lord! He
farther said, When I went to Holland, you know
not what sins, snares, and miseries I might have
fallen into, nor whether we should ever meet
again; but now you know whither I am going,
and that we shall certainly have a joyful meeting.
He said, Pray give my particular recommendations
to all my friends, with acknowledgments for all
their kindness. I advise them all to make sure
of an interest in Christ, for he is the only comfort
when we come to die.

" 'One of the prisoners seemed to be troubled
at the manner in which they were to die; to whom
he said, I bless God that I am reconciled to it all.
Just as he was going to Lyme, he wrote these few
lines to a friend, being hardly suffered to stay so
long:—I am going to launch into eternity, I hope
and trust, into the arms of my blessed Redeemer;
to whom I commit you, and all my dear relations.
My duty to my dear mother, and love to all my
sisters, and the rest of my friends.

" ' WILLIAM HEWLING.'

" As they passed through the town of Dorchester to Lyme, multitudes of people beheld
them with great lamentations, admiring his deportment at parting with his sister. Passing on
the road, his discourse was exceedingly spiritual,
taking occasion from everything to speak of the
glory they were going to. Looking at the country as they passed, he said, ' This is a glorious

creation ; but what then is the paradise of God to which we are going! It is but a few hours, and we shall be there, and be for ever with the Lord !'

"At Lyme, just before they went to die, reading John xiv. 18, he said to one of his fellow-sufferers, ' Here is a sweet promise for us, *I will not leave you comfortless, I will come unto you.* Christ will be with us to the last.' A friend taking leave of him, he said, ' Farewell till we meet in heaven. Presently I shall be with Christ. Oh, I would not change condition with any one in this world! I would not stay behind for ten thousand worlds !'

" To another who asked him how he did, he said, ' Very well, blessed be God.' And farther asking him whether he could look death in the face with comfort now it approached so near, he said, ' Yes, I bless God I can with great comfort. God hath made this a good night to me : my comforts are much increased since I left Dorchester.' Then taking leave of him, he said, ' Farewell, I shall see you no more.' To which he replied, ' How, see me no more ? Yes, I hope to meet you in glory.' To another, who was with him to the last, he said, ' Pray remember my dear love to my brother and sister, and tell them I desire they would comfort themselves that I am gone to Jesus, and we shall quickly meet in Zion above.'

" Afterwards he prayed for about three quarters of an hour with the greatest fervency, exceedingly blessing God for Jesus Christ, adoring the riches of his grace in him, in all the glorious fruits of it towards him, praying for the peace of the church

22

of God and of these nations in particular; all with
such eminent assistance of the Spirit of God as
convinced, astonished, and melted into pity the
hearts of all present, even the most malicious adversaries, forcing tears and expressions from them;
some saying they knew not what would become
of them after death, but it was evident *he* was
going to great happiness.

"When just departing out of the world, with a
joyful countenance he said, 'Oh, now my joy and
comfort is that I have a Christ to go to;' and so
sweetly resigned his spirit to Christ, on the 12th
of September, 1685.

"An officer who had shown so malicious a
spirit as to call the prisoners devils, when he was
guarding them down, was now so convinced, that
he afterwards told a person of quality that he
never was so affected as by his cheerful carriage
and fervent prayer, such as he believed was never
heard, especially from one so young; and added,
'I believe that if the lord chief justice had been
there, he would not have let him die.' The sheriff
having given his body to be buried, although it
was brought from the place of execution without
any notice given, yet very many of the town, to
the number of two hundred, came to accompany
him; and several young women of the best of the
town laid him in his grave in Lyme church-yard,
September 13, 1685.

"After this event his sister wrote to her mother:—'Although I have nothing to acquaint my
dear mother withal, but what is most afflictive to

sense, both as to the determination of God's will and as to my present apprehension concerning my brother Benjamin who still remains; yet there is such an abundant consolation mixed in both, that I only wanted an opportunity to pay this duty; God having wrought so glorious a work on both their souls, revealing Christ in them, that death is become their friend.   My brother William having already, with the greatest joy, declared to those that were with him to the last, that he would not change conditions with any that were to remain in this world, and he desired that his relations would comfort themselves that he is gone to Christ.   My brother Benjamin expects not long to continue in this world, and is quite willing to leave it when God shall call; being fully satisfied that God will choose what is best for him and for us all.   By these things God doth greatly support me, and I hope you also, my dear mother, which was and is my brother's great desire.   There is still room to pray for one; and God having so answered, though not in kind, we have encouragement still to wait on him.

'Honored mother,

'Your dutiful daughter.'

"When I came to Taunton to Mr. Benjamin Hewling, he had received the news of his brother's being gone to die with so much comfort and joy, and afterwards of the continued goodness of God in increasing it to the end, on which he expressed himself to this effect—We have no cause to fear death, if the presence of God be with us, there is no evil in it, the sting being taken away. It is nothing but our ignorance of the glory the saints pass into by death which makes it appear dark to ourselves or our relations. If in Christ, what is this world that we should desire an abode in it? It is all vain and unsatisfying, full of sin and misery. He also intimated his own cheerful expectations soon to follow, discovering then and all along great seriousness and sense of spiritual and eternal things, complaining of nothing in his present circumstances but want of a place of retirement to converse more uninterruptedly with God and his own soul ; saying that his lonely time in Newgate was the sweetest in his whole life. He said God had sometime before struck his heart, when he thought of the hazard of his life, to some serious sense of his past life, and the great consequences of death and eternity ; showing him that they were the only happy persons who had secured their eternal state, the folly and madness of the ways of sin and his own thraldom therein, with his utter inability to deliver himself, also the necessity of Christ for salvation. He said he was not without terror and amazement for some time when he had the sight of unpardoned sin and eternity before him. But God wonderfully opened to him the riches of free grace in Christ Jesus for poor sinners to flee to, enabling him to look alone to a crucified Christ for salvation. He said this blessed work was in some measure carried on upon his soul amidst all his business and hurries in the army, but never sprung forth so fully and sweetly till his close confinement in Newgate. There he saw Christ and all spiritual objects more clearly, and embraced them more strongly; there he experienced the blessedness of a reconciled state, the excellency of the way of holiness, the delightfulness of communion with God, which re- mained with deep and apparent impressions on his own soul, which he frequently expressed with ad- miration of the grace of God towards him.

"Perhaps my friends, said he, may think this the saddest summer of my life; but, I bless God, it hath been the sweetest and happiest of it all; nay, there is nothing else that deserves the name of happiness. I have sought satisfaction from the things of this world, but I never found it. But now I have found rest for my soul in God alone.

"Oh how great is our blindness by nature; till God opens our eyes we can see no excellency in spiritual things, but spend our precious time in pursuing shadows, and are deaf to all the invita- tions of grace and glorious offers of the gospel. How just is God in depriving us of that we so much slighted and abused. Oh, his infinite pa- tience and goodness, that after all he should sanc- tify any methods to bring a sinner to himself! Oh, electing love! distinguishing grace! What great cause have I to admire and adore it! What an amazing consideration is the suffering of Christ for sin to bring us to God! His suffering from wicked men was exceedingly great; but alas, what was that to the sorrows of his soul under the in- finite wrath of God! This mystery of grace and love is enough to swallow up our thoughts to all eternity.

"As to his own death, he would often say, he saw no reason to expect any other. I know God is infinitely able to deliver, and am sure he will do it, if it be for his glory and my good. In which, I bless God, I am fully satisfied. It is all my desire that he would choose for me, and then I am sure it will be best, whatever it be. For truly unless God have some work for me to do in the world for his service and glory, I see nothing else to make life desirable. In the present state of affairs, there is nothing to cast our eyes upon but sin, sorrow, and misery; and were things ever so agreeable to our desires, it is but the world still, which will never be a resting place. Heaven is the only state of rest and happiness; there we shall be perfectly free from sin and temptation, and enjoy God without interruption for ever.

"Speaking of the disappointment of their expectations in the work they had undertaken, he said, With reference to the glory of God, the prosperity of the Gospel, and the delivery of the people of God, we have great cause to lament it; but for that outward prosperity which would have accompanied it, it is of small moment in itself. As it would not satisfy, so neither could it be abiding; for at longest, death would have put an end to it all. Also adding, Nay, perhaps we might have been so foolish as to be taken with part of it, to the neglect of our eternal concerns; and then I

am sure our present circumstances are incalcula-
bly better.

"He frequently expressed great concern for
the glory of God, and affection to his people, saying, If my death may advance God's glory, and
hasten the deliverance of his people, it is enough.
Saying it was a great comfort to him to think of
so great a privilege as that of having an interest
in all their prayers.   In his conversation he particularly delighted in those persons in whom he
saw most holiness shining; also great pity to the
souls of others, saying that the remembrance of
our former vanity may well cause compassion towards others in that state.   In his conversation he
prompted them to seriousness, telling them that
death and eternity were such weighty concerns
that they deserved the utmost attention of our
minds; for the way to receive death cheerfully is
to prepare for it seriously; and if God should
please to spare our lives, surely we have the same
reason to be serious, and spend our remaining
days in his fear and service.   He also took great
care that the worship of God, which they were in
a capacity of maintaining there, might be duly
performed; as reading, praying, and singing of
psalms, in which he evidently took great delight.

"For those three or four days before their
deaths, when there was a general report that no
more should die, he said, I do not know what
God hath done, contrary to our expectations.   If
he doth prolong my life, I am sure it is all his
own, and by his grace I will wholly devote it to

him. But on the 29th of September, about ten or
eleven at night, we found the deceitfulness of this
report, they being then told that they must die
the next morning, which was very unexpected as
to the suddenness of it. But herein God glorified
his power, grace, and faithfulness, in giving suitable support and comfort by his blessed presence,
which appeared upon my coming to him at that
time, and finding him greatly composed. He said,
Though men design to surprise, God doth and
will perform his word, to be a very present help in
trouble.

" The next morning, when I saw him again,
his cheerfulness and comfort were much increased,
waiting for the sheriff with the greatest sweetness
and serenity of mind; saying, Now the will of
God is determined, to whom I have referred it,
and he hath chosen most certainly what is best!
Afterwards, with a smiling countenance, he discoursed of the glory of heaven, remarking with
much delight the third, fourth, and fifth verses of
the twenty-second of the Revelations :—And there
shall be no more curse ; but the throne of God
and of the Lamb shall be in it, and his servants
shall serve him, and they shall see his face, and
his name shall be in their foreheads; and there
shall be no night there, and they shall need no
candle, nor light of the sun ; and they shall reign
for ever and ever. Then he said, Oh, what a
happy state is this! Shall we be loth [unwilling]
to go and enjoy this ?

" He then desired to be read to him, 2 Cor. v.

1, 2. For we know that if our earthly house of
this tabernacle were dissolved, we have a building
of God, a house not made with hands, eternal in
the heavens, etc. His hope and comfort still increasing, with the assurance of an interest in that
glorious inheritance to the possession of which he
was now going, he said death was more desirable
than life, and he would rather die than live any
longer here.

"As to the manner of his death, he said, When
I have considered others under these circumstances,
I have thought it very dreadful; but now God
hath called me to it, I bless him that I have quite
other apprehensions of it. I can now cheerfully
embrace it as an easy passage to glory; and
though death separates from the enjoyment of
each other here, it will be but for a very short
time, and then we shall meet in such enjoyments
as now we cannot conceive of, and for ever rejoice
in each other's happiness.

"Then reading the Scriptures and musing with
himself, he intimated the great comfort which God
conveyed to his soul in it; saying, Oh, what an
invaluable treasure is this blessed word of God!
In all conditions here is a store of strong consolation! A friend desiring his Bible, he said, No:
this shall be my companion to the last moment of
my life.

"Thus praying together, reading, meditating,
and conversing of heavenly things, they waited for
the sheriff, who, when he came, void of all pity or
civility, hurried them away, scarcely suffering them

to take leave of their friends. Notwithstanding this, and the bitter mourning of all about them, the joyfulness of his countenance was increased. Thus he left the prison, and thus he appeared in the sledge, where they sat about half an hour before the officers could force the horses to draw; at which they were greatly enraged, there being no visible obstruction from weight or way. At last the mayor and sheriff haled them forwards themselves, Balaam-like, driving the horses.

"When they came to the place of execution, which was surrounded with spectators, many that waited their coming, said, that when they saw him and them come with such cheerfulness and joy, and evidence of the presence of God with them, it made death appear with another aspect. They first embraced each other with the greatest affection; then two of the elder persons praying audibly, they joined with great seriousness. Then he required leave of the sheriff to pray particularly; but he would not grant it, and only asked him whether he would pray for the king. He answered, 'I pray for all men.' He then requested that they might sing a hymn. The sheriff told him it must be with the rope about their necks; which they cheerfully accepted, and sung with such heavenly joy and sweetness that many who were present said, that it both broke and rejoiced their hearts. Thus in the experience of the delightfulness of praising God on earth, he willingly closed his eyes on a vain world, to pass to that eternal enjoyment, on September 30, 1685.

"All present of all sorts were exceedingly affected and amazed. Some officers who had before insultingly said, Surely these persons have no thoughts of death, but will find themselves surprised by it, now acknowledged that they saw he and they had something extrordinary within, which carried them through with so much joy. Others said that they were so convinced of their happiness, that they would be glad to change conditions with them. The soldiers in general, and all others, lamented exceedingly, saying, it was so sad a thing to see them so cut off that they scarcely knew how to bear it. Some of the most malicious in the place, from whom nothing but railing was expected, said, as they were carried to their grave in Taunton church, 'These persons have left sufficient evidence that they are now glorified spirits in heaven.' A great officer also in the king's army has often been heard to say, 'If you would learn to die, go to the young men of Taunton.' Much more was uttered by these good men, which showed the blessed frame of their hearts, to the glory of divine grace. But this is what occurs to memory.

"Mr. Benjamin Hewling, about two hours before his death, wrote the following letter, which showed his great composure of mind :—

"'HONORED MOTHER,

"'That news which I know you have a great while feared, and we expected, I must now acquaint you with ; that notwithstanding the hopes you gave in your two last letters, warrants are come for my execution, and within these few hours I expect it to be performed.

"'Blessed be the Almighty God, who gives comfort and support in such a day! How ought we to magnify his holy name for all his mercies, that when we were running on in a course of sin he should stop us in our full career, and show us that Saviour whom we had pierced, and out of his free grace enable us to look upon him with an eye of faith, believing him able to save to the uttermost all such as come to him! Oh, admirable long-suffering patience of God; that when we were dishonoring his name, he did not take that time to bring honor to himself by our destruction? But he delighteth not in the death of a sinner, but had rather he should turn to him and live; and he hath many ways of bringing his own to himself. Blessed be his holy name, he has taught my heart in some measure to be conformable to his will, which worketh patience, and patience experience, and experience hope, which maketh not ashamed.

"'I bless God that I am not ashamed of the cause for which I lay down my life; and as I have engaged in it, and fought for it, so now I am going to seal it with my blood. The Lord will still carry on the same cause which hath been long on foot; and though we die in it and for it, I question not but in his own good time he will raise up other instruments more worthy to carry it on to the glory of his name, and the advancement of his church and people.

"'Honored mother, I know there has been

nothing left undone by you or my friends for the saving of my life, for which I return many hearty acknowledgements to yourself and to them all; and it is my dying request to you and them, to pardon all undutifulness and unkindness in every relation. Pray give my duty to my grandfather and grandmother; service to my uncles and aunts; and my dear love to all my sisters; to every relation and friend a particular recommendation. Pray tell them all how precious an interest in Christ is when we come to die; and advise them never to rest in a Christless state. For if we are his, it is no matter what the world do to us; they can but kill the body, and blessed be God, for the soul is out of their reach. I question not but their malice wishes the damnation of that, as well as the destruction of the body, which has too evidently appeared by their deceitful flattering promises.

" 'I commit you all to the care and protection of God, who has promised to be a Father to the fatherless, and a husband to the widow, and to supply the want of every relation. The Lord God of heaven be your comfort under these sorrows, and your refuge from those miseries which we may easily foresee coming upon poor England, and the poor distressed people of God in it. The Lord carry you through this vale of tears with a resigning submissive spirit; and at last bring you to himself in glory; where I question not but you will meet your dying son,

'BENJAMIN HEWLING.' "

23

Mr. Kiffin adds to this statement, "Only for myself it was a great comfort to me, and is to observe what testimony they left behind of that blessed interest they had in the Lord Jesus, and their humble and holy confidence of their eternal happiness.

"One thing I think it necessary to observe, that at the trial of William Hewling, the Lord Chief Justice Jefferies was pleased in public court, to tell him, that his grandfather did as well deserve that death, which he was likely to suffer, as they did. Which I mention to that end, that thereby it may be seen what an eye they had upon me for my ruin, if the Lord, who hath watched over me for good, had not prevented."

The relative who has been described as attending these lovely young men in the west, and from whom Mr. Kiffin received his account, was their sister, Hannah Hewling, who, about a year afterwards, married Major Henry Cromwell, and who died in 1731. When all other means had failed, she determined to present a petition to the king. For this purpose she was introduced by Lord Churchill, afterwards Duke of Marlborough. While they waited in the ante-chamber for admittance, standing near the chimney-piece, Lord Churchill assured her of his most hearty wishes for the success of her petition. "But," he added, "Madam, I dare not flatter you with any such hopes, for that marble is as capable of feeling compassion as the king's heart."

Noble says, " It has been said in most of the

accounts that have been published, that Lord Chief Justice Jefferies always treated Hannah Hewling according to his usual custom, with the greatest brutality; but this is not true; for Jefferies always treated her with the greatest politeness and respect. This fact, however, does not much soften the horrors of his general character. Jefferies had a relation from whose fortune he had formed great expectations; and as this relation was an intimate acquaintance of the Hewlings, he exerted himself very warmly with him on their behalf. He repeatedly protested to the chief justice, that the continuance of his friendship together with every benefit he might hope to result from it, depended entirely on his using every endeavor to save the Hewlings. This, Jefferies declared that he did; but he always said that the king was inexorable.

"For many reasons," adds Noble, "it would be improper to omit what Mr. Hewling Luson has said of these two young men. 'The two unfortunate brothers, Benjamin and William Hewling, were the only males of their name, and of their family, which was in the highest esteem and popularity among the staunch whigs and dissenting Protestants, at that time so numerous and respectable in the city. Their parts were excellent, and their education was the best that could be given them; their morals were spotless, their piety exemplary; their zeal against popery, the ardor of their courage in the field, and the manly meekness, and devout resignation of their deportment to the last, under their sufferings, concurred with their youth, (the one twenty-one, and the other not quite twenty,) and the uncommon beauty and gracefulness of their persons, to place them the first in the list which was at that time called *The Western Martyrology*, and to render the severity of their fate most pitied of any who fell a sacrifice to the popish vengeance of James, though there were some other sentences much more unjust.' "

We cannot willingly close this account without a touching anecdote of Mr. Kiffin, the venerable grandfather of these excellent young men. Shortly before his abdication, James determined, after having arbitrarily deprived the city of London of its charters, to change its magistracy, and to put some of the dissenters into office. He privately sent to Kiffin to wait upon him at court. When he arrived there, he found many lords and gentlemen. The king immediately came up, and addressed him with all the little grace he was master of. He talked of his favor to the dissenters in the court style of the time, and concluded with telling the old man that he had put him down in his new charter as an alderman. " Sire," replied Kiffin, " I am a very old man, and have withdrawn myself from all kind of business for some years past; and am incapable of doing any service in such an affair to your majesty in the city. Besides, Sire," —the old man went on, fixing his eyes steadfastly on the king, while the tears ran down his cheeks —" the death of my grandsons gave a wound to my heart which is still bleeding, and never will close but in the 'grave." The king was greatly struck by the manner, the spirit, and the freedom of this rebuke, so unexpected but so just. An entire silence followed, while the king, chagrined and mortified, as indicated in his countenance, showed that he shrunk from the horrid remembrance. He soon, however, recovered himself enough to say, " Mr. Kiffin, I shall find a balsam for that sore ;" and then immediately turned about to a lord in waiting. Of course Mr. Kiffin never again heard from the king.

CHAPTER V.

ANNE ASKEW.

THIS distinguished lady is very truly said, by Mr. C. B. Tayler, to have been the most interesting victim of the fires of Smithfield. We have indeed a sad story to tell of this gentle and delicate woman. She was the intimate friend and companion of the lovely queen Catherine Parr, and was singled out by the crafty bishop Gardiner and others, as well as by the popish ladies of the court, hoping that through her they might find an accusation against the queen, for holding the faith and principles of the Reformation.

Anne Askew, as we learn from the second volume of "*The Pictorial History of England,*" by Messrs. Craik and Macfarlane, was associated with Joan Boucher, of whom we shall speak in our next article, in the good work of circulating books and tracts in the court of Henry VIII. Joan escaped burning till the following reign, but, like her friend, Anne Askew, she was persecuted and imprisoned by the tyrannical and hypocritical monarch. The probability that these two friends entertained the same views on the subject of baptism,

(270)

seems confirmed by uncontradicted tradition, and the fact that no other body of Christians ever seems to have claimed either the one or the other. We feel no difficulty, therefore, in placing Anne Askew among the so-called "fanatical Anabaptists," of whose religious views the lower house of convocation complained to the sovereign, "as prevalent errors that demanded correction."

Anne was the youngest daughter of Sir William Askew, of Kelsey, in Lincolnshire; her eldest sister had been engaged to marry a gentleman of the name of Kyme, a harsh and bigoted Catholic; but the sister died, and she was compelled by her father to take her sister's place, and become the wife of that gentleman. It was indeed a most unhappy marriage for Anne. Her education had been superior to that usually given even to the nobility in those days, and she possessed a strong and enlightened mind; indeed she presented a striking contrast to her morose and narrow-minded husband.

She seems to have been distinguished for piety from her earliest years, and to have searched and prized the holy Scriptures, which had made her wise unto salvation. Her love of the truth, as it is found in its purity and freshness in the word of inspiration, gave great displeasure to her husband, by whom she was cruelly driven from her home One of the accusations against her was, "that she was the devoutest woman he had ever known, for she began to pray always at midnight, and continued for some hours in that exercise."

Travelling to London to sue for a divorce from her tyrannical husband, his persecution and that of the popish priests followed her, and she soon fell into the snares they had laid for her. Full of piety and of Christian simplicity, she dreamt of no evil in the circles in which she moved. Anne Askew—for she had resumed her maiden name— was filled with the piety induced by the Holy Spirit. Her thorough knowledge of Holy Scripture, the hold which it had obtained of her heart, the influence which it exercised upon her conduct, the sweetness which it breathed over her manners, all combined to win for her the affection of those noble and pious ladies who formed the circle of the queen's society, who was herself said to be her friend, to have received books from her, and to have returned many a kind message. It has been said that probably a more unguarded and fearless spirit existed in this meek and gentle lady than in any other follower of Christ of her sex, rank, and the age in which she lived.

Soon, however, did she find that all the holy familiar intercourse she held on various occasions with the godly ladies of the court must cease; and that her attachment to the writings and memory of holy men must be locked up as inviolate secrets in her own bosom; for she was apprehended on the charge of holding heretical opinions against the six articles, with especial reference to the sacrament of the Lord's supper, and was committed to prison. Her conduct from that time presented a remarkable combination of lofty self-possession,

and touching simplicity and sweetness—of firmness, constancy, and a ready wit, according to the
true acceptation of that word; and all these qualities were in perfect keeping in her whole character
and conduct, and made her at the same time one
of the most feminine and courageous of her sex.

On the part of her enemies two objects were
plainly manifest in all the examinations to which
they subjected her—the first was to make her
criminate herself, the second to lead her to criminate the queen, and those of her ladies who were
suspected of holding "the new learning," as the
eternal truths of the gospel were called by the
Catholics.

Few women have so dearly and so truly won
the title of heroine, in the highest sense of the
word, as the poor persecuted martyr, Anne Askew.
Few have possessed a presence of mind so unsup-
ported by human strength, or even so little encouraged by human friends, as this young lady.
The wisdom and discretion which she exhibited
in answering the insidious questions, and baffling
the crafty designs of her enemies, were no less remarkable than her clear and accurate knowledge
of the word of God, and her resolute spirit in cleav-
ing to it. And thus she met and surmounted all
the difficulties to which she was exposed, in one
conference after another, with the most skilful and
subtle of the Popish party; and every one who
entered into an encounter with her, was com-
pletely foiled by her truth, her simplicity of wisdom, her patience, and her calm trust in God.

Her piteous story is enough to melt the sternest man to tears, were it not that the heart must throb, and the cheek burn at the disgraceful consciousness that Englishmen and English prelates, could be found base and bad enough to make that gentle lady the victim of their diabolical malice.

She was examined concerning her opinions by Christopher Dare, and Sir Martin Bowes, the then Lord Mayor of London, and their brother commissioners. With what inimitable simplicity did she reply in the conversation, which is said to have taken place between the Lord Mayor and herself: " What if a mouse were to eat the sacred bread after it was consecrated?" was the absurd question; "what shall become of the mouse, what sayest thou, thou foolish woman ?" " Nay, what say you, my lord, will become of it?" " I say that mouse is damned !" " Alas, poor mouse," was her quiet reply; and so at once all his divinity was discomfited. In one of her examinations she was asked if she had said that priests could not make the body of Christ; "I have read" she replied, "that God made man; but that man can make God, I never yet read, nor, I suppose ever shall."

She herself, in the most artless language, gives an account of her various examinations. First, she was summoned before the inquisition at Sadler's Hall, where Christopher Dare asked her if she did not believe that the sacrament hanging over the altar was the very blood of Christ. She replied by asking him, Why Stephen was stoned? to death? He said he could not tell. "No more," said she, "will I answer your vain question." Being charged with reading from a book that God dwelleth not in temples made with hands, she showed them the seventh and seventeenth chapters of the Acts of the Apostles. She was asked why she had said she would rather read five lines in the Bible than hear five masses? She confessed having said it, because the one did greatly edify her, and the other did not at all; quoting the text in the fourteenth of the first epistle to the Corinthians:—"If the trumpet give an uncertain sound, who shall prepare himself for the battle?"

On her next examination before the lord mayor, she relates:—"Then the bishop's chancellor rebuked me, and said I was much to blame for uttering the Scriptures; for St. Paul, he said, forbade women to speak, or to talk of the word of God. I answered him that I knew Paul's meaning as well as he, which is that a woman ought not to speak in the congregation, by the way of teaching. And then I asked him how many women he had seen go into the pulpit and preach? He said he never saw any. Then I said he ought to find no fault in poor women, except they offend against the law." In an interview with a priest she requested him to answer some of his own questions, when he told her "that it was against the order of the schools, that he who asked the question, should be required to answer it;" she at once told him that she was but a woman, and knew not the course of schools.

But we pass over these, and many other examinations, in which the patience of her adversaries, who could not overcome her, was exhausted. These bold and crafty men were determined to spare neither threat nor violence by which they might extort from her some word or other, as a ground of accusation against the Lady Herbert, who was the queen's sister, or the Duchess of Suffolk, and so at last Queen Catharine herself. As yet they had discovered nothing. Rich, and another of the council, came to her in the tower, where she was then confined, and demanded that she should make the disclosures which they required concerning her party, and her friends. She told them nothing. "Then," she says, "they did put me on the rack, because I confessed no ladies or gentlemen to be of my opinion; and thereon they kept me a long time, and because I lay still and did not cry, my lord chancellor and Mr. Rich took pains to rack me with their own hands till I was nigh dead." These inhuman creatures, it is recorded, provoked by her saint-like endurance, ordered the lieutenant of the tower to rack her again. He, Sir Anthony Knevett, "tendering the weakness of the woman," positively refused to do so. Then Wriothesley and Rich threw off their gowns, and threatening the lieutenant that they would complain of his disobedience to the king, "they worked the rack themselves, till her bones and joints were almost plucked asunder." When

Baptist Martyrs.

Interview of Members of the Counsel with Anne Askew in the Tower.   PAGE 276.

the lieutenant caused her to be loosed down from the rack, she immediately swooned. "Then," she writes, "they recovered me again. After that I sate two long hours reasoning with my lord chancellor on the bare floor, where he, with many flattering words, persuaded me to leave my opinion; but my Lord God, I thank his everlasting goodness, gave me grace to persevere, and will do, I hope, to the very end." And she concludes this account to her friend, by saying, "Farewell, dear friend, and pray, pray, pray."

The lieutenant of the tower, fearing Wriothesley's threats, secretly took a boat, and hastened to the king, to tell him the things he had witnessed. Henry seemed displeased at the excess of barbarity perpetrated, and dismissed the humane officer with assurances of his pardon; telling him to return, and see to his charge in the tower. There all the wardens and officials anxiously waited the result; and gave God thanks for the success of his embassy.

Lascelles, one of Anne's fellow martyrs, inquiring if it were true that she had recanted, received from her this reply:—"O friend, most dearly beloved in God, I marvel not a little what should move you to judge in me so slender a faith as to fear death, which is the end of all miseries. In the Lord I desire you not to believe of me such weakness. For I doubt it not but God will perform his works in me, like as he hath begun. 1 understand the council is not a little displeased, that it should be reported abroad that I was racked

24

in the tower. They say now, that what they did there was but to fear me; [make me afraid,] whereby I perceive they are ashamed of their uncomely doings, and fear much lest the king's majesty should have information thereof; wherefore they would have no man to noise it. Well, for their cruelty God forgive them!"

Her last hours were employed in writing a strong denial of a report which had been circulated, that she had recanted, and swerved from the truth, and she concludes her account with this beautiful prayer:—" O Lord, I have more enemies now, than there be hairs on my head! Yet, Lord, let them never overcome me with vain words, but fight thou, Lord, in my stead: for on Thee cast I my care! With all the spite they can imagine, they fall upon me, who am Thy poor creature. Yet, sweet Lord, let me not set by them that are against me; for in Thee is my whole delight. And, Lord, I heartily desire of Thee, that Thou wilt, of Thy most merciful goodness, forgive them that violence which they do, and have done unto me; open also Thou their blind hearts, that they may hereafter do that thing in Thy sight, which is only acceptable before Thee, and to set forth Thy verity aright, without all vain fantasies of sinful men. So be it, O Lord, so be it."

Unable to walk or stand from the tortures she had endured, Anne Askew was carried in a chair to Smithfield, and when brought to the stake was fastened to it by a chain which held up her body, and one who saw her there describes her as " hav-

Baptist Martyrs.

Burning Place, Smithfield, London.—Burning of Anne Askew.   Page 278.

ing an angel's countenance, and a smiling face."
She had three companions in her last agonies, fel-
low-martyrs with herself, John Lascelles, a gentleman of the court and household of king Henry,
John Adams, a tailor, and Nicholas Belenian, a
minister of Shropshire. The apostate priest Shax-
ton preached the sermon, to which Anne Askew
gave diligent attention, assenting when he spoke
truth, and when he erred, detecting and exposing
it. The concourse of spectators was so great, that
a space was obliged to be railed in to keep off the
pressure. The three Throckmortons, near kins-
men of the queen, and members of her household,
drew near to comfort Anne and her three companions, but were warned that they were marked
men, and were entreated to withdraw.

While these things were going on, at a short
distance, elevated on a high judicial seat, immediately under St. Bartholomew's church, sat
Wriothesley, the tormenting Lord Chancellor of
England, the old duke of Norfolk, the old earl of
Bedford, the Lord Mayor, and several others.
Guilt always makes men fearful, and when these
men heard that some gunpowder was thrown upon
the bodies of the martyrs, they showed no small
alarm, lest the faggots might thereby be driven
towards them. At length, however, the facts being fully ascertained by the earl of Bedford, their
alarm ceased.

At the very last, a written pardon from the king
was offered to Anne Askew, upon condition that
she would recant. The fearless lady turned away

her eyes and would not look upon it. She told them that she came not there to deny her Lord and Master. The fire was ordered to be put under her, and her companions, who, in like manner had each refused a pardon, by the Lord Mayor; "and thus," to use the words of John Foxe, "the good Anne Askew, with these blessed martyrs, having passed through so many torments, having now ended the long course of her agonies, being encompassed with flames of fire as a blessed sacrifice unto God, she slept in the Lord, A. D. 1546, leaving behind her a singular example of Christian constancy for all men to follow." *Her crime was the denial of the Mass.* "So this," she wrote, "is the heresy that I hold, and for it must suffer death." She kept the faith to her God, she kept the faith to her friends, for she betrayed no one, enduring shame and agony with meek unshaken constancy. O none but Christ, none but Christ could have made the weakness of a delicate woman so strong,— the feebleness of a mortal creature so triumphant!

And thus the square of Smithfield, which was made in the reign of Henry I., "a lay stall of all ordure or filth," and the place of execution for felons and other transgressors, has become not only drenched with the blood of martyrs, but hallowed by the faith and patience of the saints, by the witness of their good confessions, and by the breath of their dying prayers and praises.

JOAN BOUCHER.

JOAN BOUCHER, or as she is more frequently called, *Joan of Kent*, of high parentage, and engaged in the court of Henry VIII., was unquestionably a Baptist. Uninterrupted and uncontradicted tradition reports her as a member of the Baptist church, then meeting at Canterbury and Eythorne, and which still flourishes in the latter village, near the south-eastern extremity of England, a few miles from Dover, and about sixteen miles from Canterbury, where not a few of her friends endured the fire of martyrdom.

Strange as it may appear to some of our readers, in 1547 was established a Protestant inquisition, of which Cranmer and Latimer, who were themselves in after years martyrs, and other men of great eminence, were commissioners. Only eighteen days after the commission was issued, Joan Boucher was arraigned for heresy before this body, and her sentence formally pronounced. From Cranmer's own archiepiscopal register we learn that he himself sat as principal judge on this sad occasion, assisted by Latimer and three others, as the king's "proctors, inquisitors, judges, and commissaries."

Joan Boucher had been an active distributor of the proscribed translation of the New Testament by Tyndale. The court of Henry was the scene of her zealous labors, where she often introduced

the sacred volumes unsuspected, tying, as Strype
tells us, the precious books by strings to her apparel.   Although well acquainted with the Scriptures, she could not read them ; no uncommon
calamity in that day, even among people of rank.
Much of her time, Foxe tells us, was occupied in
visiting the prisons, wherein were incarcerated her
companions in tribulation, whom it was her custom
perpetually and bountifully to assist.

But there was one supposed error which was
sufficient to expose her to the poisonous breath of
calumny, and to the burning flame.   For this she
had to appear before the inquisitors, " in the chapel
of the blessed Mary in St. Paul's."   The examinations were long, the judges learned, and apparently
desirous to save her from the stake ; but she could
not, she would not be convinced that she held any
heresy, or anything in opposition to the truth.
Neither threatenings nor entreaties moved her ;
but a good conscience made her bold.   At length
she uttered language which it grieved her judges
to hear, but which smote their consciences with
its telling truth.   "It is," said she, "a goodly
matter to consider your ignorance.   It is not long
ago since you burned Anne Askew for a piece of
bread, and yet you came yourselves soon after to
believe and profess the same doctrine for which
you burned her.   And now, forsooth, you will
burn me for a piece of flesh, and in the end you
will come to believe this also, when you have read
the Scriptures, and understood them."

With, professedly, " the fear of God before his

eyes," and with invocation of the name of Christ, the "reverend father in Christ, Thomas, arch- bishop of Canterbury," with the full approbation of his colleagues, proceeded to pronounce her doom. The sentence contained her crime and its punishment. "You believe that the Word was made flesh in the virgin, but that Christ took flesh of the virgin you believe not; because the flesh of the virgin being the outward man sinfully gotten, and born in sin, but the Word by the consent of the inward man of the virgin was made flesh. This dogma, with obstinate, obdurate, and per- tinacious mind, you affirm, and not without much haughtiness of mien. With wonderful blindness of heart, to this you hold; therefore, for your demerits, obstinacy, and contumacy, aggravated by a wicked and damnable pertinacity, being also unwilling to return to the faith of the church, you are adjudged a heretic, to be handed to the secular power, to suffer in due course of law, and finally the ban of the great excommunication is upon you." The inquisitors completed the labors of the day, by announcing to Edward, the youthful sovereign, through their president, that they had decreed her separation from the Lord's flock as a diseased sheep. "And since," said they, "our holy mother, the church, hath nought else that she can do on this behalf, we leave the said heretic to your royal highness, and to the secular arm, to suffer her deserved punishment."

Considerable delay, however, occurred before the execution of the sentence. We may give the reformers credit for an earnest desire to lead Joan Boucher to more correct views, but must not withhold an expression of just abhorrence at the bloody deed, and at the hateful principle on which they acted. They had adopted an unsound basis for their reformation, and its necessary result was oppression of conscience. The exercise of freedom of thought and judgment upon Scripture truth was impossible. Ridley, of London, and Goodrich, of Ely, were specially active in their endeavors to reclaim her; to whom must be added, Cranmer, Latimer, Lever, Whitehead, and Hutchinson.

A year within three days was passed in these unavailing efforts. Her constancy remained unshaken. On the 27th of April, the council issued their warrant to the lord chancellor to make out a writ for her execution; and Cranmer is said, by Foxe, to have been most urgent with the young king to affix the sign manual to the cruel document. The youthful king hesitated. Cranmer argued from the law of Moses, by which blasphemers were to be stoned to death; this woman, he said, was guilty of impiety in the sight of God, which a prince, as God's deputy, ought to punish. The youthful king said to Cranmer, "My lord, will you send her soul to hell?" But his majesty was compelled to yield, and saying "If it be an error, you, my lord, shall answer it to God." With tears, the royal signature was appended. Rogers, the first martyr of Mary's reign, also thought that she ought to be put to death, and when urged with the cruelty of the deed, replied,

" that burning alive was no cruel death, but easy enough." He was the first man called in the reign of Mary to test the truth of his own remark.

The bishops had resolved that Joan Boucher should die, and on the 2d of May, 1550, she appeared at the stake in Smithfield. Here further efforts were made to shake her confidence. To Bishop Scory was allotted the duty of preaching to the sufferer, and to the people on the occasion. " He tried," says Strype, " to convert her; she scoffed, and said he lied like a rogue, and bade him, ' Go read the Scriptures.' " By this language we understand an indignant rejection of the shameful misrepresentations which in that hour of trial were made of her faith. She closely adhered to those words of truth which were her joy and strength, in the moments of her dying agony. She loved and adored the holy and immaculate Lamb of God.

Were it desirable, it might easily be shown that Joan Boucher did not believe or teach the errors laid to her charge. She differed from the Catholics chiefly in believing that the mother of Jesus, like all other merely human beings, was tainted with sin.

MRS. PREST.

Few things are more difficult in reading "John Foxe's *Martyrology*" than to distinguish between Baptists and others. Nothing was more common than to brand an appeal to the Scriptures as the only infallible standard of truth, or an assertion of the full rights of conscience, and other things of a similar character, as "*anabaptistical errors*," without any regard to their views and conduct as to the ordinance of baptism. And again, John Foxe partook fully of the prejudices of the good men of his day against the Baptists, and whenever he could, throughout his work, he defended martyrs from the supposed crime. As he has not vindicated the good woman of whom we now speak from the charge, but tells us that in several examinations she was called "*an Anabaptist*," there can be no doubt that we may place her on our list.

This poor woman resided near Launceston, in Cornwall. "She was," says Foxe, "as simple a woman to see to as any man might behold; of a very little and short stature; somewhat thick; and almost fifty years of age. She had a cheerful and lively countenance; most patient in her words and answers; sober in apparel, meat, and drink; and would never be idle; a great comfort to those who conversed with her; good to the poor; and

(286)

even when in her troubles would never accept money from any one; 'for,' she would say, 'I am going to a city where money bears no mastery; and while I am here God has promised to feed me.'" By a diligent attention to the sermons of pious ministers, probably in the days of king Edward, and hearing good books read, (for she herself could not read,) she had gained such an acquaintance with the Scriptures, that she could readily tell where any passage alluded to might be found; and very powerfully felt the truth on her heart.

Her husband and children were strongly attached to the superstitions of popery; and frequently compelled her to attend mass, visit the confessional, and assist in processions. For some time she submitted to these impositions; but as her convictions of their sinfulness increased, the burden of an accusing conscience became intolerable. She prayed earnestly for divine direction and support; and at length resolved to sacrifice all her earthly comforts rather than submit to practices which she was now convinced were antichristian and idolatrous. She communicated her determination to her family; "and grew," as Foxe expresses it, "in contempt with her husband and children." She then thought it to be her duty, in order to keep a clear conscience, to sepa rate herself from her family, and commit herself to the care of Providence. Accordingly she left her home; and moving about from place to place, obtained a livelihood by spinning. She omitted no opportunity of declaring her sentiments on religious subjects, especially on the popish doctrine of transubstantiation.

After some time, she was brought again to her husband; but whether by persuasion or force does not appear. She had not, however, been long at home, before her neighbors, having sent information to the bishop of Exeter, had her conveyed before him for examination. On this occasion, the following conversation took place, the particulars of which were communicated to the historian by those who heard it.

BISHOP.—Thou foolish woman, I hear say that thou hast spoken certain words against the most blessed sacrament of the altar, the body of Christ. Fie, for shame! Thou art an unlearned person, and a woman. Wilt thou meddle with such high matters, which all the doctors cannot define? Wilt thou talk of so high mysteries? Keep to thy work and meddle with thy own concerns. It is no woman-matter, to be prated about while carding and spinning. If it be as I am informed, thou art worthy to be burned.

MRS. PREST.—My lord, I trust your lordship will hear me speak.

BISHOP.—Yea, marry: therefore I sent for thee.

MRS. PREST.—I am a poor woman and live by my hands; getting a penny honestly; and of that I get, I give part to the poor.

BISHOP.—That is well done. Art thou not a man's wife?

Mrs. Prest.—I have a husband and children, and yet I have them not. So long as I was at liberty, I refused neither husband nor children. But now, standing as I do, in the cause of Christ and his truth; where I must either forsake Christ or my husband, I am content to cleave only to Christ, my heavenly spouse, and renounce the other. For my Saviour has said, "He that leaveth not father or mother, brother or sister, or husband, or wife, for my sake, cannot be my disciple."

Bishop.—Christ spake that of the holy martyrs, who died because they would not sacrifice to false gods.

Mrs. Prest.—Surely, sir; and I will rather die than I will worship that foul idol, which, with your mass, you make a god.

Bishop.—Dare you say that the sacrament of the altar is a foul idol?

Mrs. Prest.—Yea, truly: there never was such an idol as your sacrament is made by your priests; and commanded to be worshiped of all men, with many fantastic fooleries: when Christ did command it to be eaten and drank in remembrance of his most blessed death for our redemption

Bishop.—Alas! poor woman, thou art deceived.

Mrs. Prest.—If you will give me leave, I will declare a reason why I will not worship the sacrament.

Bishop.—Marry, say on. I am sure it will be goodly gear.

25

Mrs. Prest.—Truly such gear as I will lose this poor life of mine for.

Bishop.—Then you will die a martyr, good-wife?

Mrs. Prest.—Indeed: if denying to worship that *bready* god be my martyrdom, I will suffer it with all my heart.

Bishop.—Say thy mind.

Mrs. Prest.—I will demand of you, whether you can deny your own creed, which says that Christ perpetually sits at the right hand of his Father, both body and soul, till he come again? or whether he be there as our Advocate, and intercedes for us with God his Father? If it be so, he is not here on earth in a piece of bread. If he be not here; and if he do not dwell in temples made with hands, why do we seek him here? If he did offer his body once for all, why make you a new offering? If, with one offering, he made all perfect, why do you, with a false offering, make all imperfect? If he be to be worshipped in spirit and truth, why do you worship a piece of bread? If he be eaten and drank in faith and truth, and if his flesh be not profitable to be among us, why do you say that you seek his body and flesh, and that it is profitable for the body and soul? Alas! I am a poor woman! but rather than I would do as you do, I would live no longer. I have said, sir.

Bishop.—I promise you you are a jolly Protestant. I pray you, in what schools have you been brought up?

Mrs. Prest.—I have, upon the Sundays, visited

the sermons, and there have I learned such things as are so fixed in my breast, that death shall not separate them.

BISHOP.—O, foolish woman! Who would waste his breath on thee, or such a woman as thou art? But how chances it that thou wentest away from thy husband? If thou wert an honest woman, thou wouldst not have left thy husband and children, and run about the country like a fugitive.

MRS. PREST.—Sir, I labored for my living; and as my Master, Christ, counsels me, when I was persecuted in one city, I fled to another.

BISHOP.—Who persecuted thee?

MRS. PREST.—My husband and my children. For when I would have them leave idolatry and worship God in heaven, they would not hear; but rebuked and ill-treated me. I fled not for whoredom or theft; but because I would not be a partaker with him and his children of that foul idol the mass. And wheresoever I was, as oft as I could upon Sundays and holidays, I made excuses not to go to the popish church, but to the true church.

BISHOP.—The true church! what dost thou mean?

MRS. PREST.—Not your popish church, full of idols and abominations; but where two or three are gathered together in the name of God; to that church will I go as long as I live.

BISHOP.—Belike then you have a church of your own. Well; let this mad woman be put down to prison, until we send for her husband.

MRS. PREST.—No. I have but one husband,

who is here already, in this city and prison; from whom I will never depart.

The conclusive and rational answers of this simple woman perplexed the bishop and his officers; who seemed at first unwilling to proceed to extremities. They pretended to consider her as out of her senses; though certainly no marks of insanity can be discovered in her examinations. They therefore directed the jailer to permit her to go about the town as she pleased; in hope, probably, that she would either abscond, or commit some act of extravagance, which might sanction harsher measures. But they were disappointed. She employed her time diligently in the prison, in doing the work of a servant, and in spinning; but continued to bear her constant testimony against the Catholics; especially against their favorite doctrine of the mass.

Shortly after, they sent for her husband, who offered to take her home, if she would renounce her heretical opinions; but this she steadily refused to do, declaring that she could not betray the cause of her Saviour, for which she now stood before the bishop and his priests. Several of the Romish clergy undertook to persuade her to acknowledge the real presence of the body of Christ in the sacrament; but to all their arguments she replied, "It is nothing but very bread and wine; and you ought to be ashamed to say, that a piece of bread, which ferments and moulds, and which may be eaten by mice, or burnt in the fire, is changed by man into the natural body of Christ.

God's own body will not be so handled, nor kept in prison in boxes and cups. Let it be your god; it shall not be mine. My Saviour sits at the right hand of God, and doth pray for me." They told her that the devil had deceived her; "No," said she, "I trust that the living God hath opened my eyes, and caused me to understand the right use of the blessed sacrament, which the true church doth use, but the false church doth abuse."

At this point of the discussion, an old friar stepped forward and asked her, "What do you say of the holy pope?" Her reply was, "I say, that he is Antichrist and the devil." At this answer they all very heartily laughed. "Nay," continued she, "you have more need to weep than to laugh; and to be sorry that ever you were born to become the chaplains of that harlot of Babylon. I defy him and all his falsehoods. Get you away from me, you only trouble my conscience. You would have me follow your doings; I will first lose my life. I pray you begone." After much more fruitless conversation, finding her inflexible, the priests left her.

In one of her walks, which, as we have already said, she was allowed to take about the town, she entered a church, and seeing a Dutch sculptor, busily engaged in fitting some new noses upon some of the graven images which had been disfigured in king Edward's days, she told him that he was madly engaged. In a high rage he called her a harlot, "Nay," retorted she, "thy images are harlots, and thou art their follower; for does

25*

not God say, 'Ye go a whoring after strange
gods?' This conversation was immediately reported to the bishop, who instantly sent for her,
and committed her to close confinement.

During her imprisoment, she was visited by a
number of respectable and pious persons. Among
the rest came a wealthy and pious lady, highly
accomplished, and strongly disposed towards the
truth. To her Mrs. Prest recited the creed; and
when she came to the words, "he ascended into
heaven," she paused, and bade her visitor to seek
his body in heaven, not upon earth; telling her
plainly that God dwelleth not in temples made
with hands; and that the sacrament was intended
for nothing else but to be a remembrance of the
sufferings and death of Christ; whereas, as the
priests used it, it was but an idol, and far away
from any remembrance of Christ's body. The
lady, on returning to her husband, said that in all
her life she never heard a woman of such simplicity and plainness of appearance "talk so godly,
so perfectly, so sincerely, and so earnestly." Adding, "Insomuch, if God were not with her, she
could not speak such things, which I am not able
to answer, though I can read, and she cannot.'

At last, her persecutors having exhausted all
their powers of argument to shake her constancy,
but in vain, brought her before the court; and railing at her as an Anabaptist, delivered her over to
the civil magistrate, who sent her from one prison
to another, and endeavored to persuade her to recant; telling her, among other things, that she

was but an unlearned woman, and could not understand these high matters." "I am nothing more," was her answer, "Yet with my death I am content to be a witness of Christ's death. I pray you make no more delay with me; my heart is fixed, and I will never turn to their superstitious doings." The bishop said that she was led by the devil; and in every possible form did they seek to irritate and gain an advantage over her, but all was entirely in vain.

The sentence was then read to her—that she should be burnt in the flames till she was consumed. As soon as she heard it, she lifted up her eyes and her voice towards heaven, and said, "I thank thee, my Lord and God. This day have I found what I have long sought for." This was followed by the general mocking and derision of the whole court; but the constant martyr stood unmoved and cheerful. The court again told her, that if she would recant and turn from her errors, her life should be spared. Her ready and decided reply was, "Nay, that I will never do; God forbid that I should lose the life eternal for this carnal and short life. I will never turn from my Heavenly husband to my earthly one; from the fellowship of angels to mortal children. If my husband and children be faithful, then I am still theirs. God is my father, my mother, my brother, my sister, my friend most faithful."

She was then delivered to the sheriff; and in the midst of an immense crowd of spectators was led to the place of execution, outside of the walls

of the city of Exeter. Here again the Romish
priests assaulted her, but she refused to listen to
anything they wished to say, and begged them not
to disturb her any more. While being tied to the
stake, and while the flames were all around her,
she displayed a holy and cheerful courage. Her
last prayer was, "God be merciful to me, a sinner." Thus did she die, exhibiting a most noble
example of faith and constancy, united with Christian simplicity and humility. Her holy Redeemer
was present while she glorified him in the fire of
martyrdom, and conveyed her immortal spirit to
his own throne, eternally to participate in his joy.

MRS. ELIZABETH GAUNT.

THE Rye-house Plot, as it was called, stands associated in English history with acts of atrocious cruelty, perpetrated under color of the administration of justice. It was said to contemplate the assassination of Charles II. ; but of this there is no evidence. To adopt the words of the Right Honorable Charles James Fox:—"That which is most certain in this affair is, that the persons accused committed no overt act, indicating the imagining of the king's death, even according to the most strained construction of the statute of Edward III. ; much less was any such act legally proved against them. And the conspiracy to levy war was not treason, except by a recent statute of Charles II., the prosecutions upon which were limited to a certain time, which, in these cases had elapsed ; so that it is impossible not **to** assent to the opinion of those who have ever stigmatized the condemnation and execution of Lord William Russell as the most flagrant violation of law and justice. The proceedings in Sidney's case were still more grossly unjust. Thus Russell and Sidney fell, two names that will, it is hoped, be for ever dear to every patriotic English [and American] heart. When their memory shall cease to be an object of respect and veneration, it requires no

spir t of prophecy to foretell that liberty will be
fast approaching to its final consummation.''

The halo of glory which rests on the names of
these eminent men has made less conspicuous
some who are still worthy of grateful remembrance. These were times—like some that preceded them—in which were persecutions of persons of no ordinary worth.

———"Who lived unknown,
Till persecution dragged them into fame,
And chased them up to heaven."

Such was Elizabeth Gaunt, a Baptist in humble
life, who was charged with harboring a man, with
his family, named Burton, suspected of being concerned in the Rye-house plot. That he was a vile
scoundrel, who assumed, for his own wicked purposes, the cloak of Nonconformity, there is every
reason to believe; of which indeed there is sufficient proof in his becoming king's evidence
against the woman who afforded him shelter, and
who had twice saved his life.

The question is, had *she* incurred any guilt?
She might be innocent, though a multitude had
violated the existing laws. Of such plain facts,
however, her judge,—the infamous Jefferies—had
entirely lost sight, and he engrossed to himself
not merely the power of a tyrant-judge, but the
right of a succumbent and abject jury. He saw
that there was no proof that Elizabeth Gaunt
knew anything of Burton's being engaged in
the so-called conspiracy, or was even aware of

his name being found in any proclamation. His only *proper* course, therefore, was to tell this to the jury, and to leave them to pronounce her acquitted. But what was a *proper* course to him,— a man of furious passions, exasperated by habitual intemperance,—a man who rioted in cruelty, and had a fiendish delight in pronouncing the sentence of death? Though in the eye of the law that woman was innocent, and though witnesses were ready to attest her virtues, he forbade them to be called, directed the jury to find her guilty, and then consigned her to the agonies of the stake. We will, however, listen to the statement given of the whole affair, by bishop Burnet: —

"There was in London one Gaunt, a woman that was an Anabaptist, who spent a great part of her life in acts of charity, visiting the jails, and looking after the poor, of what persuasion soever they were. One of the rebels found her out, and she harbored him in her house, and was looking for an occasion of sending him out of the kingdom. He went about in the night, and came to hear what the king had said, [namely, that he would sooner pardon the rebels than those who harbored them.] So he, by an unheard of baseness, went and delivered himself up, and accused her that had harbored him. She was seized on and tried. There was no witness to prove that she knew the person she harbored was a rebel, except he himself. Her maid witnessed only that he was entertained at her house; but though her crime was that of harboring a traitor, and was proved only by this infamous witness, yet the judge charged the jury to bring her in guilty, pretending that the maid was a second witness, though she knew nothing of that which was the criminal part.

"She was condemned and burnt, as the law directs in the case of women convicted of treason. She died with a constancy even to cheerfulness, that struck all who saw it. She said, Charity was a part of her religion as well as faith; this at worst was feeding an enemy. So she hoped she had reward with him for whose sake she did this service, how unworthy soever the person was who made so ill a return for it. She rejoiced that God had honored her to be the first that suffered by fire in this reign, and that her suffering was a martyrdom for that religion which was all love. Penn, the Quaker, told me that he saw her die. She laid the straw about her for burning her speedily, and behaved herself in such a manner that all the spectators melted in tears."

She was executed, according to her sentence, at Tyburn, near London, October 23, 1685, and left a paper containing an account of the whole transaction, which she delivered into the hands of captain Richardson, then keeper of Newgate prison, in which she had been confined. It cannot be uninteresting to the reader:—

"Not knowing whether I shall be suffered, or able, because of weakenesses that are upon me, through my hard and close imprisonment, to speak at the place of execution, I have written these

few lines to signify that I am reconciled to the ways of my God towards me; though it is in ways I looked not for, and by terrible things, yet in righteousness; for having given me life, he ought to have the disposing of it, when and where he pleases to call for it. And I desire to offer up my all to him, it being my reasonable service, and also the first terms which Christ offers, that he who will be his disciple must forsake all and follow him. Therefore let none think hard, or be discouraged at what hath happened unto me; for he hath done nothing without cause in all that he hath done unto me; he being holy in all his ways, and righteous in all his works, and it is but my lot in common with poor desolate Zion at this day.

"Neither do I find in my heart the least regret at anything I have done in the service of my Lord and Master, Jesus Christ, in securing and succoring any of his poor sufferers, that have showed favor, as I thought, to his righteous cause; which cause, though it be now fallen and trampled on, yet it may revive, and God may plead it at another time more than ever he hath yet done, with all its opposers and malicious haters. And therefore, let all that love and fear him not omit the least duty that comes to hand or lies before them, knowing that now Christ hath need of them, and expects they should serve him. And I desire to bless his holy name that he hath made me useful in my generation, to the comfort and relief of many desolate ones; that the blessing of many who were ready to perish hath come upon me, and I helped to make the widow's heart leap for joy.

"And I bless his holy name that in all this, together with what I was charged with, I can approve my heart to him, that I have done his will, though it may cross man's. The Scriptures which satisfy me are these: 'Hide the outcasts; bewray not him that wandereth. Let mine outcasts dwell with thee: be thou a covert to them from the face of the spoiler. Thou shouldst not have delivered up those of his that did remain in the day of distress.' Isa. xvi. 3, 4; Obad. 12, 13, 14. But men say you must give them up, or die for it. Now whom to obey, judge ye. So that I have cause to rejoice and be exceeding glad, in that I 'suffer for righteousness' sake,' and that I am counted worthy to suffer 'for well doing;' and that God hath accepted any service from me, which hath been done in sincerity, though mixed with manifold infirmities, which he hath been pleased for Christ's sake to cover and forgive.

"And now as concerning my crime, as it is now called; alas, it was but a little one, and such as might well become a prince to forgive. But he that shows no mercy shall find none; and I may say of it in the language of Jonathan, 'I did but taste a little honey, and lo, I must die for it'—I did but relieve an unworthy, poor, distressed family, and lo, I must die for it. Well, I desire in the lamb-like nature of the gospel to forgive those that are concerned; and to say, 'Lord, lay it not to their charge!' But I fear he will not; nay, I believe, when he comes to make inquisition for blood, it will be found at the door of the furious judge; who, because I could not remember things, through my dauntedness [confusion] at Burton's wife and daughter's witness, and my ignorance, took advantage of it, and would not hear me when I had called to mind that which I am sure would have invalidated the evidence. And though he granted something of the same kind to another, he denied it to me. At that time my blood will also be found at the door of the unrighteous jury, who found me guilty on the single oath of an outlawed man ; for there was none but his oath about the money, who is no legal witness, though he be pardoned, his outlawry not being reversed, also the law requiring *two* witnesses in point of treason. As to my going with him to the place mentioned, namely, the Hope, it was by his own word before he could be outlawed, for it was about two months after his absconding. So that though he was in a proclamation, yet not for high treason, as I am informed; so that I am clearly murdered. And also bloody Mr. Atterbury, who hath so insatiably hunted after my life, though it is no profit to him, yet through the ill will he bears me, left no stone unturned, as I have ground to believe, till he brought it to this, and showed favor to Burton, who ought to have died for his own fault, and not to have bought his own life with mine. Captain Richardson, who is cruel and severe to all under my circumstances, did, at that time, without any mercy or pity, hasten my sentence, and held up my hand that it might be given. All which, together with the great one of all, [James II., who had just come to the throne, carrying on his brother's proceedings,] by whose power all these and multitudes more of cruelties are done, I do heartily and freely forgive as against me; but as it is done in an implacable mind against the Lord Jesus Christ, and his righteous cause and followers, I leave it to Him who is the avenger of all such wrong, and 'who will tread upon princes as upon mortar, and be terrible to the kings of the earth.'

"Know this also, that though you are seemingly fixed, and because of the power in your hands are weighing out your violence, and dealing with a spiteful mind, because of the old and new hatred, by impoverishing and every way distressing those you have got under you; yet unless you can secure Jesus Christ, and also his holy angels, you shall never do your business, nor shall your hand accomplish your enterprize. He will be upon you ere you are aware; and therefore that you would be wise, instructed, and learn, is the desire of her that finds no mercy from you!

"ELIZABETH GAUNT.

"P. S. Such as it is, you have from the hand of her who hath done as she could, and is sorry that she can do no better; hopes you will pity, and consider, and cover weaknesses and shortness, and anything that is wanting; and begs that none may be weakened or stumble by my lowness of spirit; for God's design is to humble and abase, that he alone may be exalted in that day. And I hope he may appear in a needful time and hour, and it may be he will reserve the best wine till the last, as he hath done for some before me. None goeth a warfare at his own charges, and the Spirit blows only where and when it listeth; and it becomes me who have so often grieved it and quenched it, to wait for and upon his motions, and not to murmur; but I may mourn, because through the want of it I honor not my God nor his blessed cause, which I have so long loved and delighted to serve; and repent of nothing but that I have served it and him no better."

In an anonymous work, published at the time, entitled " *A Display of Tyranny*," there are some remarks upon the trial of this truly worthy woman, which are highly creditable to her character. " Were my pen," says the author, " qualified to represent the due character of this excellent woman, it would be readily granted that she stood most deservedly entitled to an eternal monument of honor in the hearts of all sincere lovers of the reformed religion. All true Christians, though in some things differing in persuasion from her, found in her a universal charity and sincere friendship, as is well known to many here, and also to a multitude of the Scotch nation, ministers and others, who for conscience sake were thrust into exile from prelatic rage. These found in her a most refreshing refuge. She dedicated herself with unwearied industry to provide for their supply and support, and therein I do incline to think she out-

stripped every individual, if not the whole body of
Protestants in this city. Hereby she became exposed to the implacable fury of the papists, and
those blind tools who co-operated to promote their
accursed designs; and so there appeared little difficulty to procure a jury, as there were well-pre-
pared judges, to make her a sacrifice as a traitor
to " holy church."

CONCLUSION.

In closing a volume, the interest of which has, to its writer, increased with the increase of his labor in producing it, it cannot be improper to quote the language of the eloquent Robert Hall Thus does he write :—

"The example of these holy persons should be a reproof to the lukewarmness of many professing Christians. Can we suppose that Christianity was, in primitive times, in the same low state as at present? Were these martyrs to return again and see the general state of religion,—the practice of some in attending the theatre, where the name of God and the sanctity of religion are sported with—were they to see the rapacity of the rich, or the venom of party spirit which prevails, they would inquire, ' Where are the traces of martyrdom? Are these the successors of those who believed the world must be renounced, and that the kingdom of heaven must be taken with violence? *You* reason upon the lawfulness of amusements until you retain everything but your religion; *they* astonished the world by their sufferings, you by the portentous magnitude of your vices; *they* sought the favor of Divine Providence, and took nothing by violence but the kingdom of heaven; *you* let go immortality to secure wealth, and leave large legacies to your children or friends, at the expense of lifting up your eyes in torment in a future world.'

"Would not these be the sentiments of primitive Christians? What remains, then, but that we should examine our steps? Though we do not reach so high as they did, we may reach even higher. Martyrdom may be considered as the expression of those principles, which are, in their spirit, obligatory and common to all Christians. If we are under the influence of the world, that spirit will lead us to renounce Christianity, if it be not done already; and if we have not renounced the love of the world, it is evident that our feet will never stand in that blessed place where they sing the song of Moses and the Lamb.

"Let us not be slothful, but followers of them, who, through faith and patience, are now inheriting the promises. Let us kindle our dying lamps at these heavenly fires. Jesus Christ, the great proto-martyr, says, 'If any one will be my disciple, let him come after me.' As we expect eternal happiness, let us seek it in this way, for He has led the path."

Let us close our volume by borrowing from an old writer a

"CLUSTER OF SIMILES.

" God's children are like STARS, that look most bright
 When foes pursue them through the darkest night;
 Like TORCHES beat, they more resplendent shine ;
 Like GRAPES when pressed, they yield luxuriant wine;

Like Spices pounded, are to smell most sweet ;
Like Trees when shook, that wave but not retreat ;
Like Vines, that for the bleeding better grow ;
Like Gold, that burning makes the brighter show ;
Like Glow-worms, that shine best in dark attire ;
Like Cedar-leaves, whose odors gain by fire ;
Like the Palm-tree, whose humors force removes ;
Like Camomile, which treading on improves ;
Like everything that can withstand the test,
Are those God loves, and who love God the best."

THE END.